PENSION SHARING IN PRACTICE

SECOND EDITION

SPECIAL BULLETIN

PENSION SHARING IN PRACTICE

SECOND EDITION

SPECIAL BULLETIN

David Salter MA, LLM, Solicitor

Partner, Addleshaw Booth & Co, Leeds, Manchester and London

Family Law

2003

Published by
Jordan Publishing Limited
21 St Thomas Street
Bristol BS1 6JS

© Jordan Publishing Limited 2003
Reprinted November 2004

British Library Cataloguing-in-Publication Data
A catalogue record for this book is available from the British Library.

ISBN 0 85308 846 2

Typeset by Jordan Publishing Limited
Printed by Hobbs the Printers Ltd, Totton, Hampshire SO40 3WX

PREFACE

This Bulletin aims to offer the family law practitioner a practical guide to the operation of pension sharing in England and Wales presented in an accessible and user-friendly format. As well as highlighting some of the pitfalls which exist to ensnare the unwary, procedural tips are offered to enable the practitioner to achieve the right result at the first attempt. It is not intended to discuss pension sharing in the wider context of pensions and divorce. Such a discussion can be found elsewhere, for example, *Pensions and Insurance on Family Breakdown* (Family Law).

This book does not attempt to provide a commentary on pension sharing for the benefit of pension schemes, although trustees may find what follows useful in gaining an insight into the family lawyer's perception of the topic.

I must thank the many family lawyers, actuaries and independent financial advisers who have aired with me the practical difficulties encountered since 1 December 2000. Without this shared experience, this Bulletin would be much the poorer. Many will find within its pages problems which they can recall discussing with me. I must also thank my secretary, Vicky Fraser, who has painstakingly and uncomplainingly prepared the manuscript.

The law and practice is stated as at December 2002.

David Salter
Leeds
December 2002

CONTENTS

LIST OF LEGISLATIVE SOURCES

Child Support, Pensions and Social Security Act 2000, s 41

Finance Act 1999, s 79 and Sch 10

Child Support, Pensions and Social Security Act 2000 (Commencement No 1) Order 2000, SI 2000/2666

Divorce etc (Notification and Treatment of Pensions) (Scotland) Regulations 2000, SI 2000/1050, reg 4

Divorce etc (Pensions) Regulations 2000, SI 2000/1123

Divorce etc (Pensions) Regulations (Northern Ireland) 2000, SR 2000/210

Divorce etc (Pensions) (Scotland) Regulations 2000, Scottish SI 2000/112

Family Proceedings (Amendment) Regulations 2000, SI 2000/2267

Finance Act 1999, Sch 10, para 18 (First and Second Appointed Days) Order 2000, SI 2000/1093

Pensions on Divorce etc (Charging) Regulations 2000, SI 2000/1049

Pensions on Divorce etc (Provision of Information) Regulations 2000, SI 2000/1048

Pensions on Divorce etc (Pension Sharing) (Scotland) Regulations 2000, SI 2000/1051

Pensions on Divorce etc (Provision of Information) Regulations (Northern Ireland) 2000, SR 2000/142

Pensions on Divorce etc (Sharing) Regulations (Northern Ireland) 2000, SR 2000/143

Pension Sharing (Consequential and Miscellaneous Amendments) Regulations 2000, SI 2000/2691

Pension Sharing (Contracting Out) (Consequential Amendments) Regulations 2000, SI 2000/2975

Pension Sharing (Implementation and Discharge of Liability) Regulations (Northern Ireland) 2000, SR 2000/145

Pension Sharing (Implementation and Discharge of Liability) Regulations 2000, SI 2000/1053

Pension Sharing (Pension Credit Benefit) Regulations (Northern Ireland) 2000, SR 2000/146

Pension Sharing (Pension Credit Benefit) Regulations 2000, SI 2000/1054

Pension Sharing (Safeguarded Rights) Regulations 2000, SI 2000/1055

Pension Sharing (Safeguarded Rights) Regulations (Northern Ireland) 2000, SR 2000/147

Pension Sharing (Valuation) Regulations 2000, SI 2000/1052

Pension Sharing (Valuation) Regulations (Northern Ireland) 2000, SR 2000/144

Pensions Schemes Office Update No 62 (issued 28 April 2000)

1 THE CONCEPT EXPLAINED

1.1 Historical background

Pension sharing is now something of an old chestnut. As long ago as 1969, the Law Commission discussed the issue in its *Report on Financial Provision in Matrimonial Proceedings.*[1] The Law Commission revisited pensions in 1977, concluding that there was no need to make special provision because of the move away from life-long support for divorced wives, while conceding that reform was needed so as to give access to pension payments to wives in lengthy marriages. In 1985, the Lord Chancellor's Department proposed that only older spouses should be able to claim and the question of quantum should be left until retirement. By 1990, the Labour Party had proposed splitting pension rights on divorce in a brief analysis. However, a major milestone in the path towards reform was the report of the Pensions Management Institute/Law Society Working Party in May 1993, which recommended that the court be given the power to make a 'pensions adjustment order' directing the splitting of pension rights at the time of divorce in appropriate circumstances. Later that year, the Goode Committee report endorsed the PMI/Law Society conclusions in broad terms, but suggested that further research was needed before they were implemented.

In June 1994, the White Paper on Pensions Law Reform broadly accepted the conclusions of the PMI/Law Society Working Party and the Goode Committee report. It was anticipated that reform would come in a Matrimonial Causes Act rather than the forthcoming Pensions Bill. However, in the Lords, Baroness Hollis proposed an amendment to the Pensions Bill which introduced splitting. The then Government eventually conceded the principle of reform, but sought a compromise by suggesting what was then to be known as earmarking. This was implemented in due course as the Pensions Act 1995, s 166 with effect from 1 July 1996. After a faltering attempt to introduce 'pension splitting' by the Conservative Government in the Family Law Act 1996, s 16 (see **2.2**), the current Government announced its intention on 5 June 1997 to publish a draft Bill for consultation on what had now become known as 'pension sharing' (the two terms being interchangeable). In the summer of 1997, the Government took the innovative step of setting up a multi-disciplinary Pension Sharing Consultation Panel, involving pension lawyers and family lawyers as well as members of the relevant government departments and groups representing divorced couples, to review proposals for the detailed operation of pension sharing. All parties accepted the principle of pension sharing as set out in the White Paper *Pension Rights on Divorce*, published in February 1997.

After an abortive Pension Sharing Bill published in 1998, the Welfare Reform and Pensions Bill was published on 10 February 1999. The Social Security Select Committee examined the draft legislation and took evidence from interested parties. This wide-ranging consultation process has resulted in the main in workable legislation procedures in a highly complex area encompassing several disciplines.

---

[1]   HC 448 HMSO, 1969.

1.2   What is pension sharing?

Pension sharing enables the court to share (or, as it was formerly termed, split) a pension at the time of divorce so that (typically) the wife either becomes a member of (typically) the husband's scheme in her own right by provision of what has been termed 'shadow membership' (*'internal transfer'*) or, alternatively, takes a transfer of a designated amount into her own pension (*'external transfer'*).

1.3   The scope of the issue

Published figures show that there were 141,135 divorces (ie decrees absolute) in England and Wales in 2000.[1] Among full-time employees, 73% of men and 78% of women were members of an occupational or personal pension scheme. However, among women who worked part-time, only 33% belong to some form of pension scheme. Among the self-employed, 51% of men belong to some form of pension scheme compared to 31% of women.[2]

The issue is further set in context by appreciating that, whilst the average equity in property in 1998 was £36,000, the average pension transfer value was close to half as much again at £50,000. In 2001, 68% of households owned their house.[2]

The Government estimated, when pension sharing was introduced, that there would be 50,000 pension shares per annum. It was further estimated that 75% would be external transfers. External transfers were predicted to be the preference of the pensions industry, not simply because of the cost and administration involved in internal transfers but because trustees would be also reluctant to create a class of beneficiaries with no links to the principal employer. While the latter prediction proved to be correct, pension sharing proved to be something of a disappointment for a year or so after its introduction on 1 December 2000. Courts and pension schemes reported very few pension sharing orders being made. Independent financial advisers, who had prepared for an avalanche transfer market, were seriously disappointed. The initial low take-up is partly explained by the delays inherent in the court process in awaiting the pronouncement of decrees nisi on petitions issued after 1 December 2000. However, the more likely explanation is the cautious approach of all the relevant professions mounting the steep learning curve involved in the practical experience of pension sharing. By the autumn of 2002, pension sharing orders had become rather more commonplace, although not on the scale initially predicted by the Government. Nonetheless, the learning curve continues.

1.4   Myths and misconceptions

- No – it is not compulsory; it is only an option;

- No – pension *sharing* does not automatically mean 50%;

- No – it only applies to married couples, not to cohabitants (but see **14.3**);

- Yes – you can share a pension in payment;[3]

- Yes – you can share a pension share including a shared additional pension (a pension share derived from SERPs/S2P (see **7.2**(h), **8.6** and **8.7**));

---

[1]   Office of National Statistics.
[2]   *Living in Britain: Results from the 2000/2001 General Household Survey* (Office of National Statistics).
[3]   Including a purchased annuity (Pensions on Divorce etc (Provision of Information) Regulations 2000, SI 2000/1048, reg 3).

- Yes – the person with the benefit of the order may retire at his/her own retirement age (regardless of the age of the other party), commute part of his/her pension and make nominations.

2 A USER GUIDE THROUGH THE MAZE OF LEGISLATION

2.1 Welfare Reform and Pensions Act 1999

The Welfare Reform and Pensions Act 1999 (WRPA 1999) received Royal Assent on 11 November 1999. As well as including provision for pension sharing for divorcing couples, it makes provision for:

- the introduction of a new stakeholder pension scheme (Part I);
- a modernised system of welfare benefits (Part V).

2.2 Implementation

On 17 June 1999, the Lord Chancellor announced that it was no longer his intention to implement the reforms to divorce law contained in Part II of the Family Law Act 1996 (FLA 1996) before the end of 2000. The pension sharing provisions in WRPA 1999 are drafted in the alternative. Schedule 12 amends FLA 1996, Part II, whereas Sch 3 amends the Matrimonial Causes Act 1973 (MCA 1973). This Bulletin will consider pension sharing solely in the context of the law contained in MCA 1973, as the Lord Chancellor announced on 16 January 2001, that the Government intends to ask Parliament to repeal FLA 1996, Part II.

The pension sharing provisions of WRPA 1999 apply to petitions for divorce or nullity issued on or after 1 December 2000.[1]

The ill-fated attempt at pension splitting in the guise of a 'pension adjustment order' contained in the FLA 1996, s 16 was repealed by WRPA 1999, Sch 13, Part II.

2.3 Key features of the new legislation

The key features of WRPA 1999 are:

- retrospective implementation is not intended (see **8.1**);
- earmarking (which is renamed pension attachment) is retained as an alternative to pension sharing. WRPA 1999 includes changes designed to improve the attachment legislation (see **3.6**);
- pension sharing does not apply to judicial separations (cf pension attachment);
- pension sharing applies to SERPs/S2P (see **8.6**), but not to the basic State pension (where one party may already substitute their former partner's contribution record for their own in the event of divorce);
- pension sharing is only available by order, ie after a contested hearing under a court order or by agreement under the terms of a consent order;

---

[1] WRPA 1999 , s 85(3)(a); WRPA (Commencement No 5) Order, SI 2000/1116.

- *Brooks*-style variation of settlement orders[1] have disappeared. However, it will still be possible to apply for a variation of settlement order where the petition was issued before 1 December 2000 (even if Form A seeking the variation of settlement order is issued after that date).[2] See also **12.4**.

2.4   Structure of WRPA 1999

The parts of WRPA 1999 of interest to the family lawyer are:

- Part II: pensions and bankruptcy (ss 11–16);
- Part III: pension sharing orders:
  - orders in England and Wales (s 19 and Sch 3 (amending MCA 1973); Sch 12 (amending FLA 1996, Part II));
  - orders in Scotland (s 20);
  - amendments to pension attachment (s 21 and Sch 4);
  - extension of pension attachment to the Matrimonial and Family Proceedings Act 1984 (MFPA 1984), Part III (s 22);
  - miscellaneous and supplementary provisions including the supply of pension information, charges by pension arrangements in relation to attachment orders and interpretation (ss 23–26);
- Part IV:
  - pension sharing of rights under pension arrangements (ss 27–46 and Sch 5);
  - pension sharing of State scheme rights (ss 47–51 and Sch 6).

2.5   Other legislative sources

Other sources of primary and secondary legislation are listed in Appendix 1.

2.6   Pension debits and pension credits

(a)   How does pension sharing work?

Central to the concept of pension sharing is the creation of pension debits and pension credits. On the making of a pension sharing order, the transferor loses the percentage required to be transferred (the *pension debit*) so that his pension fund is reduced in value; the transferee acquires the right to require the pension scheme trustee or manager to credit her with that amount (the *pension credit*) so that she gains a pension fund of that value.[3] The transferee will then have an indefeasible pension in her own right.

(b)   Effect on the transferor

In all cases except those involving active members of final salary occupational pension schemes, the pension debit will be a once and for all reduction of a percentage of the accrued value of the

---

[1]   *Brooks v Brooks* [1995] 2 FLR 13, HL.
[2]   WRPA 1999, s 85(4).
[3]   Ibid, s 29(1).

fund. Each qualifying benefit (ie each benefit included in the cash equivalent calculation) must be reduced in the same proportion.[1]

Example

Pension sharing order directs a pension debit of 40% of a cash equivalent of £100,000.

£40,000 is taken from the accrued value of the member's fund. The former spouse's corresponding pension credit of £40,000 is invested separately for him/her.

However, the position is more complex in the case of an active member of a final salary occupational pension scheme.[2] The benefit is reduced by an amount representing the appropriate percentage of the benefit that was taken for the purpose of calculating the cash equivalent. The calculation is done by reference to the hypothetical negative deferred pension to which the member would have been entitled. Thus, the death in service benefit will not be reduced because such benefit does not form part of the hypothetical pension. The use of this formula is intended to prevent schemes from enjoying a windfall at the expense of the member.

Example

H is aged 50 and has a current pensionable salary of £27,000. He has accrued 20 years of service at the date of the hearing in a n/60ths scheme.

Cash equivalent transfer value (CETV) is £80,000; court makes a pension sharing order in favour of W for 45% of CETV.

Pension debit/credit is 45% of £80,000 = £36,000.

When H retires at age 60 (with 30 years' accrued service) at a final salary of £45,000, his pension will need to take account of the negative deferred pension representing £4,050 (20/60 × £27,000 × 45% = £4,050) increased in line with any required revaluation to the date of retirement. After such revaluation, the negative deferred pension increased to £6,000 by H's retirement.

H's reduced pension is:

30/60 × £45,000 = £22,500 – £6,000 (negative deferred pension) = £16,500.

A scheme actuary is prevented from calculating the pension as if the member had given up 45% (9 years' worth) of the rights to 20 years' pensionable service at the time of the divorce.

Reduction of member's pension 9/60 × £45,000 = £6,750.

Final pension £22,500 – £6,750 = £15,750.

In this example, the windfall to the scheme at the member's expense would be £750 per annum until the member dies.

WRPA 1999, s 32 makes certain amendments to the Pension Schemes Act 1993 to provide for the effect of pension sharing on the contracted out rights of a transferor.

---

[1]   WRPA 1999, s 31(1).
[2]   Ibid, s 31(2).

See **12.2** as to the effect on the transferor's restricted benefits in terms of rebuilding.

(c)   *Effect on the transferee*

	Funded scheme	*Unfunded public sector scheme*	*Unfunded private scheme*	*SERPs*
External transfer	Yes	Not allowed	Yes	Not allowed
Internal transfer	Voluntary	Yes	Voluntary	Yes

It must be understood that, because of the different actuarial assumptions applied to men and women, a female transferee receiving a pension credit of, say, 50% of a particular pension arrangement will not receive a pension equal to that of a male transferor of the same age (see **7.7**(a)).

Whether the transferee receiving the pension credit proceeds by way of an internal or external transfer, he/she will have an indefeasible pension in his/her own name and become a member in his/her own right. He/she can therefore retire at his/her normal retirement date under the terms of the pension arrangement (irrespective of the age of the transferor), take a tax-free lump sum and be able to make nominations, etc in the same way as any other pensioner. However, the transferee will only be able to make further contributions into (by way of example) a personal pension which has received an external transfer where he/she has relevant earnings; but, under WRPA 1999, a non-earner will be able to pay up to £3,600 per annum into a stakeholder pension or new-style personal pension (see **13.4**).

The issue of what the transferee may do with the pension credit and what are her rights under the transferred scheme will depend on the type of pension arrangement involved.

(i)   *Funded occupational pension schemes*

Where a scheme is a funded occupational scheme or a personal pension scheme, the person responsible for the scheme should first offer to discharge its liability to the transferee for the pension credit by making a transfer payment to a suitable scheme or arrangement of the transferee's choice. This can include conferring rights on the transferee within the scheme (an internal transfer), but an external transfer must be offered.

The transferee will be invited to make a choice as to the destination of the pension credit. If no choice is made within a specified period, the person responsible will decide. An internal transfer may only be effected if the transferee agrees or if the transferee does not provide details of an alternative scheme.[1]

Where an external transfer is chosen, the destination for the pension credit must not be disqualified as a qualifying arrangement (eg where the credit derives from a tax approved scheme, the destination must also be tax approved).[2]

The person responsible for the destination arrangement must be able and willing to accept payment in respect of the pension credit.[3]

---

[1]   WRPA 1999, Sch 5, para 1(2) and the Pension Sharing (Implementation and Discharge of Liability) Regulations 2000, SI 2000/1053, reg 7.
[2]   WRPA 1999, Sch 5, paras 1(3)(a) and 7.
[3]   WRPA 1999, Sch 5, para 1(3)(b).

(ii)   Unfunded public service schemes

The trustees or managers may only provide benefits by means of an internal transfer, unless the scheme is closed to new members, in which event the transferee may be offered membership of an alternative public service scheme specified by Regulations.[1]

(iii)   Other unfunded occupational pension schemes

When the pension credit is derived from an occupational pension scheme which is not funded and which is not a public service pension scheme, the trustees or managers have an absolute right to offer an internal transfer and the transferee has no choice. However, they may offer an external transfer providing that:

- the proposed destination is not disqualified;

- the person responsible for the destination arrangement is able and willing to accept payment in respect of the credit;

- payment is made with the consent of the person entitled to the credit or in accordance with Regulations.[2]

(iv)   Other pension arrangements

WRPA 1999, Sch 5, para 4 deals with pension credits derived from certain other pension arrangements:

- a retirement annuity contract;

- an annuity or insurance policy purchased or transferred for the purpose of giving effect to rights under an occupational scheme or a personal pension scheme (eg a s 32 buy-out policy); or

- an annuity purchased or entered into for the purpose of discharging liability in respect of a pension credit.

In relation to such arrangements, the person responsible for the scheme may offer an external transfer or (provided the transferee consents and the arrangement is not disqualified as a destination) by means of an internal transfer by entering into a policy of insurance or annuity contract with the transferee. An internal transfer in the way suggested will also be possible, even if the transferee does not consent.[3]

(v)   Safeguarded rights

GMP is the pension (or part of pension) accrued before 6 April 1997 by a member of a contracted-out scheme normally equal to that part of the State pension given up as a result of contracting out. It is the minimum level of pension which an occupational pension scheme must provide for this period of service as one of the conditions of being permitted to contract out. It is available at State retirement age and to the widow or widower of the member on his or her death at any time. Protected rights are the benefits under an appropriate personal pension (APP) (ie a personal pension scheme which provides contracted-out benefits) scheme or money purchase contracted-out scheme deriving from the minimum contribution or payments.

---

[1]   WRPA 1999, Sch 5, para 2(3) and (4).

[2]   Ibid, para 3 and Pension Sharing (Implementation and Discharge of Liability) Regulations 2000, SI 2000/1053, reg 8.

[3]   Pension Sharing (Implementation and Discharge of Liability) Regulations 2000, reg 9.

Any part of a pension credit stemming from GMPs or Protected Rights are treated slightly differently. This part of the pension credit is known as Safeguarded Rights in W's new pension derived from the pension credit and is subject to additional restrictions (eg benefits may only be taken from aged 60) to reflect the fact that they represent benefits which equate to State retirement benefits and to distinguish them from the contracted-out rights built up by members of such schemes. The intention is that the requirements for Safeguarded Rights should be broadly similar to those for contracted-out rights, for example, to ensure that they are securely protected and used for their intended purpose.[1]

(vi)   SERPs/S2P

See **8.6**.

(vii)   Internal transfers

Practitioners should beware the restrictive rules relating to the benefits available on an internal transfer, eg in the Armed Forces there are no widower's rights. Further, there are particular concerns where only an internal transfer is available, eg an unfunded public service scheme. If the pension debit is applied against a pension in payment but the person with the benefit of the pension credit has not yet attained age 60, she will not be able to draw benefits even though the application of the pension debit will have had an immediate adverse affect upon the income of her former husband. In other words, pension sharing in this situation creates an 'income gap' (see **3.3**).

See also **13.2**.

(viii)   Age for accessing pension credit benefits

The effect of WRPA 1999, s 37 and *PSO Update Number 62* dated 28 April 2000, para 27 is that, subject to DSS (DWP) requirements, pension credit rights come into payment as follows:

- Occupational pension schemes approved under the Income and Corporation Taxes Act 1988 (ICTA 1988), s 590 (mandatory approval):
  - payable between age 60 and 75;
- Occupational pension schemes approved under ICTA 1988, s 591 (discretionary approval):
  - payable between age 50 and 75, or earlier on grounds of exceptional circumstances of serious ill-health or on the grounds of incapacity where, in the case of the latter, the ex-spouse is simultaneously taking employee benefits on these grounds under the scheme in which the pension credits are held;
- Personal pensions:
  - payable between age 50 and 75;
- Retirement annuity contracts:
  - payable between age 60 and 75 or earlier than the prescribed age ranges for personal pension schemes and retirement annuity contracts on the grounds of incapacity by reference to any occupation of the ex-spouse;
- Buy-out contracts
  - Payable between age 50 and 75 except where the origin is an ICTA 1988, s 590 approved scheme.

---

[1]   See, generally, Pension Schemes Act 1993, Part IIIA (inserted by WRPA 1999, s 36); Pension Sharing (Safeguarded Rights) Regulations 2000, SI 2000/1055.

There have been suggestions that the DWP will not permit pension credit rights to come into payment before age 60. For example, it has been suggested that, if a wife transferred her pension credit rights under a pension sharing order by way of an external transfer from an occupational pension scheme into a personal pension, she would not be able to take benefits before age 60, notwithstanding the normal rule that benefits under personal pensions may be drawn from age 50.

The DWP view of the legal position remains at present as stated in *PSO Update Number 62*. However, the Department is considering amending primary legislation so that pension credit rights cannot come into payment before age 60.

Care will be required in advising on any settlement which is dependent upon the person having the benefit of the pension credit taking benefits before age 60, eg on a deferred clean break, where non-extendable term maintenance is payable to age 55 whereupon the benefits under a personal pension receiving the pension credit would then become payable.

Total commutation of the pension credit benefit is allowed before normal benefit age in the case of triviality or serious ill-health.

3 THE COURT'S POWERS

3.1 What is a pension sharing order?

WRPA 1999, s 19 and Sch 3 (which amends MCA 1973) enable the court to make pension sharing orders in England and Wales. Schedule 3, para 2 of WRPA 1999 in turn inserts a new s 21A into MCA 1973 which provides:

> '21A. – (1) For the purposes of this Act, a pension sharing order is an order which –
>
> > (a) provides that one party's –
> > > (i) shareable rights under a specified pension arrangement, or
> > > (ii) shareable state scheme rights,
> > > be subject to pension sharing for the benefit of the other party, and
> > (b) specifies the percentage value to be transferred.'

Note, therefore, certain features of this definition.

- The transfer must be expressed in percentage rather than (cf Scotland) cash terms (but that does not necessarily mean 50%/50%!).

- The pension arrangement must be named in the order.

- 'Shareable rights' are any rights under a pension arrangement (other than an excepted public service pension scheme) other than those specified by Regulations made by the Secretary of State for Social Security.[1]

- An excepted public service scheme refers only to the three Great Offices of State, ie the Prime Minister, the Lord Chancellor and the Speaker (because such pensions become payable immediately the holder leaves office and not at a future retirement age).[2] However, pension attachment orders could be made against these individuals.

- Rights specified by Regulations are widow's, widower's or dependant's benefits and equivalent pension benefits (EPBs) when those rights are the only rights held by a person under a pension scheme.[3]

- The basic State retirement pension cannot be shared; 'shareable state scheme rights' refers to SERPs/S2P. Where graduated pension rights are the only rights held by the person concerned, these may not be shared. The Graduated Pension Scheme was the predecessor to SERPs which began on 3 March 1961 and ended on 5 April 1975. Graduated pension rights which form part of SERPs/S2P may be shared.

3.2 When may a pension sharing order be made?

The power to make a pension sharing order is found in s 24B of MCA 1973 (inserted by Sch 3, para 4 of WRPA 1999), which provides:

---

[1] WRPA 1999, s 27(1) and (2).
[2] Pension Sharing (Exceptional Schemes) Order 2000, SI 2000/3088.
[3] Pension Sharing (Valuation) Regulations 2000, SI 2000/1052, reg 2.

'24B. – (1)   On granting a decree of divorce or a decree of nullity of marriage or at any time thereafter (whether before or after the decree is made absolute), the court may, on an application made under this section, make one or more pension sharing orders in relation to the marriage.'

3.3   When does the pension sharing order take effect?

The order does not take effect unless the decree on or after which it is made has been made absolute.[1] Further, a pension sharing order or a variation of a pension sharing order cannot take effect earlier than 7 days after the end of the period for filing notice of appeal against the order. The filing of a notice of appeal within time prevents the order taking effect before the appeal has been dealt with.[2]

It will be noted that the pension sharing annex (Form P1)[3] requires the practitioner to complete the date on which the pension sharing order will take effect.

It is not possible to make a deferred pension sharing order which will only take effect on the member's retirement because of the requirements imposed on pension schemes as to implementation: see **6.1**, step 12. For example, if H who is aged 60 has an occupational pension which is already in payment and W is aged 57, any pension sharing order made will bring about an immediate reduction in H's pension income but will not produce any immediate corresponding benefit to W until she attains age 60. In other words, an 'income gap' will arise. See further, **7.7**(e).

3.4   Pension sharing orders on variation applications

Someone who has the benefit of continuing periodical payments following divorce is able to apply for a (further) pension sharing order by way of capitalising that maintenance entitlement on a variation application (providing the periodical payments order is founded upon a petition for divorce/nullity issued on or after 1 December 2000).[4] A variation application does not, therefore, provide a backdoor route to retrospective pension sharing.[5] This course cannot, however, be taken against a pension that is already the subject of a pension sharing order in relation to that marriage or a pension attachment order.[6] Parties need to be aware of the potential danger that a capital clean break may not be as clean as it appears.

If a spouse has, for example, a series of personal pensions, can anything be done to reduce the risk of a later pension sharing order being made? The original consent order might contain a recital that the recipient of maintenance would not apply for any further pension sharing order in consideration of the pension sharing order(s) made on divorce. This would not be binding upon the court, but would have some evidential value. It might be possible to make a pension sharing order for a nominal percentage (but not 0%) as a form of future protection. However, consideration would need to be given to the potential costs involved. A further form of protection might be some form of pension attachment, eg in relation to death benefits under MCA 1973, s 25C. Beyond this, the party with pension rights must consider loading

---

[1]   MCA 1973, s 24B(2).
[2]   Ibid, s 24C; Divorce etc (Pensions) Regulations 2000, SI 2000/1123, reg 9.
[3]   See Appendix 5.
[4]   MCA 1973, s 31(7B)(ba) inserted by WRPA 1999, Sch 3, para 7(5); WRPA 1999, s 85(3)(b).
[5]   Cf lump sum/property adjustment orders made on variation applications: *Harris v Harris* [2001] 1 FCR 68, CA.
[6]   MCA 1973, s 24B(3)–(5). It is arguable that a specific dismissal of a pension sharing application could be construed as a pension sharing order, which would preclude a future application on a variation application.

post-divorce contributions into a pension arrangement which is already the subject of a pension sharing/attachment order because new arrangements would not enjoy the protection referred to above.

A party fearing a pension sharing order on a variation application might attempt to transfer an 'unprotected' pension into one which was already the subject of a pension sharing/attachment order. This course could be attacked under MCA 1973, s 37 (see **3.7**).

There may be a strategic advantage in delaying applying for a pension sharing order where a party is in receipt of periodical payments. The ability of the pension scheme member to increase substantially the value of his/her pension after divorce may contrast markedly with the earnings position of the potential transferee.

3.5   Pension sharing orders after overseas divorce

MFPA 1984, Part III conferred on the courts of England and Wales the power in certain circumstances to make orders for financial relief after a divorce granted in another jurisdiction. WRPA, Sch 12, paras 2–4 provides that the court may, after an overseas divorce, make an order corresponding to a pension sharing order. See further, **8.12**.

3.6   Changes to pension attachment (formerly 'earmarking')

(a)   Attachment after overseas divorce

The attachment provisions of MCA 1973, ss 25B–25D apply where the court is able to make orders for financial relief after a divorce granted in any other jurisdiction under MFPA 1984, Part III.[1]

(b)   Percentage orders

Attachment orders must express the amount of payment as a percentage.[2]

(c)   Directions to commute

MCA 1973, s 25B(7)[3] has been amended by WRPA 1999, Sch 4 so that, where there is a right of commutation under a pension arrangement, the order may require the person benefiting from the arrangement to exercise the right of commutation to any extent. Therefore, not only can the court direct a husband to commute, it is also able to direct commutation of, say, 50% of the available rights or that there be no commutation (eg where a wife wishes to depend upon a high level of attached periodical payments).

(d)   Attachment and pension sharing

An attachment order may not be made in relation to a pension arrangement which is the subject

---

[1]   WRPA 1999, s 22.

[2]   MCA 1973, s 25B(5) as inserted by WRPA 1999, s 21 and Sch 4.

[3]   This power may not be exercised for the purpose of commuting a benefit payable to the party with pension rights to a benefit payable to the other party (MCA 1973, s 25B(7A)). In other words, a direction to commute is parasitic upon the power to order an attached lump sum order and cannot create a separate benefit payable to the party without pension rights. The distinction should be noted between the use of the words 'payment for the benefit of the other party' in MCA 1973, s 25B(4) and 'payable to the other party' in MCA 1973, s 25B(7A).

of a pension sharing order.[1] The converse is also the case. In order for this restriction to apply, the prior pension sharing order must relate to the marriage in question. See **8.3**.

(e) Attachment and children

The opportunity was not seized in WRPA 1999 to remedy the lacuna in the legislation whereby no pension attachment order in relation to death benefits may be made under MCA 1973, s 25C for the benefit of a child of the family, although this appears to be what the court attempted to do in *Cordle v Cordle* [2002] 1 FLR 207, CA. This problem can only be addressed by means of an undertaking to the court in the preamble to a consent order.[2]

3.7 Avoidance of disposition orders

Pension sharing orders are within the categories of financial relief in respect of which an application may be made for an avoidance of disposition order.[3]

Examples of when such an order might be required might include the prevention of a transfer of a pension arrangement into a pension arrangement which is already subject to a prior pension attachment order (so as to prevent pension sharing) or into a pension arrangement in a foreign jurisdiction which would not cooperate with a pension sharing order made by a court in England and Wales (see **8.11**).

---

[1]   MCA 1973, ss 25B(7B)) and 5C(4).

[2]   Under some pension schemes (eg NHS), it is only possible to make a nomination in favour of a single person. Where the member wishes to protect a number of children, it will be necessary to undertake to make a nomination in favour of a newly created discretionary settlement.

[3]   MCA 1973, s 37 as amended by WRPA 1999, Sch 3, para 9.

4 THE INFORMATION YOU MUST HAVE: DISCLOSURE

4.1 The basic principles

In order to consider properly whether pension sharing is the most appropriate method of dealing with pensions on divorce, the parties and the court will require certain information, eg the value of accrued rights as well as details of the pension arrangement itself, including the arrangement's policy regarding charges and former spouse membership. It is essential that the parties – irrespective of whether pension sharing, attachment or offsetting is the eventual outcome – have access to this information as early as possible during the ancillary relief proceedings. It is also important that those responsible for pension arrangements have sufficient information in order to discharge their responsibilities where a pension sharing order is made, and that the parties are kept notified at key stages during the implementation period.

All requests for information *as to valuation* must be made by the member (and not the non-member spouse) under the Pensions on Divorce etc (Provision of Information) Regulations 2000, reg 2, but the court may intervene to order the provision of a valuation to a non-member spouse and may order a scheme to supply 'any other information relevant to any power with respect to the matters specified in WRPA, s 23(1)(a) [*financial relief under MCA 1973, Part II*]'.[1]

No request needs to be made where the member has an equivalent valuation under parallel subordinate legislation (see **7.3**(a)) within 12 months preceding the date of the first appointment.[2] However, conventional annual statements of CETV do not include the other information specified in the Pensions on Divorce (Provision of Information) Regulations 2000, although the member's spouse is in any event entitled to this information directly (see **4.2**).

If a scheme provides a cash equivalent valuation automatically every 12 months, eg on an annual benefits statement (in accordance with the Occupational Pension Schemes (Disclosure of Information) Regulations 1996,[3] an additional valuation within the 12-month period will incur a charge. Reliance upon the valuation supplied automatically will depend on the age of the valuation in question having regard to the effects of moving target syndrome (see **7.6**).

4.2 The information which must be supplied

Under the Pensions on Divorce etc (Provision of Information) Regulations 2000, reg 2, the pension scheme must provide:

- on request from the member:
  - a valuation of pension rights;
  - a statement summarising the way in which the valuation is calculated;
  - the pension benefits included in the valuation;

---

[1]   Pensions on Divorce etc (Provision of Information) Regulations 2000, SI 2000/1048, reg 2(4).
[2]   FPR 1991, r 2.70(4).
[3]   SI 1996/1655.

- whether the pension scheme intends to discharge liability for the pension credit other than by an internal transfer; and
- a schedule of charges;

- on request from the spouse of a member:
  - a statement that on request from the member (or pursuant to a court order) a valuation of pension rights will be provided to the member or, as the case may be, to the court;
  - a statement summarising the way in which the valuation is calculated;
  - the pension benefits included in the valuation;
  - whether the pension scheme offers an internal transfer and, if so, the types of benefit available;
  - whether the pension scheme intends to discharge liability for the pension credit other than by an internal transfer; and
  - a schedule of charges;

- pursuant to a court order:
  - any of the information which may be requested by the member or the member's spouse;
  - any other relevant information as indicated above.

4.3   Other information

There are other regulations requiring pension schemes to supply information to members (see **7.3**(a)), which information may be taken into account by the court.

4.4   Time-limits

Following a member's request or a court order, a valuation must be furnished:

- within 3 months beginning with the date the person responsible for the pension arrangement receives that request; or

- within 6 weeks of receiving the request, if notified that the proceedings have been commenced under the MCA 1973; or

- within such shorter period as is specified by a court order; or

- if the request for information does not include a valuation, the person responsible for the pension arrangement must furnish that information to the member, his spouse or the court (as the case may be) within one month beginning with the date of receiving the request or court order.[1]

4.5   State scheme rights

See **8.6** and **8.7**.

Use Forms BR19 and BR20: see **7.2**(h).

Similar provisions exist in relation to the provision of information regarding State scheme rights under the Sharing of State Scheme Rights (Provision of Information and Valuation) Regulations 2000.[2]

---

[1]   Pensions on Divorce etc (Provision of Information) Regulations 2000, SI 2000/1048, reg 2(5) and (6).
[2]   SI 2000/2914.

4.6 How to obtain the necessary information

It is insufficient for the party with pension rights simply to send to a pension provider section 2.16 of Form E requesting that this be completed. The reason for this is that section 2.16 is inconsistent with the information which the party with pension rights is required to request from a pension arrangement under FPR, r 2.70(2). A specimen letter to a pension arrangement setting out the information required in order to complete Form E and to comply with FPR, r 2.70(2) is shown at Appendix 2.

4.7 Charges

Pension providers will not be able to recover charges when a pension sharing order is made unless they provide the parties with a schedule of charges with the basic information required by the Pensions on Divorce etc (Provision of Information) Regulations 2000, reg 2. Further, a pension provider may not postpone implementation of the pension sharing order until its charges have been paid, unless it has given notice requiring charges to be paid in advance at a stage no later than in their response to the notification from the member that a pension sharing order may be made (see **6.1**: step 6). See generally, **11.1–11.2**.

5 IS PENSION SHARING APPROPRIATE?

5.1 Signposts as to whether pension sharing is the appropriate solution

Signposts for	Signposts against
Pension only/main resource: off-setting impossible.	Pension of comparatively small value such as not to justify costs of pension sharing: consider off-setting.
Party with pension rights seriously ill.	Young couple/short marriage: consider off-setting.
Where party with pension rights seeks to retain non-pension resources, eg the family home.	Party without pension rights likely to remarry or inherit: consider a pension attachment order, which is variable, unlike a pension sharing order, which is not.
Pension sharing order may enable a deferred clean break to be ordered using a non-extendable term maintenance order.	Foreign pension: foreign pension arrangement may not comply with pension sharing order **OR** pension fund may be accessible immediately to fund a conventional lump sum order.
Pension in payment: pension sharing will create a dependant's pension surviving the death of the transferor; attachment cannot.	Taxation: lump sum payable under a pension sharing order is tax-free; periodic pension payments are taxable at the payee's marginal rates. Contrast pension attachment: both a lump sum and periodical payments are tax free, although the attached periodical payments must be paid from the payer's net pension.
Party without pension rights aged over 50: pension benefits may be drawn immediately if required following a pension sharing order in certain circumstances.	Flexibility required to vary the order relating to pensions.
'Wait and see' approach: apply for a pension sharing order when varying periodical payments after divorce.	'Maintenance protection' required under MCA 1973, s 25C: a pension sharing order and an order under MCA 1973, s 25C may not be made against the same scheme.

5.2 Which remedy gives the most appropriate outcome?

(a) Off-setting

- Finality, if clean break.
- Enables pension member to rebuild without threat.
- 'Trade down' element in property.
- Combination of investment types (eg property +/ISAs +/endowment policies).

(b) Ongoing maintenance

- Variability.
- Non-member can benefit from later contributions to spouse's scheme.
- Member 'wins' if maintenance recipient remarries.
- Security problems on death of member spouse: term assurance +/death in service benefits.

(c) Pension attachment

- Variability.
- Security for maintenance before retirement (MCA 1973, s 25C).
- Availability of commutable lump sum.
- Uncertainty about retirement date.
- Death of member after retirement.
- Administrative difficulties between divorce and member's retirement.
- No power to attach pension income after member's death.
- Non-member can benefit from later contributions and growth.

(d) Pension sharing

- Changes take effect on divorce.
- Non-member acquires indefeasible rights unaffected by member's death or non-member's remarriage.
- More resources available to achieve clean break.
- Almost impossible to vary.
- Possible to have ongoing maintenance as well, perhaps with direction under MCA 1973, s 28(1A).
- No pension attachment under MCA 1973, s 25C.
- 'Wait and see' approach: apply for pension share when varying maintenance after divorce.
- Increase in *Mesher* orders.
- Possible death benefits for pension credit member.
- No need for either party to be kept informed of their former spouse's pension or marital status.
- Consistent with clean break objective of MCA 1973, s 25A.

6   PROCEDURE, VARIATIONS AND APPEALS

6.1   Procedure before and after a pension sharing order

Step	Action required	Source	Commentary
1	**Prayer in the petition** Include prayer for a pension sharing order in *petition* for divorce or nullity (even if only for dismissal purposes).	FPR 1991, r 2.53(1)	A prayer should be included if only for dismissal purposes. A dismissal will be required in a case where there are no shareable pension rights at the time of divorce so as to preclude the opportunity for one party to make application for a pension sharing order at a later stage. The prayer is the 'application' for the purposes of FPR 1991, r 2.70(1).
2	**Form A** Apply for a pension sharing order by notice in *Form A* specifying the terms of the order requested.	FPR 1991, r 2.61A(3)	It will usually only be possible to specify the terms of the order requested at the time of issuing a form where there has been voluntary disclosure. In this event, Form A might read: 'an order under the Matrimonial Causes Act 1973, s 24B (pension sharing) [*add pension attachment if required*] in relation to the Respondent's personal pension with Equitable Life Assurance Society policy number R1234567'. Where the information necessary to specify the terms of the order becomes subsequently available, it should be added as suggested by FPR 1991, r 2.70(6) to Form A, eg at the First Appointment.

3	**Service of Form A on pension arrangement** *Serve* copy of Form A on person responsible for the pension arrangement upon making an application for a pension sharing order or adding a request for a pension sharing order to an existing application.	FPR 1991, r 2.70(6)	If the details of the Respondent's pension arrangements are not available when Form A is served on the Respondent, thus precluding service upon the person responsible for the pension arrangement, it is recommended that the Applicant's solicitor should write to the Respondent or his/her solicitor requesting such information, putting them on notice as to costs in the event that the First Appointment cannot also be dealt with as an FDR in appropriate circumstances. Each pension arrangement potentially affected should be served including the DWP in the case of SERPs/S2P.
4	**Request for information from pension arrangement** Within 7 days of receiving notification of the date of the first appointment, the party with pension rights must *request* from each pension arrangement the *information* referred to in the Pensions on Divorce etc (Provision of Information) Regulations 2000, regs 2(2) and (3)(b)–(f), unless that party already has a valuation dated not earlier than 12 months prior to the date of the first appointment. Where a request for information has to be made, it does not relate solely to valuation but covers, eg, the availability of an internal transfer and charges. At this stage, the pension arrangement may choose to furnish the information referred to at step 6 below which must be given when Form A has been served.	FPR 1991, r 2.70(2), (4) and (5) Pensions on Divorce etc (Provision of Information) Regulations 2000, reg 2(7)	The duty arises regardless of whether Form A seeks a pension sharing or a pension attachment order. A party with pension rights may well choose to have available an up-to-date valuation because of 'moving target' syndrome (see **7.6**) even if this involves incurring an additional charge from the pension arrangement. If a party has a 'relevant valuation', it appears that there is no obligation to apply for the balance of basic information.

5	**Sending out of information to party without pension rights** Party with pension rights *sends information received to other party* together with the name and address of each pension arrangement within 7 days of receipt.	FPR 1991 , r 2.70(3)	The procedural duty to supply the relevant information regarding each pension arrangement necessary for service is only triggered by the receipt of information from the pension provider.
6	**Pre-order notification and information** Within 21 days of notification that a pension sharing order may be made, the pension arrangement must furnish certain information to the member, eg a prior attachment order, details of charges if not already supplied, whether the scheme is winding up, whether the trustees reserve the right to ask for information about a member's state of health and whether the trustees need further information about the divorcing couple before the implementation period can begin.	Pensions on Divorce etc (Provision of Information) Regulations 2000, regs 2(7) and 4	*Quaere*: Does 'notification' mean formal service of Form A or prior notification by letter?
7	**Supply of information by pension arrangement** Pension arrangement must *supply valuation* within 3 months of the request or (if needed in connection with proceedings) within 6 weeks (or such shorter period specified by the court). Where the request relates to information other than a valuation, the pension arrangement must supply that information within one month.	Pensions on Divorce etc (Provision of Information) Regulations 2000, reg 2(5)–(6)	Note the *'Heineken'* provision: the court can order the provision of 'any other information relevant to any power with respect to [ancillary relief claims under MCA 1973, Pt II]' (Pensions on Divorce etc (Provision of Information) Regulations 2000, reg 2(1)(c) and (4)).

8	**Form E** *Form E* should have attached to it any documents produced by the pension arrangement under FPR, r 2.70(2) or r 2.70(4).	FPR 1991, r 2.61B(3)(c)	Note the discrepancy between the information required by FPR 1991, r 2.70(2) and by Form E, para 2.16 (Appendix 8). It is essential that information is requested at the earliest opportunity (particularly with regard to SERPs/S2P) if documents are to be available by the date when Form E is to be filed. Where the information is not available, Form E should give the estimated date when it will be available and attach the letter to the pension arrangement and/or state the date Form BR20 was submitted.
9	**The pension sharing order and annex** The *pension sharing order* (whether by consent or not) must state that there is to be pension sharing in accordance with the *annex* or annexes to the order.	FPR 1991, r 2.70(13)–(14)	The annex sets out the information required by FPR 1991, r 2.70(14): use Practice Form P1 (Appendix 5). A separate annex is required for each pension arrangement. Does the pension sharing order include any appropriate dismissal (see step 1 and **9.2(b)**)?
10	**Action by court following making of pension sharing order** *Court sends* within 7 days of the making of the pension sharing order or of decree absolute (whichever is the later) *to pension arrangement*: • copy of decree nisi of divorce or nullity; • copy of decree absolute of divorce or nullity; • copy of pension sharing order and annex relating only to that pension arrangement.	FPR 1991, r 2.70(16)–(17)	The solicitor may wish to consider sending these documents to the pension arrangement so as to ensure the commencement of the implementation period (step 12). In any event, it will be the responsibility of the solicitor to ensure that the pension arrangement has the information prescribed by the Pensions on Divorce etc (Provision of Information) Regulations 2000, reg 5 so as to enable the implementation period to begin.

11	**Information required by pension provider** Before the trustees can implement the order, they need specific information about the parties including full names, addresses and national insurance numbers as well as information about the destination arrangement for the pension credit.	WRPA 1999, s 34(1)(b); Pensions on Divorce etc (Provision of Information) Regulations 2000, reg 5	
12	**Implementation period** Pension arrangement has 4 months in which to implement the pension sharing order beginning with the later of: (i) the date on which the order takes effect (see **3.3**); and (ii) the date on which the pension arrangement receives the relevant matrimonial documents (step 10) and the information required by the Pensions on Divorce etc (Provision of Information) Regulations 2000, reg 5 [information regarding the transferor and transferee] (step 11). The Occupational Pensions Regulatory Authority (OPRA) may extend the implementation period.	WRPA 1999, s 34(1) WPRA 1999, s 33(4); Pension Sharing (Implementation and Discharge of Liability) Regulations 2000, reg 3	Factors which may result in an extension of the implementation period include where the scheme is being wound up, is ceasing to be contracted out, has not been provided with information required to discharge liability for the pension credit, where the financial interests of the members generally will be prejudiced if the trustees implement the terms of the order within that period, or where there is a dispute as to the CETV for the purposes of WRPA 1999, s 29.

	Failure to implement within the specified time-limit may result in a civil penalty imposed by OPRA.	WRPA 1999, s 33(2)(b) and (3); Pension Sharing (Implementation and Discharge of Liability) Regulations 2000, reg 5	Up to £1,000 for an individual trustee; up to £10,000 for a corporate trustee.
13	**Regulation 7 notice** *Information after receiving pension sharing order*: within 21 days of receipt of the pension sharing order, the pension arrangement must provide the parties with a notice of charges and a list of personal information held (eg as to address). If the pension sharing order cannot be implemented, a statement to that effect must be supplied to the parties within 21 days of receipt of the pension sharing order. Alternatively, a notice of implementation must be given within 21 days of the commencement of the implementation period.	Pensions on Divorce etc (Provision of Information) Regulations 2000, reg 7	Diarise conclusion of implementation period.
14	**Notice of discharge of liability** By way of *information after implementation*, the pension arrangement must issue a notice of discharge of liability within 21 days of completing discharge of the liability in respect of the pension credit. The information required in the notice differs depending on whether, for example, the pension is in payment.	Pensions on Divorce etc (Provision of Information) Regulations 2000, reg 8	

15	**Default option** Where a member's occupational pension scheme does not wish to retain the former spouse's pension credit within the scheme and the former spouse has given no indication of the destination arrangement to which he/she wishes the credit to be transferred, the trustees may effect a transfer of the pension credit to a scheme of their choice.	WRPA 1999, s 35(1) and Sch 5; Pension Sharing (Implementation and Discharge of Liability) Regulations 2000, regs 7–9	See **8.14**.

The procedure for *pension attachment* orders is different. FPR 1991, r 2.70(7)–(12) inserts a procedural loop applicable only to pension attachment orders whereby the pension scheme can demand a copy of section 2.16 of Form E, file a statement in answer and be represented at the First Appointment. This is apparently because the onus on pension schemes is substantially greater in cases of pension attachment due to the deferred implementation process and the additional administrative demands. Curiously, FPR 1991, r 2.70(8) enables a person responsible for a pension arrangement upon whom notice of an application for a pension attachment order has been served to require the applicant to provide him with a copy of s 2.16 of *his* (ie the applicant's) Form E. This appears to be an ill-thought out hangover from the comparable provisions relating to mortgagees.

It should also be noted that there are conflicting time-limits where an application is made for a consent order for pension sharing/attachment.[1] In any event, FPR 1991, r 2.70(12) applies to pension attachment only. There is no corresponding provision relating to pension sharing save for the specific provisions in the Pensions on Divorce etc (Provision of Information) Regulations 2000, reg 4 (see step 6 above).

For further procedural requirements in connection with pension attachment, see also the Divorce etc (Pension) Regulations 2000, reg 4 (notices), reg 5 (reduction in benefits), reg 6 (change of circumstances), reg 7 (transfer of pension rights) and reg 8 (service).

---

[1]   FPR 1991, r 2.61(1)(dd) – objections to be made within 14 days of service of documents required for consent order; cf FPR 1991, r 2.70(12) – objections to be made within 21 days of service of documents required for consent order.

6.2   Consent applications

Step	Action required	Source	Commentary
1	**Notification to pension arrangement** Serve pension arrangement with proposed order.	FPR 1991, r 2.61(1)(dd)	FPR 1991, r 2.61(1)(dd) is wrongly drafted in that it cross-refers to FPR 1991, r 2.70(11) which only applies to pension attachment.
2	**File consent application** Assuming no objection is received from the pension arrangement within 14 days, lodge consent application, proposed order, relevant annex, Form M1 and reg 4 information [*see step 6 of the Procedural Table above*] at court.		Note the conflicting time periods for objections in FPR 1991, r 2.61(1)(dd) (14 days) and FPR 1991, r 2.70(12) (21 days). It is submitted that the latter does not apply to pension sharing. However, note the time-limit of 21 days under the Pensions on Divorce etc (Provision of Information) Regulations 2002, reg 4.

Form P1 (the pension sharing annex) indicates that, before making a pension sharing order, the court must be satisfied that the person responsible for the pension arrangement has furnished the information required by the Pensions on Divorce etc (Provision of Information) Regulations 2000, reg 4 and that in consequence there is power to make the pension sharing order. Regulation 4 requires information to be supplied by the person responsible for the pension arrangement as to, inter alia, possible obstacles in the face of the making of a pension sharing order, eg the winding up of the scheme or a prior pension attachment order. This information should be supplied by the person responsible for the pension arrangement within 21 days of being notified that a pension sharing order may be made.

The applicant's solicitor will, therefore, need to file at court with the application for a consent order the reg 4 information provided by the person responsible for the pension arrangement so that the court can be properly satisfied. The need for filing the actual information provided may in future be obviated by an amendment to Form M1 incorporating a certificate from the applicant's solicitor indicating that the reg 4 information has been provided and that there is in consequence power to make a pension sharing order.

It is important, therefore, to check that, after the pension arrangement has been served with Form A, it does comply with its obligations under reg 4 so that there is no delay in obtaining the consent order, which could have catastrophic consequences. Regulation 4 does, of course, also apply to pension sharing orders made after contested hearings.

6.3   Variation of pension sharing orders

A pension sharing order may not be varied after the decree has been made absolute. However, if the decree has not been made absolute and the pension sharing order has not, therefore, taken effect, a pension sharing order is now within the categories of orders capable of variation.[1]

---

[1]   MCA 1973, s 31(2)(g) as inserted by WRPA 1999, Sch 3, para 7.

An application to vary prevents the pension sharing order from taking effect before the application has been dealt with.[1] The court may only exercise the power to vary on an application made before the pension sharing order has taken effect and only if, at the time the application is made, the decree has not been made absolute.[2]

A pension sharing order may not be varied so as to take effect before decree absolute.[3]

6.4 Appeals against pension sharing orders

(a) Appeals: order not yet taken effect

Because of the nature of pension sharing orders, special provisions have been introduced to protect pension providers. The procedure for an appeal will depend upon whether or not the pension sharing order has taken effect. The court must stay all pension sharing orders for the period prescribed by the Divorce etc (Pensions) Regulations 2000, reg 9, which provides that a pension sharing order will not take effect earlier than 7 days after the end of the period for filing notice of appeal against the order. A pension sharing order may not be made so as to take effect before the end of this period.[4] No restrictions attach to such appeals and the Divorce on Pensions Regulations 2000, reg 9(2) provides that the order will not take effect until the appeal has been dealt with. It should also be borne in mind that a pension sharing order cannot in any event take effect until decree absolute.

(b) Appeals: order already taken effect

Where the order has already taken effect, the appeal will be out of time and the court will need to grant leave on the usual principles.[5] The special provisions contained in MCA 1973, s 40A (inserted by WRPA 1999, Sch 3, para 10) then apply.

- The appeal court may not set aside or vary the pension sharing order if the person responsible for a pension arrangement has acted to his detriment in reliance on the taking effect of the order.[6]

- There are similar provisions to protect the Secretary of State when the pension sharing order relates to a person's shareable State scheme rights.[7]

- When MCA 1973, s 40A(2) or (3) applies, the appeal court may make such further orders (including one or more pension sharing orders) as it thinks fit for the purpose of putting the parties into the position it considers appropriate.[8]

- Any pension sharing order made by an appeal court is subject to the same duty to stay pending the prescribed period except when the order of the appeal court is not itself subject to appeal (ie a pension sharing order made by the House of Lords).[9]

---

[1] MCA 1973, s 31(4A)(b).
[2] Ibid, s 31(4A).
[3] Ibid, s 31(4B).
[4] Ibid, s 24C(1) as inserted by WRPA 1999, s 19 and Sch 3.
[5] *Barder v Calouri* [1987] 2 FLR 480, HL.
[6] Ibid, s 40A(2).
[7] Ibid, s 40A(3).
[8] Ibid, s 40A(5).
[9] Ibid, s 40A(6).

7 VALUATION

7.1 What needs to be valued?

The member's and the spouse's rights need to be considered separately:

(a) *Spouse's rights* – in the event of death in service, a spouse will usually receive a lump sum possibly together with pension provision. In the event of death during retirement, a pension may be payable in full or at a reduced rate to the widow. The value of these rights, which will be lost upon divorce, form a proportion of the member's rights. The value of these rights may represent approximately 15%–20% of the total value of the pension scheme rights. The member may seek to argue that the value of these rights should be excluded where it could be shown that the husband is unlikely to remarry and would thus be unable to restart these benefits or where, unusually, the benefits will not restart in full on remarriage.

(b) *Member's rights* – on divorce, a spouse will lose the opportunity to enjoy the other spouse's pension and lump sum payable upon retirement.

7.2 What methods of valuation are available?

(a) Cash equivalent transfer value (CETV)

The CETV is the lump sum value in today's terms of the rights under a pension scheme which have accrued to date to the scheme member, as measured by the amount which would be available in the event of a transfer being made to an alternative pension arrangement were the member to leave service. The CETV is a statutory valuation, which does not take account of past service reserves (see (f) below) contained in defined benefit schemes, which are intended to take account of a member's salary increases.

(b) Included in CETV

- the member's retirement pension;
- the lump sum payable on death after leaving active scheme membership, but before retirement;
- the lump sum payable on retirement;
- the lump sum payable on death after retirement; and
- the spouse's pension payable on either the member's death after leaving active scheme membership but before retirement or after the member's retirement.

(c) Excluded from CETV

- death in service benefits (which in a final salary scheme are met by insurance and in a money purchase scheme by reserves in the fund at large); and

- future expectations based upon future salary increases and future pensionable service.

(d) Discretionary benefits

Discretionary benefits (which usually relate to generous early retirement terms or increases in pensions in payment) may be included in some schemes.

(e) CETV – but which CETV?

Great reliance is placed upon the CETV. But consider the following:

- Is it mathematically correct or negotiable?

- Certain pension schemes may be over-funded (eg British Coal). Recalculating the CETV may be necessary in the light of the surplus.

- Is the CETV calculated on the basis that the married member is single?

- Does the CETV reflect the availability of a guaranteed annuity rate?

- Has a market value adjuster (MVA) been applied?

- Is there any terminal bonus or demutualisation windfall?

- Does the quoted value of a personal pension include any compensation paid for mis-selling? When it became possible to transfer out of occupational pension schemes in 1988, many members misguidedly took this option and transferred into personal pensions, as a result of which they have mounted successful claims for compensation for mis-selling. The Code of Practice of the Securities and Investment Board indicates that such compensation should be paid into the personal pension (rather than as cash), if the member cannot be reinstated in the occupational scheme. It may, therefore, be worth checking whether any unresolved claim for compensation remains pending.

The CETV is the prescribed valuation methodology under the Pensions on Divorce etc (Provision of Information) Regulations 2000, reg 3. The basis for the calculation is found in a Guidance Note issued by the Institute and Faculty of Actuaries known as GN11 (Retirement Benefit Schemes – Transfer Values). Much is left to the discretion of the individual actuary and two actuaries can reach differing figures within GN11. The Pensions Act 1995 introduced a statutory minimum for cash equivalents based on the Minimum Funding Requirement (MFR). It is this statutory minimum which most actuaries adopt, even though it was meant to be an under-pinning mechanism. Most of the difficulties encountered in the usage of the CETV in pension sharing arise out of the fact that it is being used for a purpose for which it was not originally intended.

There are a number of reasons why the CETV may not present an appropriate measure of value of pension benefits in pension sharing. There may be a simple mathematical error in the calculations, which are often performed by trainee actuaries either using computer programs or manually using a proforma approved by the scheme actuary. Under the Pensions on Divorce etc (Provision of Information) Regulations 2000, reg 2(3)(b), the pension provider must provide, *inter alia*, details as to the way in which the CETV has been calculated. If workings are supplied, they may then be checked for mathematical accuracy.

In a final salary scheme, the CETV allows for revaluation on the leaving service pension by providing in broad terms increases in line with RPI up to 5% per annum. Given that earnings are generally expected to grow at a faster rate than RPI, a younger member of a pension scheme, who is expected to remain in service until retirement age, will find that his pension has been significantly undervalued.

Trustees are able to direct the scheme actuary not to include any allowance for discretionary benefits in the CETV. The discretionary benefits most commonly encountered are increases to pensions in payment and generous early retirement provisions. Ignoring such discretionary benefits can lead to a significant artificial reduction in the CETV.[1]

The effect of taxation is ignored in the calculation of the CETV and in consequence overstates the value to members close to or in retirement and understates the value for younger members. The CETV based on 'average' life expectancy will not take into account the state of the member's health. If the member is in poor health, the CETV will overstate the value of the pension.

Where a scheme is underfunded, the trustees have power to reduce the CETV so as to protect members who do not transfer out. Underfunded schemes are required to put in place a Schedule of Contributions which is expected to ensure the scheme will become fully funded on the MFR basis. The quoted CETV may not, therefore, reflect the full value if a scheme is underfunded. Conversely, a scheme may be overfunded where it is being wound up and there is a surplus. In this situation, it is likely that members' benefits will be enhanced to reflect a share of the surplus. However, any potential enhancement is unlikely to be reflected in the CETV.

Pension schemes usually provide benefits to spouses in the event of the member's death. Most schemes calculate a CETV, which is independent of marital status. However, some schemes (eg NHS) take into account marital status in calculating a CETV and, when supplying the CETV for the purposes of pension sharing on divorce, will base the CETV on the member's prospective status as a single person. The quoted CETV will artificially not include widow's benefits. Alternatively, in some unfunded public sector pension schemes (eg the Armed Forces), while the CETV does take account of the widow's benefits, it is calculated on the lower basis of the widow's pension applicable on the member's remarriage.

The above comments relate to final salary or defined benefit pension schemes. The treatment of money purchase or defined contribution schemes is much more straightforward, the cash equivalent being the value of the member's account. However, there are potential pitfalls even in this area. Valuations of with-profit arrangements may not include an allowance for accrued or terminal bonuses or the special bonuses arising by way of a windfall following demutualisation. Guaranteed annuity rates, which are offered by several providers other than Equitable Life, are unlikely to be reflected in the valuation supplied by the provider. Further, a market value adjuster (MVA) may have been applied in calculating the transfer value of a with-profits policy.

In view of the large element of discretion available to a scheme actuary in a final salary scheme over the CETV, the figure may be negotiable by instructing an actuary where this is proportionate to the size of the CETV in question. With all types of pensions, circumstances

---

[1] A CETV prepared for divorce purposes under the NHS scheme assumes that the member is single, but makes some allowance for the fact that he may have remarried by retirement.

may arise, as outlined above, where it may be appropriate for an actuary to calculate the realistic CETV, which is to be shared. The pension sharing order/annex must then express the chosen percentage of the realistic revalued CETV as a percentage of the original CETV.

(f)   Past Service Reserve

This method of valuation takes account of the fact that final salary schemes contain reserves designed to cover salary increases which reflect inflation as well as career progression. The Past Service Reserve will usually give a higher figure than the CETV. There is no legal right to request pension scheme trustees to provide such a valuation, which needs to be carried out on an individual basis with consequent costs implications. This method of valuation does not follow the approach adopted in *H v H*[1] (see **7.4**(b)).

(g)   Fund value

This method of valuation values the member's share of the fund and may be useful where the scheme involved is a SSAS. It assesses the value on an actuarial basis of the entitlement of a member if the fund were wound up, including any surpluses or deficits. The fund value may be higher than the CETV or Past Service Reserve where there is a surplus (or lower, where there is a deficit).

(h)   Valuation of State scheme rights

The relevant regulations are the Sharing of State Scheme Rights (Provision of Information and Valuation) Regulations 2000.

It is possible to obtain a retirement benefit forecast by submitting Form BR19 to the Benefits Agency, RPFA Unit, Pensions and Overseas Benefit Directorate, Newcastle upon Tyne, NE98 1YX earlier than 4 months prior to State retirement age. The forecast will provide:

- the amount of *basic pension* already earned;

- the amount of the projected *basic pension* payable at State retirement age based on contributions already made and likely future contributions;

- the amount of *SERPs/S2P* already earned;

- the amount of projected *SERPs/S2P* payable at State retirement age based on contributions already made and likely future contributions;

- in the case of a *divorced woman*, the amount of pension payable using a former spouse's NI contributions, if this will give a better pension.

By submitting Form BR20 to the Benefits Agency, RPFA Unit, Pensions and Overseas Benefit Directorate, Newcastle upon Tyne, NE98 1YX, it is possible to obtain a lump sum valuation of SERPs/S2P.

(i)   Valuation of lost widow's pension (At a Glance (2002–2003) (FLBA) Table 18)

This table enables the value of lost widow's rights to be calculated. The Divorce etc (Pensions) Regulations 1996,[2] reg 5, formerly imposed an obligation on pension schemes to specify what proportion of the CETV was attributable to the pension to which a spouse of the member would

---

[1]   [1993] 2 FLR 335.
[2]   SI 1996/1676.

be or might become entitled in the event of the member's death. This obligation is not preserved by the Divorce etc (Pensions) Regulations 2000.[1] It should be emphasised that it is not a full valuation exercise in that it does not take into account the wife's opportunity to enjoy the member's pension and lump sum (see **7.1**(b)) and, furthermore, it is computed on the basis that the husband's pension rights will continue to accrue beyond divorce until his retirement, which is a fundamentally different approach from the CETV which assumes that pensionable service ceases at the valuation date. It may, however, be argued that MCA 1973, s 25B(1)(b) requires consideration of the potential loss on the basis that reckonable service continues to normal retirement date.

(j)   Benefit projections

Benefit projections give an estimate of what the member (or his widow) will be entitled to when he takes his pension benefits.

Accrued benefit projections assume that no further contributions are made to the scheme, or in the case of a final salary scheme, no further years of service are added.

Future years/contributions projections assume that the member continues to contribute at the same level as he has in the past, or in the case of a final salary scheme, works until normal retirement age.

Beyond those broad categories, the assumptions which can be used are so varied that the projection becomes art rather than science, particularly for personal pension schemes where there are numerous alternative ways in which benefits can be taken and the member can therefore manipulate the end result. Various assumptions may affect the figures:

- the assumed rate of growth of investments;

- the retirement date chosen;

- whether a pension will escalate in payment or remain static;

- whether survivors' benefits are chosen;

- whether the member elects to commute a lump sum or take the maximum pension;

- whether a guaranteed pension is paid for a period of years after a member's death in retirement;

- whether an allowance is made for inflation so that projections are expressed at 'present date' values;

Projections cannot therefore be taken at face value.

Although they are no more than estimates, they will be necessary in cases where the pension could come into payment in the near future, and in other cases to give an indication of the real value to the member of his potential benefits.

(k)   Statement of death in service benefits

Too often overlooked, the benefits available in the event of the member's death before drawing benefits may not be included in the valuations referred to above. A separate statement of those benefits is required to complete Form E.

---

[1]   SI 2000/1123.

(l)   *Early leavers*

A pension sharing order may not be made where the member does not have a CETV because he/she has less than 2 years' qualifying service and does not, therefore, have a deferred pension entitlement. The member will usually have been entitled to repayment of contributions.

7.3   What do the regulations say?

(a)   *The prescribed valuation methodology*

The Divorce etc (Pensions) Regulations 2000, reg 3, which is subheaded valuation, simply cross-refers to the Pensions on Divorce etc (Provision of Information) Regulations 2000, reg 3 for the calculation and verification of pension benefits. This latter regulation provides for the CETV to be the prescribed method of valuation, even if the pension is in payment. The regulation provides that '... the valuation of benefits under a pension arrangement shall be calculated and verified ... in accordance with [the CETV]'. This methodology ensures that benefits to date are only taken into account on the assumption that the employee's service terminates at the valuation date. Thus, no account is taken of future service.

Where a pension is in payment, the valuation is, strictly speaking, referred to as the cash equivalent of benefits (CEB).[1]

In determining the CETV, the court may have regard to information furnished by the pension arrangement under a number of provisions (Divorce etc (Pensions) Regulations 2000, reg 3(1)(b)):

- Pensions on Divorce etc (Provision of Information) Regulations 2000;

- Occupational Pension Schemes (Disclosure of Information) Regulations 1996, SI 1996/1655, reg 5 and Sch 2 (or the Personal Pension Schemes (Disclosure of Information) Regulations 1987, SI 1987/1110); and Occupational Pension Schemes (Transfer Value) Regulations 1996, reg 11 and Sch 1 (*information to be made available to members*);

- Pension Schemes Act 1993, ss 93A or 94(1)(a) or (aa) (*right to statement of entitlement/CETV*);

- Pension Schemes Act 1993, s 94(1)(b) or the Personal Pension Schemes (Disclosure of Information) Regulations 1987, Sch 2, para 2(a) (or, where applicable, 2(b)) (*information to be made available to individuals*).

(b)   *The valuation date*

The Divorce etc (Pensions) Regulations 2000, reg 3(1)(a) provides for the court to specify in the pension sharing order a valuation day being no earlier than one year before the date of the petition and no later than the date on which the court exercises its power. In specifying the valuation day, the court may have regard to the date specified in any information furnished to it under the Divorce etc (Pensions) Regulations 2000, reg 3(1)(b) (see (a) above). Therefore, in practical terms, the court will usually specify the date of the CETV being used.

If there has been a period of separation predating the pension sharing order which exceeds a period of one year, the court can only give effect to this (if considered appropriate) by adjusting the percentage pension share ordered.

---

[1]   Pensions on Divorce etc (Provision of Information) Regulations 2002, regs 3(1)(d) and (7)–(9).

It should be noted that the Pension Sharing (Valuation) Regulations 2000 deal with valuation in the context of the implementation of pension sharing orders, for which purpose there is a separate valuation day chosen by the pension arrangement within the implementation period of the pension sharing order.[1]

See further, **7.6** (moving target syndrome).

(c) When does the CETV not apply?

The CETV will not apply to:

- benefits not within the CETV: see **7.2**(c) above;

- pensions administered outside the UK;

- unfunded unapproved retirement benefit schemes (UURBS).

7.4 What do the cases say?

(a) Introduction

There is still a dearth of case-law relating to the valuation of pension rights within ancillary relief applications. There is no decision of the High Court or above giving *direct* guidance on how the CETV should be applied by the courts.

(b) H v H[2]

Facts:

H and W were 39 and 42 respectively. H was a doctor and had 13 years' membership of the NHS pension scheme. W's solicitors obtained an accountant's report of projected future pension benefits prepared on the basis that H remained in employment, became a consultant in 4 years' time and continued to work until he was 60 or 65.

Decision:[3]

> '... in deciding what weight to give to pension rights it is more important in this case to look at the value of what has been earned during cohabitation than to look at the prospective value of what may be earned over the course of the 25 or 30 years between separation and retirement age.'

This decision was, of course, made before the coming into force on 1 August 1996 of the Divorce etc (Pensions) Regulations 1996, whereby a prescribed valuation methodology was introduced for the first time. It may still be thought to offer some useful *indirect* guidance in determining how the court should approach the use of the CETV.

(c) T v T[4]

This decision[5] offers general guidance on the operation of earmarking/attachment. In the course of his judgment, Singer J offered the following guidance on valuation (in circumstances where no CETVs were available):

---

[1] WRPA 1999, s 29(7).
[2] [1993] 2 FLR 335, *per* Thorpe J (as he then was).
[3] Ibid, at p 344.
[4] [1998] 1 FLR 1072, *per* Singer J.
[5] Along with *Burrow v Burrow* [1999] 1 FLR 508, *per* Cazalet J.

'I am satisfied (and fortified by the evidence of the actuaries) that the CETV would have been of no assistance in this case.

…

I should perhaps emphasise that these values are at best a guide, and their apparent precision (down to the nearest pound) is illusory, and the product of mathematical rather than predictive accuracy. For they necessarily incorporate various assumptions (as to the rate of future inflation before and after the pension commences in payment; an appropriate discount rate reflecting the tax-exempt environment (currently) enjoyed by the pension fund; and of course that ultimately unpredictable factor, mortality) … Thus (as has been said of a *Duxbury* fund) the only fact which can be predicted with absolute accuracy is that the prediction will turn out to be inaccurate. These figures are, therefore, at best and when it is appropriate to have to regard to them at all, a guide rather than a rule.'[1]

(d) Cowan v Cowan[2]

Note the *dicta* of Thorpe LJ (at para 69):

'… the special characteristics of the pension funds held by the husband and the wife respectively require recognition. The husband's fund is all vested and is no more and no less than a whole life fixed rate income stream. The fact that it would cost £1.19m to purchase an identical income stream allows a capitalisation for comparative purposes. But it is not truly comparable with a cash fund of £1.19m for the obvious reason that the latter is replete with options as to deployment, investment, and spending, as well as having the capacity to survive intact the owner's demise.'

(e) Maskell v Maskell[3]

Thorpe LJ developed his theme on valuation in *Cowan* in circumstances where the asset base was much smaller, the main asset being a pension with a CETV of £40,000. He held (at para 6):

'… the judge [in the court below] is making the seemingly somewhat elementary mistake of confusing present capital with the right to financial benefits on retirement, only 25% of which maximum could be taken in capital terms, the other 75% being taken as an annuity stream. He simply failed to compare like with like.'

(f) S v S (Financial Provision: Departing from Equality)[4]

The court was invited to find that H's pension fund, being the largest single part of the assets, took the case outside *White*. However, it was held that the court could not differentiate between assets in relation to their value: 'assets are assets'.

7.5 Should the court admit other evidence of valuation?

(a) Introduction

When provided with the CETV, the court must decide what use can be made of this evidence. On the one hand, the CETV cannot be treated as realisable capital, but on the other, pensions need to be viewed in the overall context of the parties' resources. Form E recognises the special status accorded to pensions by showing the total value of net assets both including and excluding pensions. Further, Form E departs from the strict methodology of the CETV by

---

[1]   *T v T* [1998] 1 FLR 1072, at pp 1077 and 1079.
[2]   [2001] 2 FLR 192, CA.
[3]   [2001] 3 FCR 296, CA. See also da Costa 'Pensions – The Maskell Approach' [2002] Fam Law 848. It is, however, submitted that the approach of only having regard to the capital element of the CETV should be approached with caution.
[4]   [2001] 2 FLR 246, Mr Peter Collier QC sitting as a deputy judge of the High Court.

requiring certain additional information, for example, 'the estimated lump sum and monthly pension payable upon retirement'. To a major extent, the usefulness of – and thus the willingness of the court to admit – other evidence of valuation will turn upon the nature of the remedy sought.

(b) Remedy sought

(i) Off-setting

It has been suggested that the calculation of an off-set can be viewed as an algebraic process to be applied to the CETV.[1] This could be viewed as an extension of the principle established in *H v H*. However, such a mathematical approach may be said to be at variance with the discretionary approach adopted in general terms in relation to family resources. It has, nonetheless, to be recognised that off-setting represents an accelerated benefit to a (wife) from liquid assets and this approach may offer some guidance as a flexible starting point.

(ii) Pension attachment

Pension attachment is by its very nature a deferred remedy. The court may, therefore, find the CETV in isolation singularly unhelpful. In order to make any meaningful order following a contested hearing, the court will need to have sight of projections of benefits payable upon retirement, usually from the pension provider, based on no further contributions being made into the scheme. Projections will not inevitably be prepared on this basis. It must always be borne in mind that all forms of attachment (including attached lump sum orders) are capable of variation.

(iii) Pension sharing

Here, the essential issue for the court to determine is what is the appropriate percentage to be applied to the CETV so as to create a pension credit for the recipient party without pension rights. The court will really need to know what pension benefits will be acquired by the party without pension rights with a pension credit of x%. This approach does not undermine the CETV as the prescribed valuation methodology, but rather invokes a second stage in the pension sharing process. It will be necessary for the person with the benefit of the pension credit in any event to consider whether he/she should take an internal or external transfer (where available) and (in the event of an external transfer) to consider the appropriate destination arrangement. The second stage indicated simply accelerates consideration of the likely benefits arising from the pension credit so as to become part of the determination process. Similarly, the member may seek to adduce evidence of the effect of the pension debit upon his future pension. This evidence should usually be available through the pension provider (in the case of an internal transfer) or through an independent financial adviser (in the case of an external transfer) rather than incurring the additional costs of instructing an actuary. Pension sharing does not have the benefit of the safety net of the variation jurisdiction enjoyed by pension attachment.

---

[1]   Burrows 'Pensions – How Much to Offset' [1999] Fam Law 556.

(c)   Summary paper: The provisions of Regulations under s 166 of the Pensions Act 1995 issued by Family Policy Division, Lord Chancellor's Department (June 1996)

The summary paper was issued to give guidance on the earmarking provisions of the Pensions Act 1995, s 166 and the Divorce etc (Pensions) Regulations 1996. To some extent, the paper is, therefore, superseded by the repeal of the 1996 Regulations and their replacement by the Divorce etc (Pensions) Regulations 2000. However, paras 14–16 of the paper, which relate to valuation, still offer useful guidance:

'Use of other methods of valuation

14   In so far as pension rights accrued up to the time when the court considers financial provision on divorce are concerned, the divorcing parties will not be permitted to use any method of valuation other than the prescribed methods. It would, however, be open to them to dispute whether the prescribed method had been correctly applied.

15   The Regulations [the Divorce etc (Pensions) Regulations 1996] will not prevent the parties providing further information as to the expectation of the pension, and will not prevent the court from taking account of that information in circumstances where it deems the Cash Equivalent Transfer Value method of valuation provides an inappropriate or inadequate indication.

16   The prescribed method cannot be used for discretionary benefits not included in the CETV or pensions administered outside England and Wales. Regulations cannot, therefore, bar other methods of valuing such pension benefits.'

(d)   Headquarters Policy Group of the Department of Social Security

The Headquarters Policy Group of the DSS set out their position on 31 August 1999 as follows:

'... it is the policy intention that in determining what is a fair split of the matrimonial assets, the Court should be able to consider other evidence in relation to the pension rights ... in addition to the Cash Equivalent Transfer Value.

... the extra evidence might persuade the court, for example, that a 50:50 split was inappropriate and that the party without pension rights should, in the interests of fairness, receive a higher proportion of the other assets.'

(e)   Family Proceedings Rules 1991

(i)   Rule 2.51B: the overriding objective

'The court must deal with the case justly by ... ensuring that the parties are on an equal footing and dealing with the case in ways which are proportionate to the amount of money involved ... to the complexity of the issues and as to the financial position of each party.'

(ii)   Rule 2.61C: expert evidence

This rule applies CPR 1998, rr 35.1–35.14 (expert evidence) (excepting CPR 1998, rr 35.5(2) and 35.8(4)(b)) to ancillary relief proceedings. Expert evidence (whether written or oral) will not be allowed unless permission has been given.[1] Permission will not be given unless the evidence is reasonably required[2] and justified in the light of the overriding objective. A joint report from a single expert will be the norm (see, however, **7.5**(g)). If the parties have not agreed on whom

---

[1]   CPR 1998, r 35.4.

[2]   Ibid, r 35.1.

should be appointed, then they must be in a position on the First Appointment or when the matter comes to be considered by the court to provide the court with a list of suitable experts or to make submissions as to the method by which the expert is to be selected.[1]

The court might make a direction in the following form:

'The parties do jointly instruct an expert [♦] to prepare a report showing the effect upon each of the parties of a pension sharing order of the following percentages, namely, x%, y% and z% made in relation to the [applicant]/[respondent]'s pension with [♦]. A letter of joint instruction shall be delivered to the expert by 4 pm on [♦] and his report shall be filed and served by 4 pm on [♦].'

(f) Human Rights Act 1998: a footnote

Might it be argued that the Pensions on Divorce etc (Provision of Information) Regulations 2000, reg 3, falls foul of Article 6 of the European Convention on Human Rights and Fundamental Freedoms 1950 (ECHR) (right to a fair trial) in so far as it seeks to restrict the evidence which may be put before the court? It seems likely that such arguments will be given short shrift following the Court of Appeal's decision in *Daniels v Walker.*[2] Lord Woolf MR held that it was essential that advisers took a responsible attitude as to when it was right to raise a point under the Human Rights Act 1998. It would be unfortunate if case management decisions involve the need to refer to human rights issues. Courts would be robust to resist any attempt to introduce such arguments. The issues may be determined by applying the overriding objective.

(g) More than one expert?

It may in any event be possible, as in *Daniels v Walker*, to persuade the court that a party should be permitted to call a further expert.[3]

7.6 Moving target syndrome

The Divorce etc (Pensions) Regulations 2000, reg 3 provides that the court is to carry out its valuation exercise at a date to be specified by the court, being not earlier than one year before the date of the petition and not later than the date of the court order. This is the date inserted in the annex to the pension sharing order. It will be the date of the CETV used by the court at the hearing for evidential purposes or by the parties in negotiations. The use of this date in Form P1 is misleading and may well be omitted in a redraft because WRPA 1999, s 29(2) goes on to provide that the pension debit and pension credit are the specified percentage in the order calculated on the 'valuation day', which in turn is defined by s 29(7) as being 'such day within the implementation period ... as the person responsible for the relevant arrangement may specify by notice in writing to the transferor and transferee'. This is a second later date used solely for implementation purposes, which must by definition postdate the pension sharing order because the implementation period is defined by the WRPA 1999, s 34(1) as being the 4-month period beginning with the later of the day on which the pension sharing order takes effect (the date of decree absolute or, if later, 21 days from the date of the pension sharing order)

---

[1] *President's Practice Direction 25 May 2000* [2000] 1 FLR 997, para 4.1.

[2] [2000] 1 WLR 1382 (ability to obtain a further expert's report where a party was dissatisfied with the report of a jointly instructed expert).

[3] See *Cosgrove v Pattison* [2001] CP Rep 68, Neuberger J, which sets out a non-exhaustive list of the factors to be taken into account by the court when considering such an application, including the amount at stake and any delay occasioned by instructing and calling the new expert.

and the first day on which the pension arrangement receives the relevant pension sharing documentation.

An example may assist in highlighting this particular pitfall. A petition for divorce is issued by W on 1 December 2000. On 14 November 2001, the court makes a pension sharing order in favour of W for 50% of the CETV of £100,000 as at (the reg 3 date of) 25 February 2000. The order is served on the pension arrangement and the implementation period begins. The arrangement specifies under WRPA 1999, s 29(7) that it has chosen 25 February 2002 as the valuation day. By 25 February 2002, the CETV has increased to £120,000. W therefore acquires a pension credit of £60,000 rather than £50,000.

To some degree, because the pension sharing annex must specify a percentage, the parties must share the benefit or the pain if there is a significant change in value between the two dates. However, particular pitfalls may arise where the court adopts an ancient date for the purposes of reg 3, eg where there has been a considerable time lapse between the date of the petition and the final ancillary relief hearing[1] or where the pensioner has several pension arrangements so that comparative valuation issues arise. Further pitfalls may arise in schemes where the asset base is volatile (eg a SSAS or a SIPP), where there are multiple funds within one scheme (eg a personal pension plan invested in a series of managed funds, some but not all of which perform well in the period between the court chosen valuation date and the scheme chosen valuation day) or where, in a final salary scheme, there is a salary increase.

A possible solution might be to adopt the following formula:

> 'whatever percentage (not being greater than 100%) shall yield a transfer of £x at the valuation day specified by the person responsible for [relevant arrangement] for the purposes of the Welfare Reform and Pensions Act 1999, s 29.'

The formula creates certainty, but to the potential detriment of one or other of the parties. Some courts have indicated their willingness to accept the formula, although it will be necessary to obtain the prior approval of the pension provider to its use. Others have shown a disinclination to do so on the ground that it represents an attempt to outflank the express requirements of MCA 1973, s 21A(1) to specify a percentage value. If the pension provider will not accept the formula, it is possible by consent for the parties to make an adjustment in cash terms – by what is a form of off-setting – under cross-undertakings in the preamble to a consent order. The amount of the adjustment, which presupposes the availability of requisite assets, will be the difference in cash value of the specified percentage between the reg 3 date and the s 29(7) date.

Another possible solution to this syndrome may be, in certain circumstances where this is possible, to switch funds which may be volatile into a safer environment (ie cash) during the period between the date of the agreement/order fixing the percentage to be shared and the actual date notified by the pension arrangement under s 29(7). This solution can only be achieved by consent, as the instruction has to come from the person with pension rights, and will require specialist advice from an independent financial adviser.

Further complications have been that some pension schemes have seen fit to attempt to implement a pension sharing order by reference to the date specified in Form P1, even though this date cannot by definition fall within the implementation period for the purposes of WRPA 1999, s 29(2), and that some courts have approved orders specifically referring to percentages of the evidential valuation referred to in the pension sharing annex.

---

[1]   Consider also the problems arising where there is a delay, first, in converting a mediated agreement into a consent order and, secondly, implementing that agreement.

Section 29 also introduces the concept of 'relevant benefits': under s 29(2), it is the specified percentage of the cash equivalent of the 'relevant benefits' on the valuation day which form the basis of the pension debit and pension credit. Under an occupational pension scheme where the transferor is in pensionable service, the 'relevant benefits' are the benefits or future benefits to which the transferor would be entitled had his pensionable service terminated immediately before the day on which the order took effect (which date is known as the 'transfer day').[1] In other circumstances, the 'relevant benefits' are the benefits or future benefits to which, immediately before the transfer day, the transferor is entitled under the terms of the relevant arrangement.[2]

7.7 What other factors are relevant to valuation?

(a) Sex

An equal division of a pension by way of pension sharing does not create equality because of the different actuarial assumptions applied to the sexes. For example, assume H and W are both aged 50. A pension sharing order is made for 50% of the CETV in favour of W, giving each party a fund of £75,000. Assuming growth at 7% net per annum and the purchase of an annuity at age 60, their gross incomes might then be as follows:

	Husband	*Wife*
Level (ie non-escalating) income	£5,900 pa	£5,200 pa
or		
RPI linked income	£4,300 pa	£3,600 pa

(b) Life expectancy

The life expectancy of the member will affect actuarial calculations. Where the life expectancy of the member is impaired, the spouse's interest will be greater.

(c) Ages of the parties

Similarly, actuarial calculations can be affected by the difference in the ages of the parties. Where a wife is much younger, her interest could be greater.

(d) Date of separation

It may be that the divorce follows a lengthy period of separation during which one party has accrued substantial pension rights. It follows from the rationale of *H v H* (see **7.4**(b)) that the relevant contributions/accrued rights are those attaching to cohabitation within marriage. The court may, therefore, be left to factor the period of separation into the percentage pension share ordered.

(e) Uniformed services

The uniformed services are the police, the armed forces, the fire service and prison officers whose service started before November 1987. The common feature of these schemes is that the

---

[1] WRPA 1999, s 29(4).
[2] Ibid, s 29(5).

retirement age is different according to whether the member stays in service until retirement or leaves service before retirement. Depending on circumstances (length of service and, in the case of the armed forces, rank), members of the armed forces can retire from age 40, the police and the fire service from age 50 and prison officers referred to above and certain members of the NHS from age 55. For example, a police officer can retire with an unreduced pension at age 50 providing he/she has 25 years' service (or before age 50 if he/she has 30 years' service). If, however, he/she leaves service before age 50 (without 30 years' service), he/she will receive a deferred pension commencing at age 60.

A CETV is calculated as if the member were leaving service on the date of calculation. Therefore, in the above example, the police officer's CETV would be calculated on the basis of retirement at age 60, which would be a significant underestimate of its true value if the officer concerned is still in service. An actuarial valuation for divorce purposes will be based on the actual expected retirement age. The wife's pension share based upon an actuarial valuation will then need to be expressed as a percentage of the quoted CETV, as already mentioned. The husband is not prejudiced because his pension debit is actuarially adjusted to reflect the fact that he has retired as expected prior to age 60.

What the court cannot do to resolve this problem is to make a deferred pension sharing order (see **3.3**). If early retirement is proximate, consideration may be given to adjourning the application for a pension sharing order. Alternatively, a 100% pension sharing order of the quoted (reduced) CETV might be combined with some measure of off-setting in order to achieve fairness.

A further problem which may be encountered with the armed forces is that a CETV may be prepared for divorce purposes which takes into account the widow's benefits, but the calculation is prepared on the lower basis of the widow's pension applicable on the member's remarriage (see **7.2**(e)).

7.8   Conclusion

The starting point for the court, where a pension sharing order is to be made, must be the CETV, which represents the prescribed valuation methodology. Because pensions must be seen within the overall context of the parties' other resources and a general application of MCA 1973, s 25, the court will wish to consider the other factors referred to in **7.7** above as well as looking at the future needs of each party which will be determined by projections from the pension provider or, more unusually, by expert evidence of the projected benefits to be derived from the percentage pension credit being urged upon the court as well as the likely future effect of the pension debit upon the member's pension. Such evidence may not be proportionate where the CETV in question is of little value in absolute terms or in relation to the parties' other resources.

8 TRAPS FOR THE UNWARY

8.1 The D-day conundrum

Pension sharing orders are, as has been seen, only available where the petition for divorce or nullity was issued on or after 1 December 2000. It is over-simplistic to suggest that husbands should have issued prior to 1 December 2000 in order to avoid pension sharing. There will be many husbands who might welcome a pension sharing order being made against them in order to facilitate a clean break. A pension sharing order will enable the pension to be accessed for these purposes.

What will happen, however, if H has issued a petition for divorce prior to 1 December 2000? If H has proceeded with that petition to decree absolute before 1 December 2000, W can only deal with pensions by solutions other than pension sharing. If, however, no decree nisi has been granted by 1 December 2000, it is open to W to issue her own second petition for divorce out of any divorce county court. No permission of the court is required. She is not obliged to proceed by way of a cross-petition in the existing proceedings where pension sharing would not be available in any event.[1] The court will then need to consider how the two suits should proceed. The court may well consider consolidating the two suits, ordering that H's petition should be designated as the lead suit as being that filed first in time. However, on the principle of relation back, this may well mean that the wife is then deprived of the remedy of pension sharing. It is, therefore, suggested that in this situation the court should direct that the petitions be heard together one immediately following the other. It would, therefore, be possible for a decree nisi to be granted on each petition on the same day. The wife could file Form A in her own divorce proceedings enabling a pension sharing order to be granted.

Where a decree nisi has already been granted on a petition for divorce issued before 1 December 2000, it is possible for the decree nisi to be rescinded so as to facilitate the issuing of a fresh petition which will confer the jurisdiction to make a pension sharing order where the application is made by consent.[2] However, this course is not permissible without the consent of both parties.[3]

See, also, Glover 'Pension Sharing Procedure' [2001] Fam Law 691, which refers to the decision in *S v S*.[4] In that case, W's petition issued on 1 December 2000 was stayed as an abuse with a direction that the husband's prior petition should be heard first as a defended petition. However, W had resiled from an agreement to issue a pre-1 December 2000 petition without saying so and subsequently tried to avoid service of H's pre-1 December 2000 petition.[5]

---

[1] A cross-petition does not constitute separate proceedings for the purposes of WRPA 1999, s 83(3)(a): *W v W (Divorce Proceedings: Withdrawal of Consent after Perfection of Order)* [2002] 2 FLR 1225, Bodey J.

[2] *S v S (Rescission of Decree Nisi: Pension Sharing Provision)* [2002] FLR 457, *per* Singer J.

[3] *H v H* [2002] 2 FLR 116, Bodey J; *Rye v Rye* [2002] 2 FLR 981, *per* Charles J. See, by way of comparison, Hallam 'Earmarking – Avoiding the 1 July 1996 Barrier' [1997] Fam Law 267.

[4] (Unreported), 26 April 2001 (Dewsbury County Court).

[5] Cf *G v G* (unreported), 2001 (Preston County Court), where the district judge pursued the conventional approach outlined above.

8.2   Multiple pension sharing orders

As MCA 1973, s 24B(1) provides, more than one pension sharing order may be made in relation to a marriage. However, a pension sharing order may not be made in relation to a pension arrangement or shareable State scheme rights, which are already the subject of a pension sharing order in relation to the marriage.[1]

Consider therefore these issues:

- the wording of the section is such that it will be possible to make a pension sharing order in relation to a pension arrangement where the pre-existing pension sharing order relates to *another* marriage: serial pension sharing;

- a pension sharing order may be made against a pension share arising out of a previous divorce/nullity;

- it is at least arguable that the wording of MCA 1973, s 24B(3)(a) is such that it may be possible to make a reverse pension sharing order, eg in favour of H, against a pension arrangement created by a pension sharing order made in favour of W in the same divorce because the pension arrangement arising from W's pension credit is separate and distinct from the pension out of which it was carved. This strategy may be considered where rebuilding is an issue (see section **12**), but could fall foul of the rule in *Furniss v Dawson*;[2]

- the making of a pension sharing order against one pension arrangement will not prevent the making of a pension sharing order at a later stage against another pension arrangement in the absence of an appropriate clean break dismissal;

- if no such dismissal is ordered, there is a powerful incentive for the person with pension rights to continue making contributions into the pension arrangement which has already been the subject of the pension sharing order rather than starting a new pension arrangement.

8.3   The interrelationship between pension sharing and pension attachment

A pension sharing order may not be made where there is in force a pension attachment order in relation to the particular pension arrangement.[3] MCA 1973, s 24B(5) is not qualified by the words 'in relation to the marriage'; the wording of the subsection is, it is submitted, such as to preclude the making of a pension sharing order where the pre-existing attachment order relating to that pension arrangement relates to any marriage.

It would appear, therefore, from the use of the words 'in force' in MCA 1973, s 24B(5) that, where the pre-existing attachment order made on a previous divorce or a judicial separation in relation to the same marriage has been discharged under MCA 1973, s 31, there is no bar on the making of a subsequent pension sharing order.

It will not be possible therefore to attach the lump sum death benefit and share the member's other rights despite the fact that pension sharing operates upon the CETV which does not include death benefits. The restriction created by MCA 1973, s 24B(5) can only be overcome by

---

[1]   MCA 1973, s 24B(3) and (4).
[2]   [1984] AC 474, HL.
[3]   MCA 1973, s 24B(5).

the use of an undertaking to the court in relation to death benefits alongside a pension sharing order (see further, **3.6**(c)).

An attachment order may not be made in relation to a pension arrangement which is the subject of a pension sharing order.[1] In order for this restriction to apply, the prior pension sharing order must relate to the marriage in question.

Summary

Prior pension sharing order relating to same marriage.	No pension sharing nor attachment order possible in relation to same pension arrangement.
Prior pension sharing order relating to previous marriage.	Pension sharing or attachment order possible in relation to same pension arrangement.
Prior attachment order relating to any marriage.	No pension sharing order possible in relation to same pension arrangement. However, pension attachment order possible in relation to same pension arrangement where prior pension attachment order made on earlier divorce.[4]

8.4   Serving the pension sharing order

County courts appear largely unaware of their obligations under FPR 1991, r 2.70(16) and (17) to send the requisite pension sharing documents to the pension arrangement. Unless this action is taken, the implementation period will not commence. Solicitors are increasingly aware of the problem and are either checking whether the court has complied with its obligations or are serving pension arrangements direct. However, some pension arrangements have indicated that they will only accept sealed documents from the court.

8.5   Pension sharing/attachment and the statutory charge

(a)   The statutory charge

The Legal Services Commission's charge arises under the Access to Justice Act 1999, s 10(7) on money or property recovered or preserved in family proceedings. Whether or not the charge applies depends on whether or not property was in issue in the proceedings; that will be determined as a matter of fact from the court order, evidence, pleadings and correspondence in the case.[2] It is subject to the exemption of the first £2,500 recovered or preserved.[3] The exemption is the first £3,000 in relation to applications made on or after 3 December 2001.[4]

(b)   Legal Services Commission Guidance

The Legal Services Commission originally published guidance on the operation of the statutory charge on pension sharing and pension attachment orders in July 2001. The Commission then took the view that, whilst all periodical payments by way of pension attachment would be

---

[1]   MCA 1973, s 25B(7B) and s 25C(4).
[2]   *Hanlon v Law Society* [1981] AC 124; [1980] 2 All ER 199.
[3]   Community Legal Service (Financial) Regulations 2000, SI 2000/516, reg 44(1)(d).
[4]   Community Legal Service (Financial) (Amendment No 3) Regulations 2001, SI 2001/3663, reg 22.

exempt from the statutory charge, it might be possible for the charge to operate on a preserved pension following an application for pension attachment/sharing, any lump sum order by way of pension attachment and upon a shared pension. The exact position would depend, in each case, on whether the original pension was affected by a statutory prohibition on assignment or charging and whether that provision had been disapplied.

Having taken the advice of leading counsel (Mr John Wardell QC), the Legal Services Commission announced in May 2002 that its revised view is that, when a court determines an application for a pension sharing or attachment order, any property recovered or preserved as a result of its determination is exempt from the statutory charge apart from any lump sum order (subject to the exemptions referred to above) payable under a pension attachment order.

8.6   SERPs/S2P

The State Second Pension (S2P) came into effect on 6 April 2002, replacing SERPs. The lump sum value CETV for someone with maximum SERPs entitlement who is approaching retirement is likely to be over £100,000. It is easy to regard SERPs as only affecting a small number of employees because most choose to contract out. However, 22% of those of working age are contributing to SERPs/S2P.

The cost of maintaining SERPs in its original form had proved too expensive and a gradual process of reduction of benefits was embarked upon. S2P is in essence nothing more than a rebranding of SERPs. Collectively, SERPs and S2P are known as the additional State pension. Those who had previously contracted out of SERPs through an appropriate personal pension may need to take advice and reconsider this decision in the light of the new regime. Any SERPs entitlement already built up is protected, both for those who have already retired and for those who have not yet reached State retirement age. S2P gives employees earning up to £24,600 (in 2002/03) a better pension than under SERPs.

A significant change is that those earning between £3,900 per annum and £10,800 per annum will be treated as if they had earned £10,800 and will receive S2P benefit accordingly. The benefit is payable even though those earning less than £4,535 do not have to pay income tax or national insurance, effectively giving them a free pension. The new regime effectively means that S2P will pay out 40% of the difference between actual earnings (subject to a minimum of £3,900) and £10,800 so that on retirement those earning £3,900 throughout their working lives would be entitled to S2P payments equivalent to 40% of £6,900 (£2,760). Benefit is linked to the years in work. For those in work only from aged 40 to retirement, the maximum payout is approximately £1,300, which is the equivalent of annuity income from a pension fund of £30,000. However, this change could produce a windfall of as much as £60,000 over a working lifetime, which is twice the size of the average personal pension fund.

S2P has also been extended to those not in paid employment (or part-time employment earning less than £3,900 per annum (in 2002/03)) because of looking after a child under the age of 6 or a person with a long-term illness or disability and to those not in paid employment because of a long-term illness or disability.

The changes will encourage husbands to employ wives within a family business on a low salary at or just in excess of £3,900 per annum. It will now be even more important for both parties to obtain a BR20 valuation so as to complete Form E. Further information on S2P may be accessed by visiting the Government Website (*www.pensionguide.gov.uk*).

8.7 Pension sharing and State scheme rights

WRPA 1999, ss 47–51, the Social Security Benefits and Contributions Act 1992, ss 55A–55C[1] and the Sharing of State Scheme Rights (Provision of Information and Valuation) Regulations 2000 deal with the sharing of State scheme rights.

Pension sharing is not available in relation to the basic State retirement pension (where the existing substitution rules apply), but is available in relation to SERPs/S2P or rights derived from a pension share in respect of previous family proceedings, which is known as a 'shared additional pension'.[2]

The transferor's SERPs/S2P is reduced by the amount of the pension debit. The transferee becomes entitled to an additional shared pension in her own right based on the credit expressed as a specified percentage of the cash equivalent on the transfer day of 'the transferor's shareable State scheme rights immediately before that day'.[3] The transfer day is the day on which the order takes effect.[4]

Entitlement to a shared additional pension is dependent upon the transferee attaining pensionable age: the transferor need not have attained State retirement age and could be younger than the transferee.

8.8 Pension sharing and death/remarriage

A pension sharing order is not affected by the death or remarriage of either party, although an application for leave to appeal out of time might be made. However, if the recipient of a pension credit dies before the liability for the pension credit has been discharged, WRPA 1999, s 35(2) and the Pension Sharing (Implementation and Discharge of Liability) Regulations 2000, reg 6 prescribe how the liability is to be discharged. In this rare situation, trustees have full discretion to discharge their liability in accordance with appropriately drafted scheme rules subject to Inland Revenue limits. The transferee is to be treated as if he/she had become a member of the pension arrangement. In some cases, it will be effected by payment of a lump sum, in others by payment of a pension or both a pension and a lump sum. Schemes may discharge their liability by entering into an annuity contract and/or an insurance contract to provide benefits for survivors. If the scheme rules do not make provision for payments of the type mentioned, the pension credit will be retained by the scheme from which it was derived.[5] If the transferee would have become a member of a personal pension, the amount of the pension credit should be paid into the deceased transferee's estate. For all of these reasons, the pension sharing order could be expressed only to take effect in the event of the recipient of the pension credit not predeceasing the transferor, where this is considered appropriate (see **9.2**(a)).

Conversely, where the person suffering the pension debit (the transferor) dies after the date on which the pension sharing order has taken effect but before its implementation, the position is governed by WRPA 1999, ss 28 and 29. Section 28 provides that WRPA 1999, s 29 applies on the

---

[1] As inserted by WRPA 1999, Sch 6.

[2] WRPA 1999, s 47(2)(b); Social Security Benefits and Contributions Act 1992, s 55A (as inserted by WRPA 1999, Sch 6).

[3] WRPA 1999, s 49(2).

[4] Ibid, s 49(6).

[5] Pensions on Divorce etc (Provision of Information) Regulations, reg 6 and the Pension Sharing (Implementation and Discharge of Liability) Regulations 2000, reg 6 (both as amended by the Pension Sharing (Consequential and Miscellaneous Amendments) Regulations 2000).

taking effect of the pension sharing order. In turn, s 29 provides that on application of s 29 the transferor's shareable rights become subject to a debit and the transferee becomes entitled to a credit of the appropriate amount. Therefore, in the situation envisaged, there has already been a pension debit at the date of death and the non-member spouse has an enforceable credit. In the case of an occupational pension scheme, the enforceable credit arises before the member's rights metamorphose into a death-in-service benefit. Where the transferor dies before the pension sharing order takes effect, that part of the order is unenforceable. For this reason, claims should not be dismissed until the pension sharing order takes effect so that the non-member spouse is left with a claim against the member's estate under the Inheritance (Provision for Family and Dependants) Act 1975, assuming the member dies domiciled in England and Wales.

8.9   Member's ill-health

The Pensions on Divorce etc (Provision of Information) Regulations 2000, regs 4(2)(i) and 5(e) allow trustees to request information about the member's state of health from the member as a precondition of implementing a pension sharing order. It is believed that the purpose of this was that, if the information showed that the member had an impaired life expectancy, this could be taken into account in calculating the pension debit/credit, thus reducing the amount payable if an external transfer was taken. However, when the revised GN11 was drafted, the Institute and Faculty of Actuaries were advised that there was nothing in the legislation which would allow an actuary to calculate the CETV for pension sharing purposes on the basis of the member's actual life expectancy rather than the normal life expectancy (which has to be used in calculating the CETV for the purposes of the Pension Schemes Act 1993). Thus, even if the pension scheme were to ask for the information about the member's state of health, the actuary would not be able to use the information in calculating the member's CETV. Trustees may, however, object to the making of a pension sharing order where, for example, the member had only a very short life expectancy and the wife was much younger on the ground that the members of the scheme as a whole would be prejudiced. It should, however, be noted that under the Pensions on Divorce etc (Provision of Information) Regulations 2000, trustees may only request information about the member's state of health if the member has been told in writing at the pre-order notification stage (see **6.1**, step 6) that the trustees may ask for medical evidence.

8.10   Pension sharing post-*White*

A full discussion of this landmark decision is beyond the scope of this Bulletin. However, the court's ability to make pension sharing orders will permit the yardstick of equality to be applied more readily without any perceived unfairness to either party. For example, it will no longer be necessary in certain circumstances for a husband to be denuded of all realisable assets on the basis that he retains his pension. Pension sharing will enable equality to be achieved both as to quantum and the nature of the assets with which each party is left.

In *T v T (Financial Relief: Pensions)*,[1] Singer J rejected the argument that provision for W from H's pension was a matter of right and entitlement by way of compensation. It is submitted that post-*White* a claim on behalf of W framed in this way would now have a greater prospect of success.

---

[1]   [1998] 1 FLR 1072.

Could it be argued that an accurate valuation is fundamental to the *fairness* of the result? It should be noted that Lord Nicholls added the pension values to the other capital values with no comment. Is this indicative of a future approach to the treatment of pensions in capital redistribution? Is no distinction to be drawn between pensions and other immediately realisable assets? It could be argued that the basis for aggregation in *White* was because the parties were aged about 60. However, is the yardstick of equality to be measured against the proposed order with no distinction being drawn between pensions and other immediately available assets? Differing post-*White* answers to this question are to be found in *Cowan*, *Maskell* and *S v S* (see **7.4**(d)–(f)).

8.11   Pension sharing and foreign pensions

The anti-alienation restrictions contained in UK pensions law do not apply to all foreign pensions, although some jurisdictions have comparable restrictions, eg former Commonwealth jurisdictions. Those with the benefit of such pensions may, in the absence of comparable provisions in the law regulating the pension in question, be able to gain access to the funds prior to the normal retirement date. It may, therefore, be possible to make an immediate conventional lump sum order.

The definition of a 'pension arrangement'[1] is sufficiently wide to enable a pension sharing order to be made against a foreign pension. Certain arrangements are disqualified as the destination for a pension credit.[2] However, the general scheme of WRPA 1999 is that an overseas arrangement within the meaning of the Contracting-Out (Transfer and Transfer Payments) Regulations 1996 will qualify as a destination arrangement.[3] In any event, the court will not exercise its discretion to make a pension sharing order relating to a foreign pension without being satisfied that the foreign pension arrangement will cooperate.[4]

Caution must be exercised at all times over pension scheme charges and legal costs in terms or proportionality, where foreign pensions are involved.

8.12   Pension sharing and foreign divorce

Because of mobility of employment, it is by no means now unusual to find that amongst the resources of a couple divorcing abroad might be a pension from an English provider. It may well be that the English provider is not prepared to recognise and implement a pension sharing order made by the foreign court. The couple may then find that there is no jurisdiction to bring proceedings for financial relief after an overseas divorce under MFPA 1984, Pt III (of which s 17(1)(b) enables a pension sharing order to be made) because there is no jurisdiction under s 15 of the Act based upon either domicile, habitual residence or a former matrimonial home in this country. It should be noted that the court may not make a pension sharing order where jurisdiction is exclusively based upon a matrimonial home in England and Wales.[5]

---

[1]   MCA 1973, ss 21A and 25D(3), Pension Schemes Act 1993, s 1 and WRPA 1999, ss 27(1) and 46(1).
[2]   WRPA 1999, Sch 5, para 7; Pension Sharing (Implementation and Discharge of Liability) Regulations 2000, SI 2000/1053, regs 12–15.
[3]   WRPA 1999, Sch 5, para 6(1).
[4]   See, eg, *Hamlin v Hamlin* [1986] 1 FLR 61.
[5]   MFPA 1984, s 20.

Where this is the case, the foreign pension sharing order will remain unenforceable and, unless it is possible for an alternative route to be pursued in the foreign proceedings, eg off-setting (where this is feasible both procedurally and in terms of the available assets), the pension in question will fall into something of a black hole. It may well be that the solution is to amend MFPA 1984, s 15 so as to extend jurisdiction where there is a pension from a provider in this jurisdiction, based upon the analogy of the jurisdiction founded upon the existence of a former matrimonial home in England and Wales. However, amendments will also be needed to MFPA 1984, s 20. Presumably, even where there is jurisdiction to make a pension sharing order under MFPA 1984, Pt III, that jurisdiction could arguably still be defeated because MFPA 1984, s 21(1) applies various provisions of the MCA 1973, Pt II to orders made under s 17 of the 1984 Act. These provisions include MCA 1973, s 24B(3)–(5), which relates to the restriction on the making of a pension sharing order where there is a prior pension sharing order, where there has been pension sharing between the parties in relation to the pension arrangement/shareable State scheme rights in relation to the marriage or where a prior pension attachment order exists in relation to the pension arrangement. It is arguable that this might embrace an order comparable to a pension sharing order made in another jurisdiction and might mean that it would not be possible to obtain, under MFPA 1984, Pt III, a mirror order for enforcement purposes in England and Wales.

8.13   Additional voluntary contributions (AVCs)

A pension sharing order made against AVCs (as opposed to FSAVCs) must be for the same percentage as the member's main scheme. The reason for this is that the pension sharing order must relate to all of the member's rights under the pension scheme.[1] Such 'member's rights' are made up of main scheme benefits, AVCs and (if the scheme is contracted-out) GMPs and Protected Rights. The same specified percentage in the pension sharing order will, therefore, apply to each such constituent part of the member's overall rights.

FSAVCs constitute a separate set of rights under a different pension scheme. Care must, therefore, be taken, when FSAVCs exist, to ensure that separate pension sharing orders are made against the FSAVCs and the main pension scheme, if this is intended. Such orders may be for differing percentages.

8.14   Default option

The person with the benefit of the pension credit may state no preference as to an internal or external transfer, may fail to identify a destination arrangement, or may request an internal transfer within a scheme which does not offer this option. The trustees must then determine a default option, either selecting an arrangement for the transfer or, indeed, transferring the pension credit internally. The position is regulated by WRPA 1999, s 35(1) and Sch 5 and the Pension Sharing (Implementation and Discharge of Liability) Regulations 2000.[2]

What are the duties of the pension provider (if any) in this default situation? There had been some concern that, in transferring the pension credit externally, trustees might be carrying out investment business under the Financial Services and Markets Act 2000. The Financial Services Authority (FSA) has confirmed, however, that this should not be the case. Another concern was

---

[1]   WRPA 1999, s 29.

[2]   SI 2000/1053, regs 7–9: see **2.6**(c).

that trustees might owe the ex-spouse a fiduciary duty, which they would breach if performing an external transfer without consent. The consensus view of pensions lawyers does not support this argument and this view has been confirmed by the DSS (now DWP) in a letter to the Association of Pensions Lawyers. While the administrators of an occupational pension scheme therefore ordinarily owe no duty of care to advise the beneficiary under the scheme, where the administrators proffered specific advice to the beneficiary, they might nevertheless assume a duty to exercise reasonable care and skill in giving such advice.[1]

The potential vehicles into which a pension credit may be transferred are limited in the absence of the consent and cooperation of the party with the benefit of the pension credit. It is thought possible to transfer only to an annuity policy or a s 32 buy-out policy because transfer options such as a personal pension will require the former spouse to sign a proposal form.

It is even arguable that the pension provider may never have to use the default option. Where the spouse with the benefit of a pension credit has consented to an external transfer, WRPA 1999, s 34(1)(b) and the Pensions on Divorce etc (Provision of Information) Regulations 2000, reg 5(c) provide that the implementation period does not begin to run until the provider has been given details of the destination arrangement. Therefore, if the spouse with the benefit of the pension credit consents to an external transfer but does not choose a destination arrangement, implementation simply does not begin. It appears possible to achieve a similar result even where the spouse with the benefit of the pension credit fails to consent to an external transfer. The Pensions on Divorce etc (Provision of Information) Regulations 2000, reg 4(2)(k) allows the pension provider to specify any information which, in addition to the reg 5 information, it will need to implement the pension sharing order. If the pension provider includes consent to an external transfer as a precondition to implementation, the joint effect of s 34(1)(b) and reg 5(e) is that the implementation period will not begin to run until consent to an external transfer is forthcoming.

8.15 Income gap syndrome

See **3.3**.

8.16 Mis-selling compensation

Compensation for mis-selling arising out of a transfer from an occupational pension scheme into a personal pension (see **7.2(e)**) will usually be paid as an increment to the value of the personal pension which receives the transfer. Care will, therefore, be needed where it is known that the party with pension rights is about to receive compensation. The party who is to receive the pension credit will not be able to benefit from the compensation unless it has been paid into the personal pension at the date notified by the pension arrangement for the purposes of WRPA 1999, s 29(7) (see **7.6**). Where this is not possible, the options open to the party without pension rights are:

- to defer the making of the pension sharing order; it is not possible to defer the order taking effect (see **3.3**); or

- where the amount of compensation is known but not paid, to deal with the matter by way of off-setting where available assets exist.

---

[1]   *Wirral Borough Council v Evans* (2001) *The Times*, February 20; 3 LGLR 30, ChD.

9 TIPS FOR THE PRACTITIONER

9.1 Completing Form A

(a) FPR 1991, r 2.61A(3) provides:

'(3) Where the applicant requests an order for ancillary relief and includes provision to be made by virtue of section 24B, 25B or 25C of the Act of 1973 the terms of the order requested must be specified in the notice in Form A.'

(b) The applicant will normally only be in a position to specify the term of the order requested if, for example, there has been prior voluntary disclosure in accordance with the ancillary relief protocol.

(c) Where there has been such voluntary disclosure, Form A might read:

'an order under the Matrimonial Causes Act 1973, ss 24B (pension sharing), 25B or 25C (pension attachment) in relation to the Respondent's personal pension with the Equitable Life Assurance Society policy number R123567.'

(d) Where this information is not available, FPR 1991, r 2.70(6) would suggest that the request for such provision should be added to an existing application for ancillary relief enabling Form A to be sent to the person responsible for the pension arrangement.

(e) A pension attachment order and a pension sharing order may not be made in relation to the same pension arrangement in the same divorce.

9.2 Drafting the order and annex

(a) Precedent for a pension sharing order

'[BY CONSENT] IT IS ORDERED that:

[1] [Unless the [Respondent]/[Petitioner] predeceases* the [Petitioner]/[Respondent] prior to the implementation of this order in which event only it shall not be carried into effect] there be provision by way of pension sharing in favour of the [Respondent]/[Petitioner] in respect of the [Petitioner]/[Respondent]'s rights under [his]/[her] pension arrangement[s] with [♦] in accordance with the [annex[es]*] to this order.'

[* See **9.2**(d) as to the annex and **8.8** as to the death of the recipient of the pension credit.]

(b) Precedent for the dismissal of pension sharing orders

'[Save as aforesaid], the application[s] of the [Petitioner]/[Respondent]/[Petitioner and the Respondent] for a pension sharing order be dismissed.'

(c) Precedent for a pension sharing order on a variation application

'There be provision by way of pension sharing in favour of the [Petitioner]/[Respondent] in respect of the [Respondent]/[Petitioner]'s rights under [his]/[her] pension arrangement[s] with [♦] in accordance with the [annex[es]] to this order WITH THE PROVISO THAT this order shall not be carried into effect in the event of the [Petitioner]/[Respondent] dying before the implementation of this order.

The order made herein by District Judge [♦] on [♦] whereby the [Respondent]/[Petitioner] do pay to the [Petitioner]/[Respondent] periodical payments at the rate of £[♦] per annum be discharged and the claims of the [Petitioner]/[Respondent] for periodical payments [and secured periodical payments] do stand dismissed and the [Petitioner]/[Respondent] shall not be entitled to make any further application in relation to the marriage under the Matrimonial Causes Act 1973, s 23(1)(a) or (b).'

This precedent assumes that all original applications for pension sharing (as well as for financial provision and property adjustment orders) were dismissed at the time the original periodical payments order was made.

(d)   The annex

Annexes 5 and 6 contain the forms of annex for pension sharing and pension attachment. These are Court Service Practice Forms P1 and P2. A slightly different version is to be found in *At a Glance* (2002/03) (FLBA), Table 20, which has been approved by the President's Ancillary Relief Advisory Group. This version omits the date at which the pension benefits are to be valued in accordance with the Divorce etc (Pensions) Regulations 2000: see **7.6**.

If the purpose of a separate pension sharing annex is to provide confidentiality for the parties, that purpose is frustrated by FPR 1991, r 2.70(16) which requires the court, inter alia, to send to the pension arrangement a copy of the 'order including provision under s 24B ...'. This requirement might be met by simply sending to the pension arrangement solely that part of the order including the relevant provision.

(e)   Practical tips

- A pension sharing order or a pension attachment order must refer to an annex.

- The annex in the practice form contains the information required by FPR 1991, r 2.70(14) (pension sharing) or FPR 1991, r 2.70(15) (pension attachment).

- There must be a separate annex for each pension arrangement.

- The annex should, as a matter of good practice, deal with charges;

- The annex must specify the percentage of the transferor's rights which are to be transferred in a specified scheme as at the valuation date.

- The pension sharing order cannot take effect until the later of decree absolute or 7 days after the end of the period for filing notice of appeal.

9.3   Form PR4[1]: tracing request

Under the Register of Occupational and Personal Pension Schemes Regulations 1997, reg 6, anyone who is, may be or may become entitled to benefit under a former pension scheme, or any person acting on the beneficiary's behalf, may make a tracing request. The search prompted by the tracing request application, for which there is no fee, is undertaken by reference to the name of the scheme or the former employers and not by reference to the scheme member's name. Thus, a search in the Registry by this means will not enable a party to ascertain whether the other spouse is a member of a particular scheme or what benefits may have accrued to that

---

[1]   This was the number formerly allocated to the tracing request application, which is now numberless.

party, but will enable the claimant to trace (given information about the scheme or as to the other spouse's employment history) the trustees or administrators of a scheme so that appropriate enquiries may be made.

A separate request must be made in relation to each scheme.[1]

9.4 Form BR20: how to get a State earnings related pension scheme (SERPs) valuation

See **7.2**(h).

9.5 Drafting *Calderbank* offers

Consider the following points when preparing a *Calderbank* offer.

- Make sure you have valuations/projections at an early stage so as not to delay negotiations.

- Do not forget SERPs/S2P – an answer to Form BR20 will not come quickly.

- Remember to express the pension share as a percentage of the CETV on a given date so as to make the offer capable of conversion into a consent pension sharing order.

- However, this data in isolation is unconvincing. A *Calderbank* offer will be more persuasive if supported by projections from an IFA showing the pension benefits which are likely to accrue to the payee as part of the analysis of whether that party's long-term needs will be met.

- Correspondingly, it may also be persuasive to show by further projections the effect of the pension debit upon the payer.

- Do not forget to deal with all charges (ie those of the pension provider, IFA and actuary (as appropriate)) as well as conventional legal costs in the *Calderbank* proposal.

9.6 Keeping the work proportionate

(a) Tunnel vision

It must not be thought that pension sharing is a panacea for every manner of pension problem encountered upon marriage breakdown. It is simply an additional weapon in the court's armoury.

Do not develop pension tunnel vision. It is simply one aspect of ancillary relief as a whole. Consider the pension problem in the round within the context of MCA 1973, s 25.

(b) The three basic questions

Ask yourself these questions.

- What is the best solution to the pensions problem in this particular case (see section **5**)?

- If the answer is pension sharing, should the client opt for an internal transfer (if available) or an external transfer?

---

[1] See Appendix 3.

- If the client opts for an external transfer, what is the appropriate destination arrangement?

9.7   Explaining the pros and cons: a model advice letter

There can be no substitute for advising a client fully in writing about the various factors which will influence the client's decision as to whether or not to proceed by way of pension sharing. Obviously, such advice must be tailored to meet the needs of the individual case. A model advice letter covering the salient points which will influence the decision is to be found at Appendix 7.

9.8   Pension sharing and taxation: equalisation of post-retirement income

A commuted lump sum payable under a pension sharing order is tax free. The pension income payable to a person with the benefit of a pension credit arising from a pension sharing order is taxable in the normal way. In other words, payments made to the person with the benefit of the pension sharing order are treated in the same way as conventional pension payments. If, however, H retains his pension benefits and pays maintenance (eg under a pension attachment order) to W, he may be liable to higher rate band taxation, although the payments as attached periodical payments will be tax free in the hands of W. In contrast, where H consents to a pension sharing order(s) under which the post-retirement income is equalised, both parties may remain within the basic rate band. To put this in context, it has been estimated that the cost to the Treasury in lost income tax as a result of the payment of two pensions instead of one is an estimated £1.3bn.

9.9   Return to sender: the boomerang effect

Where a pension sharing order is made in favour of W, consideration might be given to the possibility of a consent order incorporating an undertaking by W to pay the death benefits arising out of her pension credit to H in the event that she predeceases him (assuming [neither] she [nor he] has remarried). A similar result could be achieved by a pension attachment order in favour of H under MCA 1973, s 25C. However, such an order cannot be made contemporaneously with the original pension sharing order because there will be no pension to attach until such time as the pension sharing order has been implemented.

10 STATUTORY PROTECTION ON BANKRUPTCY

10.1 Will a pension vest in the trustee in bankruptcy?

(a) The problem

It had been held that benefits under a pension effected by a bankrupt before his bankruptcy, but which became payable after his discharge, do not amount to property acquired after the bankruptcy under the Insolvency Act 1986, s 307. The benefits were treated as choses in action, which comprised property belonging to the bankrupt at the commencement of the bankruptcy and accordingly vested in the trustee. On retirement, they were payable to the trustee in bankruptcy and not to the discharged bankrupt himself.[1] However, in *Rowe v Sanders*, it was held that the discharged bankrupt was entitled to the rights which were attributable to his service after bankruptcy since those contributions had been made in the mistaken belief that the pension rights remained vested in him and it would be inequitable for the trustee to take the benefit of such contributions.

A further problem arose because occupational pension schemes usually contain protective provisions called forfeiture clauses, which provide that on bankruptcy a member's benefits are forfeited and held on discretionary trusts for a class of beneficiaries consisting of the bankrupt, his spouse and close dependants. Typically, the trustees of the occupational pension scheme paid any benefits to the bankrupt spouse until discharge and then recommenced payments to the bankrupt. The trustee in bankruptcy would not, therefore, even be able to obtain pension payments made before discharge.[2] In contrast, similar forfeiture clauses in personal pensions might not have proved valid, as they may have fallen foul of the general principle that an individual cannot contract out of the insolvency legislation.

(b) The solution

The position is resolved by WRPA 1999, ss 11–14 and Sch 13. Section 11 provides statutory protection on bankruptcy for pension rights in approved schemes by excluding such rights from the bankrupt's estate. Under s 12, unapproved pension rights are capable of protection in the same way in prescribed circumstances, for example, where other pension benefits the bankrupt is likely to receive are inadequate to meet his reasonable needs and those of his dependants. By virtue of s 14, the trustees or managers of a scheme are no longer able to forfeit pension rights on a member's bankruptcy. Section 13 applies ss 11–12 to Scotland. The Welfare Reform and Pensions Act 1999 (Commencement No 7) Order 2000[3] brought s 11(1), (2), (3) and (11) and s 13(1) and (2) into force on 29 May 2000 and the problem identified in *Re L* has, therefore, only continued to be litigated in relation to bankruptcies which occurred before that

[1]   *Re L (A Bankrupt)* [1997] 2 FLR 660; *Krasner v Dennison* [2000] 3 All ER 234, CA; *Jones v Patel and the London Borough of Brent* [2001] Pens LR 217, CA; *Rowe v Sanders* [2002] 2 All ER 800 (Note), [2002] Pens LR 367.
[2]   *Re Trusts of the Scientific Investment Pension Plan* [1998] 2 FLR 761 (where benefits payable under an occupational pension scheme were forfeited on bankruptcy and so did not vest in the trustee).
[3]   SI 2000/1382.

date. Section 11(12) was brought into force on 1 December 2000. The balance of these provisions were brought into force on 6 April 2002.[1]

It has also been argued, following submissions made in *Harper v O'Reilly and Harper*,[2] that a pension lump sum subject to an attachment order would not in any event vest in a trustee in bankruptcy under the Insolvency Act 1986, s 283(5) as 'property comprised in a bankrupt's estate' which is 'subject to the rights of any person other than the bankrupt'.[3]

10.2 Attacks upon pension sharing orders by trustees in bankruptcy

A trustee in bankruptcy may attack an order made in ancillary relief proceedings, eg in relation to the family home, as a transaction at an undervalue or a preference.[4] Against this background, WRPA 1999, Sch 12, paras 70–71 amended the Insolvency Act 1986 by introducing new provisions (ss 342D, 342E and 342F) dealing with the recovery of *unfair contributions* in pension sharing cases by means of restoration orders. These provisions came into force on 6 April 2002.[5]

A pension sharing transaction is to be taken to be capable of being a transaction entered into at an undervalue only so far as it is a transfer of so much of the *appropriate amount* as is recoverable.[6] Similarly, such a transaction is capable of being a preference given to the transferee only so far as it is a transfer of so much of the appropriate amount as is recoverable.[7] The appropriate amount means the specified percentage of the CETV which is to be transferred under the pension sharing order.[8] The question of whether any pension sharing transaction is recoverable is to be decided in accordance with the Insolvency Act 1986, s 342D(4)–(8). The determination process involves a number of steps.

First, the court must determine the extent to which the transferor's rights under the shared arrangement appear to have been the fruits of *personal contributions* made by or on behalf of the transferor.[9] Where the transferor's rights under the shared arrangement are to any extent the fruits of personal contributions, the court must next determine the extent to which those rights represent *unfair contributions* in the sense that their making has unfairly prejudiced the transferor's creditors.[10] In determining whether the transferor has made unfair contributions, the court must consider, in particular, whether any of the personal contributions were made for the purpose of putting assets beyond the reach of the transferor's creditors, and whether the total amount of any personal contributions represented, at the time the pension sharing transaction was made, by rights under pension arrangements was an amount which is excessive in view of the transferor's circumstances when those contributions were made.[11] If it appears to the court that the extent to which the transferor's rights under the shared arrangement were the fruits of unfair contributions is such that the transfer of the appropriate amount could have been made out of rights which were not the fruits of unfair contributions, then the appropriate amount is not recoverable.[12] If it appears to the court that the transfer could not have been

---

[1]   WRPA (Commencement No 13) Order 2002, SI 2002/153.
[2]   [1997] 2 FLR 816.
[3]   See Spon-Smith 'Pension Lump Sums and Bankruptcy' [2000] Fam Law 498.
[4]   Insolvency Act 1986, ss 339–341.
[5]   WRPA (Commencement No 13) Order 2002, SI 2002/153.
[6]   Insolvency Act 1986, s 342D(1).
[7]   Ibid, s 342D(2).
[8]   Ibid, s 342D(9).
[9]   Ibid, s 342D(4).
[10] Ibid, s 342D(5).
[11] Ibid, s 342D(8).
[12] Ibid, s 342D(6).

wholly so made, then the appropriate amount is recoverable to the extent to which it appears to the court that the transfer could not have been so made.[1] If the court proceeds to find that (part of) the appropriate amount is recoverable, it will then make a finding that the transaction was either entered into at an undervalue or was a preference. Under the Insolvency Act 1986, ss 342E and 342F, the trustee in bankruptcy has a right to obtain payment from the person responsible for the destination arrangement.

It should be noted that there is also a process for the recovery of excessive pension contributions in the Insolvency Act 1986, ss 342A–342C,[2] which also came into force on 6 April 2002. This process could apply in a non-pension sharing situation where excessive pension contributions have been made by a person who becomes bankrupt. However, the scheme of the recovery provisions is that recourse will be had first to contributions which do not represent the pension debit.

---

[1]   Insolvency Act 1986, s 342D(7).
[2]   Inserted by WRPA 1999, s 15.

11 CHARGES

11.1 Charges by pension schemes

(a) Sources

The key sources are WRPA 1999, s 23(1)(d) (*recovery of prescribed charges*), s 24 (*charges in relation to earmarking orders*), s 41 (*charges in relation to pension sharing orders*) and the Pensions on Divorce (Charging) Regulations 2000.[1]

(b) General principle: the parties pay

The general principle is that the divorcing couple should bear the cost of pension sharing and not the scheme itself[2] except in relation to shareable State scheme rights. However, there is a need to balance the ability of pension arrangements to recover charges with the need for the parties to have full details of any charges before a pension sharing order is made. For this reason, pension arrangements, which fail to provide the parties with a schedule of charges with the basic information required by the Pensions on Divorce (Provision of Information) Regulations 2000, reg 2, will not be able to recover charges when a pension sharing order is made.[3] Pension arrangements must set out in the schedule of charges details of any specific charges they intend to recover, eg the ongoing administration of a pension credit on an internal transfer.[4]

The initial start up costs of compliance and any rule amendments will be at the expense of the pension arrangement generally. Pension arrangements will not be able to charge for information which would be available free under disclosure requirements (see **7.3**(a)). For example, trustees will not be able to charge for a valuation unless it is required within a shorter period than 3 months or the member has already received a quotation under the existing disclosure and transfer regulations[5] within the past 12 months.

(c) Limit on charges

WRPA 1999, ss 23, 24 and 41 allow the Government to regulate the limit on charges which pension arrangements may recover in respect of pensions and divorce. The Government has not placed specific limits on charges. However, the Pensions on Divorce (Charging) Regulations 2000 require all charges to be reasonable and linked to the costs associated with each individual case.[6] The Occupational Pension Schemes (Internal Dispute Resolution Procedures) Regulations 1996 and the Personal and Occupational Pension Schemes (Pension Ombudsman) Regulations 1996 have been widened to enable former spouses who qualify for a

---

[1] SI 2000/1049.
[2] WRPA 1999, s 41(1).
[3] Pensions on Divorce (Charging) Regulations 2000, reg 2.
[4] Ibid.
[5] See **7.3**(a).
[6] Regulation 5.

pension credit to obtain clarification about a pension arrangement's charges and to dispute unreasonable charges.[1]

The recommended scale of charges from the National Association of Pension Funds (NAPF) suggests a charge of £150 for an additional CETV quotation and up to £750 to cover all administration costs from receipt of the pension sharing order to the completion of pension payments, where the scheme member has not yet retired. Where the pension is already in payment, the recommended valuation charge is up to £500 and up to £750 to cover all administration costs from receipt of the pension sharing order to completion of pension payments or (in the alternative) to settle an external transfer up to £300.[2]

(d)   Provision for charges in the pension sharing order

A pension sharing order may specify who is to bear the charges;[3] if the order is silent and no agreement is reached between the couple about charges, the scheme member will bear the charges.[4]

(e)   When can a charge be made?

The Pensions on Divorce (Charging) Regulations 2000, reg 3(1) sets out the items where pension arrangements can recover charges, ie under the Pensions on Divorce (Provision of Information) Regulations 2000, reg 2 (*basic information*), reg 4 (*provision of information in response to a pre-order notification*) and reg 10 (*provision of information after receipt of an earmarking order*). Regulation 3(2) lists the items of information for which a charge cannot be made, eg basic information under the Pensions on Divorce etc (Provision of Information) Regulations 2000, reg 2(2) and (3), including a valuation where there has been no valuation supplied within the previous 12 months (unless the information is required in less than 3 months or the member has reached normal retirement age on or before the date of the request or the court order for the provision of the information or is due to reach normal retirement age within 12 months of such date).

(f)   Methods of recovery

It is permissible for a pension arrangement to postpone implementation until its charges have been paid. However, for this to apply, the trustees must have given notice that they require charges to be paid in advance at a stage no later than in their response to the notification from the member that a pension sharing order may be made (see **6.1**: step 6). In these circumstances, the trustees must issue a notice of postponement to the member and former spouse no later than 21 days after receipt of the pension sharing order, which notice reminds the parties that charges are to be paid in advance.[5]

In certain circumstances, the pension arrangement may deduct the costs directly from the pension credit (before it is transferred out or converted into an internal benefit and, in the case of an internal transfer, additional charges may be made to cover scheme expenses at a later stage), from the accrued rights of the member or, if the pension is in payment, from the member's pension benefits.[6] These methods have an obvious cashflow advantage, particularly

---

[1]   Child Support, Pensions and Social Security Act 2000, s 53(7)(a).
[2]   Further details may be obtained from the NAPF, NIOC House, 4 Victoria Street, London SW1H 0NX (telephone: 0207 808 1300); *Pension Sharing on Divorce Made Simple* (£10 to non-members).
[3]   WRPA 1999, s 41(3)(a).
[4]   Ibid, s 41(3)(b).
[5]   Ibid, s 41(2)(a) and the Pensions on Divorce (Charging) Regulations 2000, reg 7.
[6]   Ibid, s 38(2)(c) and Pensions on Divorce (Charging) Regulations 2000, reg 9.

in a publicly funded case. However, they may only be employed if a pension sharing order is actually made and not where charges are incurred in negotiations which do not lead to the making of a pension sharing order. The parties may pay the charges in cash if they so wish.

Pension arrangements may insist on payment before providing any information for which a charge can be made,[1] unless the information is sought pursuant to a court order.

The Pensions on Divorce (Charging) Regulations 2000, reg 8 provides that, where one party to a pension sharing order pays the charges on behalf of the other, those charges may be recoverable as a debt by the party who made payment. This may be necessary as a last resort by the party benefiting from the pension sharing order in order to prevent postponement of implementation.

(g) Charges for attachment

The Pensions on Divorce (Charging) Regulations 2000, reg 10 sets out the procedures for the recovery of charges following the making of an attachment order closely following the previous provisions.

11.2 The global picture

It should be borne in mind that not only the charges of the pension arrangement, but also legal costs and those of any actuaries or IFAs involved, must be taken into account in assessing the viability of pension sharing as a solution. Further, where one party has a variety of pension arrangements, it will be cheaper to make a single pension sharing order against one of those arrangements than to make orders against all for a lower percentage. Against this strategy – dictated by mitigating charges – is the risk faced by the transferor (if the arrangement against which the order is made performs well in comparison to those retained): the transferee will usually avoid this risk by an external transfer.

---

[1]   Pensions on Divorce (Charging) Regulations 2000, SI 2000/1049, reg 4(1).

12 REBUILDING

12.1 Restrictions on contributions

The net effect of implementation of a pension sharing order upon a pension scheme member will be reduced benefits. A member may, therefore, wish to know how he can rebuild pension rights to restore his position. This can be done by making AVCs to the scheme and those earning up to £30,000 per annum (excluding controlling directors) may also pay up to £3,600 per annum into a stakeholder or new-style personal pension. However, there is a limit of 15% of the member's taxable remuneration on the aggregate of regular contributions and AVCs which qualify for tax relief in the case of occupational pension schemes. This limit was not relaxed by WRPA 1999. Different, but similar, restrictions based upon a sliding scale limit tax-effective contributions to retirement annuity contracts and personal pensions. Beyond these restrictions, the member must look to other – non-pension – investment vehicles (such as ISAs) in order to rebuild.

12.2 Restrictions on benefits

Restrictions on *contributions* are not the only relevant Inland Revenue limitation so far as occupational pension schemes are concerned. There is also a limitation upon the *benefits* which may be provided by an Inland Revenue approved pension scheme (eg broadly, in the case of an occupational pension scheme, two-thirds of final salary subject to the earnings cap (£97,200 for 2002/2003)). Generally, the Inland Revenue will require the benefits lost to the member by reason of the pension sharing order to be taken into account in calculating his/her Inland Revenue maximum benefit limits as part of what are known as his/her *retained benefits*. In a money purchase scheme, the amount of the pension debit is increased up to the date when the member draws his pension at the rate of return achieved by the member on his/her remaining fund or, where it is not possible to use the actual investment yield, a rate of 8.5% per annum will be assumed. The resulting capital fund is then turned into a pension equivalent by applying a suitable annuity rate appropriate to the member's retirement date.

However, by way of Inland Revenue concession, benefits lost will be disregarded where earnings amount to no more than 25% of the earnings cap (£24,300 for 2002/2003)[1] in calculating both the maximum pension and lump sum payable. The concession only applies to those earning less than £24,300 in the year of assessment immediately preceding the year in which the dissolution or annulment occurred and does not create an 'exempt band'. The effect of this concession will be that the transferor will be free to rebuild his/her pension towards the maximum permitted, but within the 15% annual limit on employee contributions. The concession is applied at the point indicated above, even if the transferor earns more than 25% of the earnings cap at a later stage or changes employment. The concession does not apply to controlling directors (and to those who have been controlling directors within 10 years of the date of divorce).

---

[1] *PSO Update No 62*, 28 April 2000.

12.3   Restrictions on former spouse

Where a wife is, for example, a member of a pension scheme in her own right, she can receive an Inland Revenue maximum pension from that scheme in addition to the benefits from the pension credit. Where such a wife remarries after the pension sharing order and then dies, her widower can receive an Inland Revenue maximum dependant's pension in addition to any benefits arising from the deceased wife's pension credit. These exemptions enabling the pension credit not to count towards Inland Revenue limits only apply if the pension credit rights in the occupational pension scheme are treated separately from those arising *qua* employee/member or *qua* widow of an employee/member.

12.4   Is *Brooks* really dead?

The use of a *Brooks*-style settlement achieved by consent by means of an undertaking (given that a *Brooks* variation of settlement order is no longer available in relation to petitions issued on or after 1 December 2000[1]) may enable a husband to rebuild his pension to the original level in that the husband's permitted maximum pension will not be affected in the way that it would be by a pension sharing order.[2] This is an area where the advice of a skilled independent financial adviser will be required.

12.5   Reverse pension sharing orders

See **8.2**.

---

[1]   WRPA 1999, s 85(4) and Sch 3, para 3.
[2]   See Campbell 'Pension Sharing in Practice' [2002] Fam Law 35.

13 FINANCIAL ADVICE: THE ROLE OF THE EXPERT

13.1 Pension sharing and investment business

The effect of the Financial Services and Markets Act 2000 (FSMA 2000), of which Part XX deals with professional firms, has been to change the regime for the regulation of investment business for, inter alia, solicitors with effect from 1 December 2001. On that date, the FSA became the sole body with power to authorise solicitors' firms to provide 'regulated activities'; The Law Society's powers as a recognised professional body ceased. However, The Law Society has become a 'designated professional body' (DPB), which will allow solicitors' firms to provide certain limited 'regulated activities' without being authorised by the FSA. The statutory definition of 'regulated activities' is still wide enough to embrace some activities in fields such as family law.

From 1 December 2001, solicitors' firms who provide any form of mainstream investment business – formerly *discrete investment business* – need to be authorised directly by the FSA. Firms which wish to restrict their activities to non-mainstream work – broadly what was *non-discrete investment business* – may avoid FSA authorisation by staying within the ambit of the new DPB regime. This allows solicitors to provide non-mainstream investment activities. All DPBs will be supervised by the FSA. DPBs must have rules designed to secure that 'in providing a particular professional service to a particular client, the member carries on only regulated activities which arise out of, or are complementary to, the provision by him of that service to the client'. The Solicitors' Investment Business Rules 1995 have ceased to exist as has the need for solicitors' firms to have an investment business certificate issued by The Law Society. The new rules made by the Council of The Law Society as the DPB are the Solicitors' Financial Services (Scope) Rules 2001. A firm which breaches the new rules may be committing a criminal offence under s 23 of FSMA 2000.

The family lawyer needs to take particular care when dealing with the life policies or pension credits arising out of pension sharing orders. If in any doubt, the solicitor should refer investment business to an independent financial adviser (IFA), unless directly authorised by the FSA. The assignment or conversion (eg to a single life) of a life policy is likely to be within the new exemption as will the solicitor advising on the overall settlement involving a life policy or pension sharing. However, the arrangement of the sale or surrender of a life policy should be referred to an IFA, as should the investment of a pension credit by way of an external transfer in the absence of direct FSA authorisation. It should be borne in mind that breaches of FSMA 2000 or the Solicitors' Financial Services (Scope) Rules 2001 are quite independent of any issue of solicitors' negligence.

13.2 The role of the IFA

The IFA has a key role to play alongside the family lawyer in the operation of pension sharing. The advice of the IFA will first be needed upon the wisdom of taking an internal transfer (for which reason family lawyers will feel more comfortable with hourly charges rather than a purely commission-based charging structure) and secondly, where an external transfer is chosen, on a suitable destination arrangement for the pension credit. This latter function will embrace the provision of projections indicating the pension benefits which will be acquired by the party without pension rights with a pension credit of x/y/z%. Such projections need to be carefully prepared so as to be expressed in current financial terms and based upon no further contributions/salary accruals. Projections may also be needed showing the effect of the pension debit on the party with pension rights.

Under the Solicitors' Financial Services (Scope) Rules 2001, a solicitor must obtain the client's consent to retain commission received. It should also be borne in mind that, under the Data Protection Act 1998, the client's consent must be obtained for the transmission of personal data to a third party, for example, an IFA. A solicitor will usually seek such consent by asking the client at the outset to endorse a copy of a retainer letter. However, in the case of health data, express written consent must be obtained.

Care should be taken to ensure that any commission generated by a new pension arrangement chosen as the destination for the pension credit is not applied in such a way as to remove Inland Revenue approval from the arrangement in question, which would make the arrangement vulnerable to attack by a trustee in bankruptcy (see **10.2**) and would result in tax relief granted being reclaimed by the Inland Revenue. This will not occur where (part of) the commission is rebated into the pension arrangement.[1]

A suitable IFA can be located by contacting the Society of Financial Advisers (SOFA), 20 Aldermanbury, London EC2V 7HY (telephone: 020 7417 4798). Such an IFA should be G60 qualified. G60 is one of the modules of the Advanced Financial Planning Certificate (AFPC) of the Chartered Insurance Institute. It is also a stand-alone qualification. Unless a financial adviser is G60 qualified, he/she cannot conduct pension transfer business. An IFA who does not hold the qualification must get another G60 qualified IFA to sign off a pension transfer. G60 is a degree-level qualification, but is not by any means solely concerned with pension sharing on divorce.

An IFA may be called upon to advise the person with the benefit of a pension credit as to what the precise benefits are on an internal transfer.

Consider the following:

- what death benefits are available for the transferee, eg can the transferee nominate a dependant to receive a widow's/widower's pension or lump sum from the new pension benefits (often this is not possible);

- whether early retirement is available (eg the Government Actuary has confirmed that, in the uniformed services, although the original member can take early retirement, the transferee cannot and will have to wait until age 60 to retire);

- whether further contributions can be paid;

- what the eventual pension income will be either with or without further contributions or with or without commutation.

---

[1]   See, generally, *PSO Update 64*, 16 June 2000.

13.3 The role of the actuary

Given the death of the *Brooks*-style variation of settlement order, there seems little doubt the continuing role of the actuary is now restricted. However, the role will be significant in a number of cases. Here are a few examples of where an actuary might be needed:

- where pension(s) is/are the main resource either in isolation or in the context of the parties' overall wealth;

- where there is a lack of concurrency between cohabitation within marriage and membership of the pension scheme, eg because of a significant period of separation prior to divorce or because the member joined the pension scheme for a significant period prior to marriage;

- where either party is a member of the police, prison service, fire service or armed forces pension schemes, where benefits payable to an early leaver are of substantially less value than the benefits payable to a member who continues in service to retirement.

13.4 Use of stakeholder pensions

It is envisaged that stakeholder pensions will become popular as a destination for pension credits because of the limit on charges. If personal pensions restructure their charges so as to become more competitive, the range of available personal pensions (as compared with the limited range of stakeholder pensions) will become an important factor in making the ultimate choice. However, the ability of a non-working wife who puts a pension credit into a stakeholder pension or new-style personal pension to make continuing contributions from her maintenance income of up to £3,600 per annum (at a net cost of £2,808 per annum (£234 per month) given that pension contributions will be made net of notional basic rate tax from April 2001) is also a significant consideration.

14 THE FUTURE

14.1 *Pickering Report*/Government Green Paper

The *Pickering Report* commissioned by the Government on the simplification of pensions law was published on 11 July 2002. Among its recommendations are some dealing specifically with pensions and divorce:

- abolition of pension attachment because of the uncertainties involved, while recognising that the court may regard attachment as the most appropriate option in certain circumstances;

- simplification of pension sharing rules;

- bringing into line the conditions for receipt of benefits under pension sharing arrangements with those for other types of scheme member;

- the removal of restrictions on the share derived from contracted out rights.

The Government published a Green Paper *Simplicity, Security and Choice: Working and Saving for Retirement* on 17 September 2002, having considered the *Pickering Report* (as well as the *Sandler Review* of medium and long-term retail investment set up by the Chancellor of the Exchequer and the Inland Revenue's review of the simplification of the tax rules relating to pensions), addressing the pensions crisis involving a £27 billion gap between savers' expectations of retirement income and the reality, as many final salary schemes close to new members. Chapter 7 of the Green Paper addresses issues affecting women, work and pensions. These proposals should be monitored as they will impact significantly on the treatment of pension rights on divorce.

14.2 State Pension Credit Act 2002

The Act received Royal Assent on 25 June 2002. Its provisions are due to come into effect from October 2003.

Pension credit is made up of two separate components:

- a guarantee credit; and

- a savings credit.

The guarantee credit will replace the current minimum income guarantee (MIG). It will ensure a minimum guaranteed income for pensioners so they need not live on less than £100 per week (£154 per week for pensioner couples). It will be paid to claimants (men and women) from age 60, but between 2010 and 2020 the age will rise to 65 based on the date of birth of the claimant in the same way as the State pension age for women will rise over the same period. The savings credit is designed to reward claimants, from age 65, who have modest levels of 'qualifying income' which takes their income over the 'savings credit threshold' (ie the basic State pension). 'Qualifying income' means income from either the state retirement pension or from occupational or personal pension schemes. In other words, pensioners with modest savings will no longer lose a pound in their benefit for every pound of pensions or other savings they have built up.

Intrusive weekly means tests are abolished. From age 65, most awards will instead be set for 5 years with pensioners only having to report significant changes in their circumstances. In general, increases in income during this fixed period (known as the 'assessed income period') will be ignored.

For all purposes, the pension credit calculation will ignore the amount of any capital held by the claimant which is less than £6,000. If capital of more than £6,000 is held, the excess over £6,000 will be deemed to provide qualifying income to the pensioner at the rate of 10%. The rule excluding pensioners with £12,000 or more of capital is abolished.

Pension credit represents an important new resource to watch out for where a couple are approaching retirement.

14.3   Cohabitants

In July 2002, the Law Commission published its report *Sharing Homes: A Discussion Paper*. Disappointingly, the Commission concluded, having attempted to clarify when a person who has made contributions to a shared home might obtain an interest where there is no declaration of trust in his/her favour, that:

> 'It is not possible ... to devise a statutory scheme for the ascertainment and quantification of beneficial interests in the shared home which can operate fairly and evenly across the diversity of domestic circumstances which are now to be encountered.'

In the last parliamentary session, two Private Members' Bills were introduced by Lord Lester QC and Jane Griffiths, MP (The Civil Partnership Bill and the Relationships (Civil Registration) Bill). Lord Lester's Bill proposed the creation of a separate system of civil partnership by registration between persons over 16, one of whom is resident in the UK. Such a partnership could be opted into by couples of the same or opposite sex. The effect of entering into a civil partnership would be that the law governing property and maintenance of the partners would closely reflect that governing married couples. A civil partnership would be capable of dissolution by court order.

The Bill of Jane Griffiths envisaged a system whereby registration of the relationship would result in the couple having exactly the same rights and responsibilities as afforded to married couples under current legislation. Indeed, provision was made that any application for financial relief on dissolution (subject to any pre-registration agreement about property rights) should be decided 'on the same terms as an application by a spouse in divorce proceedings'.

In response to the Private Members' Bills, the Cabinet Office convened a working group to consider the impact of registration of civil partnerships across all relevant government departments. The potential cost of recognising partners in public sector pension schemes was viewed as key concern. Lord Lester has decided, for the moment, not to take his Bill further so as to give the Government the opportunity to complete its inter-departmental review and to formulate its position. On 6 December 2002, Barbara Roche, the Social Exclusion Minister, announced the Government's intention to publish a consultation paper in the summer of 2003 on proposals for the registration of civil partnerships limited to same-sex couples.

Any form of civil registration is likely, therefore, to give registered partners rights in relation to pensions on a relationship breakdown as well as extending death benefits to registered partners. Approximately half of the pension schemes in the UK already make reference to unmarried partners, and most refer to pensions or 'dependants' at the discretion of the trustees. Inland Revenue rules would need to be changed, however, to allow pension schemes to make specific provision for same-sex partners as of right. While a survivor's pension is usually paid automatically to a spouse, in some occupational, but few public sector schemes, a pension can be paid to a surviving same-sex partner, but only at the trustees' discretion on proof of financial dependency upon the deceased.

APPENDIX 1

LEGISLATION

Matrimonial Causes Act 1973[1]

****

Part II
Financial Relief for Parties to Marriage and Children of Family[2]

Financial provision and property adjustment orders

****

[21A   Pension sharing orders

(1)   For the purposes of this Act, a pension sharing order is an order which –

   (a)   provides that one party's –

   (i)   shareable rights under a specified pension arrangement, or

   (ii)   shareable state scheme rights,

   be subject to pension sharing for the benefit of the other party, and

   (b)   specifies the percentage value to be transferred.

(2)   In subsection (1) above –

   (a)   the reference to shareable rights under a pension arrangement is to rights in relation to which pension sharing is available under Chapter I of Part IV of the Welfare Reform and Pensions Act 1999, or under corresponding Northern Ireland legislation,

   (b)   the reference to shareable state scheme rights is to rights in relation to which pension sharing is available under Chapter II of Part IV of the Welfare Reform and Pensions Act 1999, or under corresponding Northern Ireland legislation, and

   (c)   'party' means a party to a marriage.][3]

Ancillary relief in connection with divorce proceedings etc

****

24[4]   Property adjustment orders in connection with divorce proceedings etc

(1)   On granting a decree of divorce, a decree of nullity of marriage or a decree of judicial separation or at any time thereafter (whether, in the case of a decree of divorce or of nullity of marriage, before or after the decree is made absolute), the court may make any one or more of the following orders, that is to say –

---

[1]   Act reference: 1973 c 18.
   Royal assent: 23 May 1973.
   Long title: An Act to consolidate certain enactments relating to matrimonial proceedings, maintenance agreements, and declarations of legitimacy, validity of marriage and British nationality, with amendments to give effect to recommendations of the Law Commission.

[2]   Note that no pension sharing order may be made under section 24B of the Matrimonial Causes Act 1973 if the proceedings in which the decree is granted were begun before 1 December 2000, or under section 31(7B) if the marriage was dissolved by a decree granted in proceedings so begun (Welfare Reform and Pensions Act 1999, s 85(3), with effect from 1 December 2000 (Welfare Reform and Pensions Act 1999 (Commencement No 5) Order 2000, SI 2000/1116)).

[3]   Section inserted: Welfare Reform and Pensions Act 1999, s 19, Sch 3, paras 1, 2, with effect from 1 December 2000 (Welfare Reform and Pensions Act 1999 (Commencement No 5) Order 2000, SI 2000/1116).

[4]   Commencement: 1 January 1974 (SI 1973/1972).

(a)　　an order that a party to the marriage shall transfer to the other party, to any child of the family or to such person as may be specified in the order for the benefit of such a child such property as may be so specified, being property to which the first-mentioned party is entitled, either in possession or reversion;

(b)　　an order that a 'settlement' of such property as may be so specified, being property to which a party to the marriage is so entitled, be made to the satisfaction of the court for the benefit of the other party to the marriage and of the children of the family or either or any of them;

(c)　　an order varying for the benefit of the parties to the marriage and of the children of the family or either or any of them any ante-nuptial or post-nuptial settlement (including such a settlement made by will or codicil) made on the parties to the marriage [, other than one in the form of a pension arrangement (within the meaning of section 25D below)];[1]

(d)　　an order extinguishing or reducing the interest of either of the parties to the marriage under any such settlement [, other than one in the form of a pension arrangement (within the meaning of section 25D below)];[2]

subject, however, in the case of an order under paragraph (a) above, to the restrictions imposed by section 29(1) and (3) below on the making of orders for a transfer of property in favour of children who have attained the age of eighteen.

(2)　　The court may make an order under subsection (1)(c) above notwithstanding that there are no children of the family.

(3)　　Without prejudice to the power to give a direction under section 30 below for the settlement of an instrument by conveyancing counsel, where an order is made under this section on or after granting a decree of divorce or nullity of marriage, neither the order nor any settlement made in pursuance of the order shall take effect unless the decree has been made absolute.

****

[24B　Pension sharing orders in connection with divorce proceedings etc

(1)　　On granting a decree of divorce or a decree of nullity of marriage or at any time thereafter (whether before or after the decree is made absolute), the court may, on an application made under this section, make one or more pension sharing orders in relation to the marriage.

(2)　　A pension sharing order under this section is not to take effect unless the decree on or after which it is made has been made absolute.

(3)　　A pension sharing order under this section may not be made in relation to a pension arrangement which –

(a)　　is the subject of a pension sharing order in relation to the marriage, or

(b)　　has been the subject of pension sharing between the parties to the marriage.

(4)　　A pension sharing order under this section may not be made in relation to shareable state scheme rights if –

(a)　　such rights are the subject of a pension sharing order in relation to the marriage, or

(b)　　such rights have been the subject of pension sharing between the parties to the marriage.

---

[1]　Words inserted: Welfare Reform and Pensions Act 1999, s 19, Sch 3, paras 1, 3, with effect from 1 December 2000 (Welfare Reform and Pensions Act 1999 (Commencement No 5) Order 2000, SI 2000/1116). Note that this amendment does not have effect if the proceedings in which the decree is granted were begun before 1 December 2000 (Welfare Reform and Pensions Act 1999, s 85(4), with effect from 1 December 2000 (Welfare Reform and Pensions Act 1999 (Commencement No 5) Order 2000, SI 2000/1116).

[2]　Words inserted: Welfare Reform and Pensions Act 1999, s 19, Sch 3, paras 1, 3, with effect from 1 December 2000 (Welfare Reform and Pensions Act 1999 (Commencement No 5) Order 2000, SI 2000/1116). Note that this amendment does not have effect if the proceedings in which the decree is granted were begun before 1 December 2000 (Welfare Reform and Pensions Act 1999, s 85(4), with effect from 1 December 2000 (Welfare Reform and Pensions Act 1999 (Commencement No 5) Order 2000, SI 2000/1116).

(5)   A pension sharing order under this section may not be made in relation to the rights of a person under a pension arrangement if there is in force a requirement imposed by virtue of section 25B or 25C below which relates to benefits or future benefits to which he is entitled under the pension arrangement.

24C   Pension sharing orders: duty to stay

(1)   No pension sharing order may be made so as to take effect before the end of such period after the making of the order as may be prescribed by regulations made by the Lord Chancellor.

(2)   The power to make regulations under this section shall be exercisable by statutory instrument which shall be subject to annulment in pursuance of a resolution of either House of Parliament.

24D   Pension sharing orders: apportionment of charges

If a pension sharing order relates to rights under a pension arrangement, the court may include in the order provision about the apportionment between the parties of any charge under section 41 of the Welfare Reform and Pensions Act 1999 (charges in respect of pension sharing costs), or under corresponding Northern Ireland legislation.][1]

[25   Matters to which court is to have regard in deciding how to exercise its powers under ss 23, 24 and 24A

(1)   It shall be the duty of the court in deciding whether to exercise its powers under section 23, 24 [, 24A or 24B][2] above and, if so, in what manner, to have regard to all the circumstances of the case, first consideration being given to the welfare while a minor of any child of the family who has not attained the age of eighteen.

(2)   As regards the exercise of the powers of the court under section 23(1)(a), (b) or (c), 24 [, 24A or 24B][3] above in relation to a party to the marriage, the court shall in particular have regard to the following matters –

     (a)   the income, earning capacity, property and other financial resources which each of the parties to the marriage has or is likely to have in the foreseeable future, including in the case of earning capacity any increase in that capacity which it would in the opinion of the court be reasonable to expect a party to the marriage to take steps to acquire;

     (b)   the financial needs, obligations and responsibilities which each of the parties to the marriage has or is likely to have in the foreseeable future;

     (c)   the standard of living enjoyed by the family before the breakdown of the marriage;

     (d)   the age of each party to the marriage and the duration of the marriage;

     (e)   any physical or mental disability of either of the parties to the marriage;

     (f)   the contributions which each of the parties has made or is likely in the foreseeable future to make to the welfare of the family, including any contribution by looking after the home or caring for the family;

     (g)   the conduct of each of the parties, if that conduct is such that it would in the opinion of the court be inequitable to disregard it;

     (h)   in the case of proceedings for divorce or nullity of marriage, the value to each of the parties to the marriage of any benefit ...[4] which, by reason of the dissolution or annulment of the marriage, that party will lose the chance of acquiring.

---

[1]   Sections inserted: Welfare Reform and Pensions Act 1999, s 19, Sch 3, paras 1, 4, with effect from 1 December 2000 (Welfare Reform and Pensions Act 1999 (Commencement No 5) Order 2000, SI 2000/1116).

[2]   Words substituted: Welfare Reform and Pensions Act 1999, s 19, Sch 3, paras 1, 5(a), with effect from 1 December 2000 (Welfare Reform and Pensions Act 1999 (Commencement No 5) Order 2000, SI 2000/1116).

[3]   Words substituted: Welfare Reform and Pensions Act 1999, s 19, Sch 3, paras 1, 5(b), with effect from 1 December 2000 (Welfare Reform and Pensions Act 1999 (Commencement No 5) Order 2000, SI 2000/1116).

[4]   Amendment: Words repealed: Pensions Act 1995, s 166(2), with effect from 1 August 1996 (Pensions Act 1995 (Commencement) (No 5) Order 1996, SI 1996/1675).

(3)   As regards the exercise of the powers of the court under section 23(1)(d), (e) or (f), (2) or (4), 24 or 24A above in relation to a child of the family, the court shall in particular have regard to the following matters –

(a)   the financial needs of the child;

(b)   the income, earning capacity (if any), property and other financial resources of the child;

(c)   any physical or mental disability of the child;

(d)   the manner in which he was being and in which the parties to the marriage expected him to be educated or trained;

(e)   the considerations mentioned in relation to the parties to the marriage in paragraphs (a), (b), (c) and (e) of subsection (2) above.

(4)   As regards the exercise of the powers of the court under section 23(1)(d), (e) or (f), (2) or (4), 24 or 24A above against a party to a marriage in favour of a child of the family who is not the child of that party, the court shall also have regard –

(a)   to whether that party assumed any responsibility for the child's maintenance, and, if so, to the extent to which, and the basis upon which, that party assumed such responsibility and to the length of time for which that party discharged such responsibility;

(b)   to whether in assuming and discharging such responsibility that party did so knowing that the child was not his or her own;

(c)   to the liability of any other person to maintain the child.][1]

[25A Exercise of court's powers in favour of party to marriage on decree of divorce or nullity of marriage

(1)   Where on or after the grant of a decree of divorce or nullity of marriage the court decides to exercise its powers under section 23(1)(a), (b) or (c), 24 [, 24A or 24B][2] above in favour of a party to the marriage, it shall be the duty of the court to consider whether it would be appropriate so to exercise those powers that the financial obligations of each party towards the other will be terminated as soon after the grant of the decree as the court considers just and reasonable.

(2)   Where the court decides in such a case to make a periodical payments or secured periodical payments order in favour of a party to the marriage, the court shall in particular consider whether it would be appropriate to require those payments to be made or secured only for such term as would in the opinion of the court be sufficient to enable the party in whose favour the order is made to adjust without undue hardship to the termination of his or her financial dependence on the other party.

(3)   Where on or after the grant of a decree of divorce or nullity of marriage an application is made by a party to the marriage for a periodical payments or secured periodical payments order in his or her favour, then, if the court considers that no continuing obligation should be imposed on either party to make or secure periodical payments in favour of the other, the court may dismiss the application with a direction that the applicant shall not be entitled to make any future application in relation to that marriage for an order under section 23(1)(a) or (b) above.][3]

[25B Pensions

(1)   The matters to which the court is to have regard under section 25(2) above include –

(a)   in the case of paragraph (a), any benefits under a pension [arrangement][4] which a party to the marriage has or is likely to have, and

---

[1]   Section substituted: Matrimonial and Family Proceedings Act 1984, s 3, with effect from 12 October 1984 (s 47(1)).

[2]   Words substituted: Welfare Reform and Pensions Act 1999, s 19, Sch 3, paras 1, 6, from 1 December 2000 (Welfare Reform and Pensions Act 1999 (Commencement No 5) Order 2000, SI 2000/1116).

[3]   Section inserted: Matrimonial and Family Proceedings Act 1984, s 3, with effect from 12 October 1984 (s 47(1)).

[4]   Word substituted: Welfare Reform and Pensions Act 1999, s 21, Sch 4, paras 1(1), (2), with effect from 1 December 2000 (Welfare Reform and Pensions Act 1999 (Commencement No 5) Order 2000, SI 2000/1116).

(b)   in the case of paragraph (h), any benefits under a pension [arrangement][1] which, by reason of the dissolution or annulment of the marriage, a party to the marriage will lose the chance of acquiring,

and, accordingly, in relation to benefits under a pension [arrangement],[2] section 25(2)(a) above shall have effect as if 'in the foreseeable future' were omitted.

(2)   ...[3]

(3)   The following provisions apply where, having regard to any benefits under a pension [arrangement],[4] the court determines to make an order under section 23 above.

(4)   To the extent to which the order is made having regard to any benefits under a pension [arrangement],[5] the order may require the [person responsible for][6] the pension [arrangement][7] in question, if at any time any payment in respect of any benefits under the [arrangement][8] becomes due to the party with pension rights, to make a payment for the benefit of the other party.

[(5)   The order must express the amount of any payment required to be made by virtue of subsection (4) above as a percentage of the payment which becomes due to the party with pension rights.][9]

(6)   Any such payment by the [person responsible for the arrangement] –[10]

(a)   shall discharge so much of [his][11] liability to the party with pension rights as corresponds to the amount of the payment, and

(b)   shall be treated for all purposes as a payment made by the party with pension rights in or towards the discharge of his liability under the order.

(7)   Where the party with pension rights [has a right of commutation under the arrangement, the order may require him to exercise it to any extent];[12] and this section applies to [any payment due in consequence of commutation][13] in pursuance of the order as it applies to other payments in respect of benefits under the [arrangement].[14]

[(7A)   The power conferred by subsection (7) above may not be exercised for the purpose of commuting a benefit payable to the party with pension rights to a benefit payable to the other party.

(7B)   The power conferred by subsection (4) or (7) above may not be exercised in relation to a pension arrangement which –

---

[1]   Word substituted: Welfare Reform and Pensions Act 1999, s 21, Sch 4, paras 1(1), (2), with effect from 1 December 2000 (Welfare Reform and Pensions Act 1999 (Commencement No 5) Order 2000, SI 2000/1116).

[2]   Word substituted: Welfare Reform and Pensions Act 1999, s 21, Sch 4, paras 1(1), (2), with effect from 1 December 2000 (Welfare Reform and Pensions Act 1999 (Commencement No 5) Order 2000, SI 2000/1116).

[3]   Subsection omitted: Welfare Reform and Pensions Act 1999, ss 21, 88, Sch 4, paras 1(1), (3), Sch 13, Pt II, with effect from 1 December 2000 (Welfare Reform and Pensions Act 1999 (Commencement No 5) Order 2000, SI 2000/1116).

[4]   Word substituted: Welfare Reform and Pensions Act 1999, s 21, Sch 4, paras 1(1), (4), with effect from 1 December 2000 (Welfare Reform and Pensions Act 1999 (Commencement No 5) Order 2000, SI 2000/1116).

[5]   Word substituted: Welfare Reform and Pensions Act 1999, s 21, Sch 4, paras 1(1), (5)(a), with effect from 1 December 2000 (Welfare Reform and Pensions Act 1999 (Commencement No 5) Order 2000, SI 2000/1116).

[6]   Words substituted: Welfare Reform and Pensions Act 1999, s 21, Sch 4, paras 1(1), (5)(b), with effect from 1 December 2000 (Welfare Reform and Pensions Act 1999 (Commencement No 5) Order 2000, SI 2000/1116).

[7]   Word substituted: Welfare Reform and Pensions Act 1999, s 21, Sch 4, paras 1(1), (5)(a), with effect from 1 December 2000 (Welfare Reform and Pensions Act 1999 (Commencement No 5) Order 2000, SI 2000/1116).

[8]   Word substituted: Welfare Reform and Pensions Act 1999, s 21, Sch 4, paras 1(1), (5)(a), with effect from 1 December 2000 (Welfare Reform and Pensions Act 1999 (Commencement No 5) Order 2000, SI 2000/1116).

[9]   Subsection substituted: Welfare Reform and Pensions Act 1999, s 21, Sch 4, paras 1(1), (6), with effect from 1 December 2000 (Welfare Reform and Pensions Act 1999 (Commencement No 5) Order 2000, SI 2000/1116).

[10]   Words substituted: Welfare Reform and Pensions Act 1999, s 21, Sch 4, paras 1(1), (7)(a), with effect from 1 December 2000 (Welfare Reform and Pensions Act 1999 (Commencement No 5) Order 2000, SI 2000/1116).

[11]   Words substituted: Welfare Reform and Pensions Act 1999, s 21, Sch 4, paras 1(1), (7)(b), with effect from 1 December 2000 (Welfare Reform and Pensions Act 1999 (Commencement No 5) Order 2000, SI 2000/1116).

[12]   Words substituted: Welfare Reform and Pensions Act 1999, s 21, Sch 4, paras 1(1), (8)(a), with effect from 1 December 2000 (Welfare Reform and Pensions Act 1999 (Commencement No 5) Order 2000, SI 2000/1116).

[13]   Words substituted: Welfare Reform and Pensions Act 1999, s 21, Sch 4, paras 1(1), (8)(b), with effect from 1 December 2000 (Welfare Reform and Pensions Act 1999 (Commencement No 5) Order 2000, SI 2000/1116).

[14]   Word substituted: Welfare Reform and Pensions Act 1999, s 21, Sch 4, paras 1(1), (8)(c), with effect from 1 December 2000 (Welfare Reform and Pensions Act 1999 (Commencement No 5) Order 2000, SI 2000/1116).

(a)   is the subject of a pension sharing order in relation to the marriage, or

(b)   has been the subject of pension sharing between the parties to the marriage.

(7C)   In subsection (1) above, references to benefits under a pension arrangement include any benefits by way of pension, whether under a pension arrangement or not.]']²

[25C   Pensions: lump sums

(1)   The power of the court under section 23 above to order a party to a marriage to pay a lump sum to the other party includes, where the benefits which the party with pension rights has or is likely to have under a pension [arrangement]³ include any lump sum payable in respect of his death, power to make any of the following provision by the order.

(2)   The court may –

(a)   if the [person responsible for the pension arrangement in question has]⁴ power to determine the person to whom the sum, or any part of it, is to be paid, require [him]⁵ to pay the whole or part of that sum, when it becomes due, to the other party,

(b)   if the party with pension rights has power to nominate the person to whom the sum, or any part of it, is to be paid, require the party with pension rights to nominate the other party in respect of the whole or part of that sum,

(c)   in any other case, require the [person responsible for the pension arrangement]⁶ in question to pay the whole or part of that sum, when it becomes due, for the benefit of the other party instead of to the person to whom, apart from the order, it would be paid.

(3)   Any payment by the [person responsible for the arrangement]⁷ under an order made under section 23 above by virtue of this section shall discharge so much of [his]⁸ liability in respect of the party with pension rights as corresponds to the amount of the payment.

[(4)   The powers conferred by this section may not be exercised in relation to a pension arrangement which –

(a)   is the subject of a pension sharing order in relation to the marriage, or

(b)   has been the subject of pension sharing between the parties to the marriage.]⁹]¹⁰

[25D   Pensions: supplementary

[(1)   Where –

(a)   an order made under section 23 above by virtue of section 25B or 25C above imposes any requirement on the person responsible for a pension arrangement ('the first arrangement') and the party with pension rights acquires rights under another pension arrangement ('the

---

1   Subsections inserted: Welfare Reform and Pensions Act 1999, s 21, Sch 4, paras 1(1), (9), with effect from 1 December 2000 (Welfare Reform and Pensions Act 1999 (Commencement No 5) Order 2000, SI 2000/1116).

2   Section inserted: Pensions Act 1995, s 166(1), with effect from 16 July 1996 (Pensions Act 1995 (Commencement No 7) Order 1996, SI 1996/1853).

3   Word substituted: Welfare Reform and Pensions Act 1999, s 21, Sch 4, paras 2(1), (2), with effect from 1 December 2000 (Welfare Reform and Pensions Act 1999 (Commencement No 5) Order 2000, SI 2000/1116).

4   Words substituted: Welfare Reform and Pensions Act 1999, s 21, Sch 4, paras 2(1), (3)(a)(i), with effect from 1 December 2000 (Welfare Reform and Pensions Act 1999 (Commencement No 5) Order 2000, SI 2000/1116).

5   Word substituted: Welfare Reform and Pensions Act 1999, s 21, Sch 4, paras 2(1), (3)(a)(ii), with effect from 1 December 2000 (Welfare Reform and Pensions Act 1999 (Commencement No 5) Order 2000, SI 2000/1116).

6   Words substituted: Welfare Reform and Pensions Act 1999, s 21, Sch 4, paras 2(1), (3)(b), with effect from 1 December 2000 (Welfare Reform and Pensions Act 1999 (Commencement No 5) Order 2000, SI 2000/1116).

7   Words substituted: Welfare Reform and Pensions Act 1999, s 21, Sch 4, paras 2(1), (4)(a), with effect from 1 December 2000 (Welfare Reform and Pensions Act 1999 (Commencement No 5) Order 2000, SI 2000/1116).

8   Words substituted: Welfare Reform and Pensions Act 1999, s 21, Sch 4, paras 2(1), (4)(b), with effect from 1 December 2000 (Welfare Reform and Pensions Act 1999 (Commencement No 5) Order 2000, SI 2000/1116).

9   Subsection inserted: Welfare Reform and Pensions Act 1999, s 21, Sch 4, paras 2(1), (5), with effect from 1 December 2000 (Welfare Reform and Pensions Act 1999 (Commencement No 5) Order 2000, SI 2000/1116).

10   Section inserted: Pensions Act 1995, s 166(1), with effect from 16 July 1996 (Pensions Act 1995 (Commencement No 7) Order 1996, SI 1996/1853).

new arrangement') which are derived (directly or indirectly) from the whole of his rights under the first arrangement, and

(b)   the person responsible for the new arrangement has been given notice in accordance with regulations made by the Lord Chancellor,

the order shall have effect as if it had been made instead in respect of the person responsible for the new arrangement.][1]

(2)   [The Lord Chancellor may by regulations] –[2]

(a)   in relation to any provision of sections 25B or 25C above which authorises the court making an order under section 23 above to require the [person responsible for a pension arrangement][3] to make a payment for the benefit of the other party, make provision as to the person to whom, and the terms on which, the payment is to be made,

[(ab)   make, in relation to payment under a mistaken belief as to the continuation in force of a provision included by virtue of section 25B or 25C above in an order under section 23 above, provision about the rights or liabilities of the payer, the payee or the person to whom the payment was due,][4]

(b)   require notices to be given in respect of changes of circumstances relevant to such orders which include provision made by virtue of sections 25B and 25C above,

[(ba)   make provision for the person responsible for a pension arrangement to be discharged in prescribed circumstances from a requirement imposed by virtue of section 25B or 25C above,][5]

(c), (d) ...[6]

[(e)   make provision about calculation and verification in relation to the valuation of –

(i)   benefits under a pension arrangement, or

(ii)   shareable state scheme rights,

for the purposes of the court's functions in connection with the exercise of any of its powers under this Part of this Act.][7]

...[8]

[(2A)   Regulations under subsection (2)(e) above may include –

(a)   provision for calculation or verification in accordance with guidance from time to time prepared by a prescribed person, and

(b)   provision by reference to regulations under section 30 or 49(4) of the Welfare Reform and Pensions Act 1999.

(2B)   Regulations under subsection (2) above may make different provision for different cases.

---

[1]   Subsection substituted: Welfare Reform and Pensions Act 1999, s 21, Sch 4, paras 3(1), (2), with effect from 1 December 2000 (Welfare Reform and Pensions Act 1999 (Commencement No 5) Order 2000, SI 2000/1116).

[2]   Words substituted: Welfare Reform and Pensions Act 1999, s 21, Sch 4, paras 3(1), (3)(a), with effect from 1 December 2000 (Welfare Reform and Pensions Act 1999 (Commencement No 5) Order 2000, SI 2000/1116).

[3]   Words substituted: Welfare Reform and Pensions Act 1999, s 21, Sch 4, paras 3(1), (3)(b), with effect from 1 December 2000 (Welfare Reform and Pensions Act 1999 (Commencement No 5) Order 2000, SI 2000/1116).

[4]   Paragraph inserted: Welfare Reform and Pensions Act 1999, s 21, Sch 4, paras 3(1), (3)(c), with effect from 1 December 2000 (Welfare Reform and Pensions Act 1999 (Commencement No 5) Order 2000, SI 2000/1116).

[5]   Paragraph inserted: Welfare Reform and Pensions Act 1999, s 21, Sch 4, paras 3(1), (3)(d), with effect from 1 December 2000 (Welfare Reform and Pensions Act 1999 (Commencement No 5) Order 2000, SI 2000/1116).

[6]   Paragraphs omitted: Welfare Reform and Pensions Act 1999, ss 21, 88, Sch 4, paras 3(1), (3)(e), Sch 13, Pt II, with effect from 1 December 2000 (Welfare Reform and Pensions Act 1999 (Commencement No 5) Order 2000, SI 2000/1116).

[7]   Paragraph substituted: Welfare Reform and Pensions Act 1999, s 21, Sch 4, paras 3(1), (3)(f), with effect from 1 December 2000 (Welfare Reform and Pensions Act 1999 (Commencement No 5) Order 2000, SI 2000/1116).

[8]   Words omitted: Welfare Reform and Pensions Act 1999, ss 21, 88, Sch 4, paras 3(1), (3)(g), Sch 13, Pt II, with effect from 1 December 2000 (Welfare Reform and Pensions Act 1999 (Commencement No 5) Order 2000, SI 2000/1116).

(2C)   Power to make regulations under this section shall be exercisable by statutory instrument which shall be subject to annulment in pursuance of a resolution of either House of Parliament.][1]

[(3)   In this section and sections 25B and 25C above –

'occupational pension scheme' has the same meaning as in the Pension Schemes Act 1993;

'the party with pension rights' means the party to the marriage who has or is likely to have benefits under a pension arrangement and 'the other party' means the other party to the marriage;

'pension arrangement' means –

(a)   an occupational pension scheme,

(b)   a personal pension scheme,

(c)   a retirement annuity contract,

(d)   an annuity or insurance policy purchased, or transferred, for the purpose of giving effect to rights under an occupational pension scheme or a personal pension scheme, and

(e)   an annuity purchased, or entered into, for the purpose of discharging liability in respect of a pension credit under section 29(1)(b) of the Welfare Reform and Pensions Act 1999 or under corresponding Northern Ireland legislation;

'personal pension scheme' has the same meaning as in the Pension Schemes Act 1993;

'prescribed' means prescribed by regulations;

'retirement annuity contract' means a contract or scheme approved under Chapter III of Part XIV of the Income and Corporation Taxes Act 1988;

'shareable state scheme rights' has the same meaning as in section 21A(1) above; and

'trustees or managers', in relation to an occupational pension scheme or a personal pension scheme, means –

(a)   in the case of a scheme established under a trust, the trustees of the scheme, and

(b)   in any other case, the managers of the scheme.

(4)   In this section and sections 25B and 25C above, references to the person responsible for a pension arrangement are –

(a)   in the case of an occupational pension scheme or a personal pension scheme, to the trustees or managers of the scheme,

(b)   in the case of a retirement annuity contract or an annuity falling within paragraph (d) or (e) of the definition of 'pension arrangement' above, the provider of the annuity, and

(c)   in the case of an insurance policy falling within paragraph (d) of the definition of that expression, the insurer.][2]][3]

****

Variation, discharge and enforcement of certain orders etc

31[4]   Variation, discharge etc of certain orders for financial relief

(1)   Where the court has made an order to which this section applies, then, subject to the provisions of this section [and of section 28(1A) above],[1] the court shall have power to vary or discharge the order

---

[1]   Subsections inserted: Welfare Reform and Pensions Act 1999, s 21, Sch 4, paras 3(1), (4), with effect from 1 December 2000 (Welfare Reform and Pensions Act 1999 (Commencement No 5) Order 2000, SI 2000/1116).

[2]   Subsections substituted: Welfare Reform and Pensions Act 1999, s 21, Sch 4, paras 3(1), (5), with effect from 1 December 2000 (Welfare Reform and Pensions Act 1999 (Commencement No 5) Order 2000, SI 2000/1116).

[3]   Section inserted: Pensions Act 1995, s 166(1), with effect from 16 July 1996 (Pensions Act 1995 (Commencement No 7) Order 1996, SI 1996/1853).

[4]   Commencement: 1 January 1974 (SI 1973/1972).

or to suspend any provision thereof temporarily and to revive the operation of any provision so suspended.

(2)   This section applies to the following orders, that is to say –

(a)   any order for maintenance pending suit and any interim order for maintenance;

(b)   any periodical payments order;

(c)   any secured periodical payments order;

(d)   any order made by virtue of section 23(3)(c) or 27(7)(b) above (provision for payment of a lump sum by instalments);

[(dd)   any deferred order made by virtue of section 23(1)(c) (lump sums) which includes provision made by virtue of –

(i)   section 25B(4), or

(ii)   section 25C,

(provision in respect of pension rights);][2]

(e)   any order for a settlement of property under section 24(1)(b) or for a variation of settlement under section 24(1)(c) or (d) above, being an order made on or after the grant of a decree of judicial separation;

[(f)   any order made under section 24A(1) above for the sale of property].[3]

[(g)   a pension sharing order under section 24B above which is made at a time before the decree has been made absolute.][4]

[(2A)   Where the court has made an order referred to in subsection (2)(a), (b) or (c) above, then, subject to the provisions of this section, the court shall have power to remit the payment of any arrears due under the order or of any part thereof.][5]

[(2B)   Where the court has made an order referred to in subsection (2)(dd)(ii) above, this section shall cease to apply to the order on the death of either of the parties to the marriage.][6]

(3)   The powers exercisable by the court under this section in relation to an order shall be exercisable also in relation to any instrument executed in pursuance of the order.

(4)   The court shall not exercise the powers conferred by this section in relation to an order for a settlement under section 24(1)(b) or for a variation of settlement under section 24(1)(c) or (d) above except on an application made in proceedings –

(a)   for the rescission of the decree of judicial separation by reference to which the order was made, or

(b)   for the dissolution of the marriage in question.

[(4A)   In relation to an order which falls within paragraph (g) of subsection (2) above ('the subsection (2) order') –

(a)   the powers conferred by this section may be exercised –

(i)   only on an application made before the subsection (2) order has or, but for paragraph (b) below, would have taken effect; and

---

Words substituted: Matrimonial and Family Proceedings Act 1984, s 6, with effect from 12 October 1984 (s 47(1)).

[2]   Paragraph inserted: Pensions Act 1995, s 166(3), with effect from 1 August 1996 (Pensions Act 1995 (Commencement) (No 5) Order 1996, SI 1996/1675).

[3]   Words inserted: Matrimonial Homes and Property Act 1981, s 8(2)(a), with effect from 1 October 1981 (Matrimonial Homes and Property Act 1981 (Commencement No 1) Order 1981, SI 1981/1275).

[4]   Paragraph inserted: Welfare Reform and Pensions Act 1999, s 19, Sch 3, paras 1, 7(1), (2), with effect from 1 December 2000 (Welfare Reform and Pensions Act 1999 (Commencement No 5) Order 2000, SI 2000/1116).

[5]   Subsection inserted: Administration of Justice Act 1982, s 51, with effect from 1 January 1983 (s 76(11)).

[6]   Subsection inserted: Pensions Act 1995, s 166(3)(b), with effect from 1 August 1996 (Pensions Act 1995 (Commencement No 5) Order 1996, SI 1996/1675).

(ii)   only if, at the time when the application is made, the decree has not been made absolute; and

(b)   an application made in accordance with paragraph (a) above prevents the subsection (2) order from taking effect before the application has been dealt with.

(4B)   No variation of a pension sharing order shall be made so as to take effect before the decree is made absolute.

(4C)   The variation of a pension sharing order prevents the order taking effect before the end of such period after the making of the variation as may be prescribed by regulations made by the Lord Chancellor.][1]

(5)   [Subject to subsections (7A) to [(7G)][2] below and without prejudice to any power exercisable by virtue of subsection (2)(d), (dd) [, (e) or (g)][3] above or otherwise than by virtue of this section,][4] no property adjustment order [or pension sharing order][5] shall be made on an application for the variation of a periodical payments or secured periodical payments order made (whether in favour of a party to a marriage or in favour of a child of the family) under section 23 above, and no order for the payment of a lump sum shall be made on an application for the variation of a periodical payments or secured periodical payments order in favour of a party to a marriage (whether made under section 23 or under section 27 above).

(6)   Where the person liable to make payments under a secured periodical payments order has died, an application under this section relating to that order [(and to any order made under section 24A(1) above which requires the proceeds of sale of property to be used for securing those payments) may be made by the person entitled to payments under the periodical payments order][6] or by the personal representatives of the deceased person, but no such application shall, except with the permission of the court, be made after the end of the period of six months from the date on which representation in regard to the estate of that person is first taken out.

[(7)   In exercising the powers conferred by this section the court shall have regard to all the circumstances of the case, first consideration being given to the welfare while a minor of any child of the family who has not attained the age of eighteen, and the circumstances of the case shall include any change in any of the matters to which the court was required to have regard when making the order to which the application relates, and –

(a)   in the case of a periodical payments or secured periodical payments order made on or after the grant of a decree of divorce or nullity of marriage, the court shall consider whether in all the circumstances and after having regard to any such change it would be appropriate to vary the order so that payments under the order are required to be made or secured only for such further period as will in the opinion of the court be sufficient [(in the light of any proposed exercise by the court, where the marriage has been dissolved, of its powers under subsection (7B) below)][7] to enable the party in whose favour the order was made to adjust without undue hardship to the termination of those payments;

(b)   in a case where the party against whom the order was made has died, the circumstances of the case shall also include the changed circumstances resulting from his or her death.][8]

---

[1]   Subsections inserted: Welfare Reform and Pensions Act 1999, s 19, Sch 3, paras 1, 7(1), (3), with effect from 1 December 2000 (Welfare Reform and Pensions Act 1999 (Commencement No 5) Order 2000, SI 2000/1116).

[2]   Subsection reference substituted: Welfare Reform and Pensions Act 1999, s 19, Sch 3, paras 1, 7(1), (4)(a), with effect from 1 December 2000 (Welfare Reform and Pensions Act 1999 (Commencement No 5) Order 2000, SI 2000/1116).

[3]   Words in italics substituted: Welfare Reform and Pensions Act 1999, s 19, Sch 3, paras 1, 7(1), (4)(b), with effect from 1 December 2000 (Welfare Reform and Pensions Act 1999 (Commencement No 5) Order 2000, SI 2000/1116).

[4]   Words inserted: Family Law Act 1996, s 66(1), Sch 8, para 16(5)(a), with effect from 1 November 1998 (Family Law Act 1996 (Commencement) (No 3) Order 1998, SI 1998/2572).

[5]   Words inserted: Welfare Reform and Pensions Act 1999, s 19, Sch 3, paras 1, 7(1), (4)(c), with effect from 1 December 2000 (Welfare Reform and Pensions Act 1999 (Commencement No 5) Order 2000, SI 2000/1116).

[6]   Words substituted: Matrimonial Homes and Property Act 1981, s 8(2)(b), with effect from 1 October 1981 (Matrimonial Homes and Property Act 1981 (Commencement No 1) Order 1981, SI 1981/1275).

[7]   Words inserted: Family Law Act 1996, s 66(1), Sch 8, para 16(6)(b), with effect from 1 November 1998 (Family Law Act 1996 (Commencement) (No 3) Order 1998, SI 1998/2572).

[8]   Subsection substituted: Matrimonial and Family Proceedings Act 1984, s 6, with effect from 12 October 1984 (s 47(1)).

[(7A) Subsection (7B) below applies where, after the dissolution of a marriage, the court –

    (a)   discharges a periodical payments order or secured periodical payments order made in favour of a party to the marriage; or

    (b)   varies such an order so that payments under the order are required to be made or secured only for such further period as is determined by the court.

(7B)   The court has power, in addition to any power it has apart from this subsection, to make supplemental provision consisting of any of –

    (a)   an order for the payment of a lump sum in favour of a party to the marriage;

    (b)   one or more property adjustment orders in favour of a party to the marriage;

    [(ba)   one or more pension sharing orders;][1]

    (c)   a direction that the party in whose favour the original order discharged or varied was made is not entitled to make any further application for –

        (i)   a periodical payments or secured periodical payments order, or

        (ii)   an extension of the period to which the original order is limited by any variation made by the court.

(7C)   An order for the payment of a lump sum made under subsection (7B) above may –

    (a)   provide for the payment of that sum by instalments of such amount as may be specified in the order; and

    (b)   require the payment of the instalments to be secured to the satisfaction of the court.

(7D)   [Section 23(6)][2] above apply where the court makes an order for the payment of a lump sum under subsection (7B) above as they apply where it makes such an order under [section 23][3] above.

(7E)   If under subsection (7B) above the court makes more than one property adjustment order in favour of the same party to the marriage, each of those orders must fall within a different paragraph of section 21(2) above.

(7F)   Sections 24A and 30 above apply where the court makes a property adjustment order under subsection (7B) above as they apply where it makes such an order under [section 24][4] above.][5]

[(7G)   Subsections (3) to (5) of section 24B above apply in relation to a pension sharing order under subsection (7B) above as they apply in relation to a pension sharing order under that section.][6]

(8)   The personal representatives of a deceased person against whom a secured periodical payments order was made shall not be liable for having distributed any part of the estate of the deceased after the expiration of the period of six months referred to in subsection (6) above on the ground that they ought to have taken into account the possibility that the court might permit an application under this section to be made after that period by the person entitled to payments under the order; but this subsection shall not prejudice any power to recover any part of the estate so distributed arising by virtue of the making of an order in pursuance of this section.

(9)   In considering for the purposes of subsection (6) above the question when representation was first taken out, a grant limited to settled land or to trust property shall be left out of account and a grant

---

[1]   Paragraph inserted: Welfare Reform and Pensions Act 1999, s 19, Sch 3, paras 1, 7(1), (5), with effect from 1 December 2000 (Welfare Reform and Pensions Act 1999 (Commencement No 5) Order 2000, SI 2000/1116).

[2]   Modified until such time as Family Law Act 1996, Pt II comes into force: Family Law Act 1996 (Commencement) (No 3) Order 1998, SI 1998/2572, with effect from 1 November 1998.

[3]   Modified until such time as Family Law Act 1996, Pt II comes into force: Family Law Act 1996 (Commencement) (No 3) Order 1998, SI 1998/2572, with effect from 1 November 1998.

[4]   Modified until such time as Family Law Act 1996, Pt II comes into force: Family Law Act 1996 (Commencement) (No 3) Order 1998, SI 1998/2572, with effect from 1 November 1998.

[5]   Subsections inserted: Family Law Act 1996, s 66(1), Sch 8, para 16(7), with effect from 1 November 1998 (Family Law Act 1996 (Commencement) (No 3) Order 1998, SI 1998/2572).

[6]   Subsection inserted: Welfare Reform and Pensions Act 1999, s 19, Sch 3, paras 1, 7(1), (6), with effect from 1 December 2000 (Welfare Reform and Pensions Act 1999 (Commencement No 5) Order 2000, SI 2000/1116).

limited to real estate or to personal estate shall be left out of account unless a grant limited to the remainder of the estate has previously been made or is made at the same time.

[(10)   Where the court, in exercise of its powers under this section, decides to vary or discharge a periodical payments or secured periodical payments order, then, subject to section 28(1) and (2) above, the court shall have power to direct that the variation or discharge shall not take effect until the expiration of such period as may be specified in the order.][1]

[(11)   Where –

(a)   a periodical payments or secured periodical payments order in favour of more than one child ('the order') is in force;

(b)   the order requires payments specified in it to be made to or for the benefit of more than one child without apportioning those payments between them;

(c)   a *maintenance assessment* [-][2] ('*the assessment* [-][3]') is made with respect to one or more, but not all, of the children with respect to whom those payments are to be made; and

(d)   an application is made, before the end of the period of 6 months beginning with the date on which *the assessment* [-][4] was made, for the variation or discharge of the order,

the court may, in exercise of its powers under this section to vary or discharge the order, direct that the variation or discharge shall take effect from the date on which *the assessment* [-][5] took effect or any later date.

(12)   Where –

(a)   an order ('the child order') of a kind prescribed for the purposes of section 10(1) of the Child Support Act 1991 is affected by a *maintenance assessment* [-];[6]

(b)   on the date on which the child order became so affected there was in force a periodical payments or secured periodical payments order ('the spousal order') in favour of a party to a marriage having the care of the child in whose favour the child order was made; and

(c)   an application is made, before the end of the period of 6 months beginning with the date on which the *maintenance assessment* [-][7] was made, for the spousal order to be varied or discharged,

the court may, in exercise of its powers under this section to vary or discharge the spousal order, direct that the variation or discharge shall take effect from the date on which the child order became so affected or any later date.

(13)   For the purposes of subsection (12) above, an order is affected if it ceases to have effect or is modified by or under section 10 of the Child Support Act 1991.

---

[1]   Subsection inserted: Matrimonial and Family Proceedings Act 1984, s 6, with effect from 12 October 1984 (s 47(1)).

[2]   Words in italics prospectively substituted by Child Support, Pensions and Social Security Act 2000, s 26, Sch 3, para 3(1), (3)(a), from a date to be appointed.
New text = 'maintenance calculation'.

[3]   Words in italics prospectively substituted by Child Support, Pensions and Social Security Act 2000, s 26, Sch 3, para 3(1), (3)(b), from a date to be appointed.
New text = 'the calculation'.

[4]   Words in italics prospectively substituted by Child Support, Pensions and Social Security Act 2000, s 26, Sch 3, para 3(1), (3)(b), from a date to be appointed.
New text = 'the calculation'.

[5]   Words in italics prospectively substituted by Child Support, Pensions and Social Security Act 2000, s 26, Sch 3, para 3(1), (3)(b), from a date to be appointed.
New text = 'the calculation'.

[6]   Words in italics prospectively substituted by Child Support, Pensions and Social Security Act 2000, s 26, Sch 3, para 3(1), (3)(a), from a date to be appointed.
New text = 'maintenance calculation'.

[7]   Words in italics prospectively substituted by Child Support, Pensions and Social Security Act 2000, s 26, Sch 3, para 3(1), (3)(a), from a date to be appointed.
New text = 'maintenance calculation'.

(14) Subsections (11) and (12) above are without prejudice to any other power of the court to direct that the variation of discharge of an order under this section shall take effect from a date earlier than that on which the order for variation or discharge was made.][1]

[(15) The power to make regulations under subsection (4C) above shall be exercisable by statutory instrument which shall be subject to annulment in pursuance of a resolution of either House of Parliament.][2]

****

[*Consent orders*

33A[3] Consent orders for financial provision on property adjustment

(1) Notwithstanding anything in the preceding provisions of this Part of this Act, on an application for a consent order for financial relief the court may, unless it has reason to think that there are other circumstances into which it ought to inquire, make an order in the terms agreed on the basis only of the prescribed information furnished with the application.

(2) Subsection (1) above applies to an application for a consent order varying or discharging an order for financial relief as it applies to an application for an order for financial relief.

(3) In this section –

'consent order', in relation to an application for an order, means an order in the terms applied for to which the respondent agrees;

'order for financial relief' means an order under any of sections 23, 24, 24A [, 24B][4] or 27 above; and

'prescribed' means prescribed by rules of court.][5]

****

Miscellaneous and supplemental

37[6] Avoidance of transactions intended to prevent or reduce financial relief

(1) For the purposes of this section 'financial relief' means relief under any of the provisions of sections 22, 23, 24, [24B,][7] 27, 31 (except subsection (6)) and 35 above, and any reference in this section to defeating a person's claim for financial relief is a reference to preventing financial relief from being granted to that person, or to that person for the benefit of a child of the family, or reducing the amount of any financial relief which might be so granted, or frustrating or impeding the enforcement of any order which might be or has been made at his instance under any of those provisions.

(2) Where proceedings for financial relief are brought by one person against another, the court may, on the application of the first-mentioned person –

(a) if it is satisfied that the other party to the proceedings is, with the intention of defeating the claim for financial relief, about to make any disposition or to transfer out of the jurisdiction or otherwise deal with any property, make such order as it thinks fit for restraining the other party from so doing or otherwise for protecting the claim;

---

[1] Subsections inserted: Maintenance Orders (Backdating) Order 1993, SI 1993/623, with effect from 5 April 1993.
[2] Subsection inserted: Welfare Reform and Pensions Act 1999, s 19, Sch 3, paras 1, 7(1), (7), with effect from 1 December 2000 (Welfare Reform and Pensions Act 1999 (Commencement No 5) Order 2000, SI 2000/1116).
[3] Commencement: 1 January 1974 (SI 1973/1972).
[4] Reference inserted: Welfare Reform and Pensions Act 1999, s 19, Sch 3, paras 1, 8, with effect from 1 December 2000 (Welfare Reform and Pensions Act 1999 (Commencement No 5) Order 2000, SI 2000/1116).
[5] Section inserted: Matrimonial and Family Proceedings Act 1984, s 7, with effect from 12 October 1984 (s 47(1)).
[6] Commencement: 1 January 1974 (SI 1973/1972).
[7] Reference inserted: Welfare Reform and Pensions Act 1999, s 19, Sch 3, paras 1, 9, with effect from 1 December 2000 (Welfare Reform and Pensions Act 1999 (Commencement No 5) Order 2000, SI 2000/1116).

(b)   if it is satisfied that the other party has, with that intention, made a reviewable disposition and that if the disposition were set aside financial relief or different financial relief would be granted to the applicant, make an order setting aside the disposition;

(c)   if it is satisfied, in a case where an order has been obtained under any of the provisions mentioned in subsection (1) above by the applicant against the other party, that the other party has, with that intention, made a reviewable disposition, make an order setting aside the disposition;

and an application for the purposes of paragraph (b) above shall be made in the proceedings for the financial relief in question.

(3)   Where the court makes an order under subsection (2)(b) or (c) above setting aside a disposition it shall give such consequential directions as it thinks fit for giving effect to the order (including directions requiring the making of any payments or the disposal of any property).

(4)   Any disposition made by the other party to the proceedings for financial relief in question (whether before or after the commencement of those proceedings) is a reviewable disposition for the purposes of subsection (2)(b) and (c) above unless it was made for valuable consideration (other than marriage) to a person who, at the time of the disposition, acted in relation to it in good faith and without notice of any intention on the part of the other party to defeat the applicant's claim for financial relief.

(5)   Where an application is made under this section with respect to a disposition which took place less than three years before the date of the application or with respect to a disposition or other dealing with property which is about to take place and the court is satisfied –

(a)   in a case falling within subsection (2)(a) or (b) above, that the disposition or other dealing would (apart from this section) have the consequence, or

(b)   in a case falling within subsection (2)(c) above, that the disposition has had the consequence,

of defeating the applicant's claim for financial relief, it shall be presumed, unless the contrary is shown, that the person who disposed of or is about to dispose of or deal with the property did so or, as the case may be, is about to do so, with the intention of defeating the applicant's claim for financial relief.

(6)   In this section 'disposition' does not include any provision contained in a will or codicil but, with that exception, includes any conveyance, assurance or gift of property of any description, whether made by an instrument or otherwise.

(7)   This section does not apply to a disposition made before 1st January 1968.

****

[40A   Appeals relating to pension sharing orders which have taken effect

(1)   Subsections (2) and (3) below apply where an appeal against a pension sharing order is begun on or after the day on which the order takes effect.

(2)   If the pension sharing order relates to a person's rights under a pension arrangement, the appeal court may not set aside or vary the order if the person responsible for the pension arrangement has acted to his detriment in reliance on the taking effect of the order.

(3)   If the pension sharing order relates to a person's shareable state scheme rights, the appeal court may not set aside or vary the order if the Secretary of State has acted to his detriment in reliance on the taking effect of the order.

(4)   In determining for the purposes of subsection (2) or (3) above whether a person has acted to his detriment in reliance on the taking effect of the order, the appeal court may disregard any detriment which in its opinion is insignificant.

(5)   Where subsection (2) or (3) above applies, the appeal court may make such further orders (including one or more pension sharing orders) as it thinks fit for the purpose of putting the parties in the position it considers appropriate.

(6)   Section 24C above only applies to a pension sharing order under this section if the decision of the appeal court can itself be the subject of an appeal.

(7)   In subsection (2) above, the reference to the person responsible for the pension arrangement is to be read in accordance with section 25D(4) above.][1]

****

Part IV
Miscellaneous and Supplemental

****

52[2]   Interpretation

(1)   In this Act –

... [3]

'child', in relation to one or both of the parties to a marriage, includes an illegitimate ...[4] child of that party or, as the case may be, of both parties;

'child of the family', in relation to the parties to a marriage, means –

(a)   a child of both of those parties; and

(b)   any other child, not being a child who [is placed with those parties as foster parents][5] by a local authority or voluntary organisation, who has been treated by both of those parties as a child of their family;

'the court' (except where the context otherwise requires) means the High Court or, where a county court has jurisdiction by virtue of [Part V of the Matrimonial and Family Proceedings Act 1984],[6] a county court;

... [7]

'education' includes training.

['*maintenance assessment* [-][8]' has the same meaning as it has in the Child Support Act 1991 by virtue of section 54 of that Act as read with any regulations in force under that section].[9]

(2)   In this Act –

(a)   references to financial provision orders, periodical payments and secured periodical payments orders and orders for the payment of a lump sum, and references to property adjustment orders, shall be construed in accordance with section 21 above;

---

[1]   Section inserted: Welfare Reform and Pensions Act 1999, s 19, Sch 3, paras 1, 10, with effect from 1 December 2000 (Welfare Reform and Pensions Act 1999 (Commencement No 5) Order 2000, SI 2000/1116).

[2]   Commencement: 1 January 1974 (SI 1973/1972).

[3]   Definition 'adopted' repealed: Children Act 1975, s 108(1)(b), Sch 4, with effect from 1 January 1976.

[4]   Words repealed: Children Act 1975, s 108(1)(b), Sch 4, with effect from 1 January 1976.

[5]   Words substituted: Children Act 1989, s 108(4), Sch 12, para 33, with effect from 14 October 1991 (Children Act 1989 (Commencement and Transitional Provisions) Order 1991, SI 1991/828).

[6]   Words substituted: Matrimonial and Family Proceedings Act 1984, s 46(1), Sch 1, para 16, with effect from 28 April 1986 (Matrimonial and Family Proceedings Act 1984 (Commencement No 3) Order 1986, SI 1986/635).

[7]   Definition 'custody' repealed: Children Act 1989, s 108(7), Sch 15, with effect from 14 October 1991 (Children Act 1989 (Commencement and Transitional Provisions) Order 1991, SI 1991/828).

[8]   Words in italics prospectively substituted by Child Support, Pensions and Social Security Act 2000, s 26, Sch 3, para 3(1), (4), from a date to be appointed.
New text = 'maintenance calculation'.

[9]   Words inserted: Maintenance Orders (Backdating) Order 1993, SI 1993/623, with effect from 5 April 1993.

[(aa)   references to pension sharing orders shall be construed in accordance with section 21A above; and][1]

(b)   references to orders for maintenance pending suit and to interim orders for maintenance shall be construed respectively in accordance with section 22 and section 27(5) above.

(3)   For the avoidance of doubt it is hereby declared that references in this Act to remarriage include references to a marriage which is by law void or voidable.

(4)   Except where the contrary intention is indicated, references in this Act to any enactment include references to that enactment as amended, extended or applied by or under any subsequent enactment, including this Act.

****

---

[1]   Paragraph substituted for word 'and': Welfare Reform and Pensions Act 1999, s 19, Sch 3, paras 1, 11, with effect from 1 December 2000 (Welfare Reform and Pensions Act 1999 (Commencement No 5) Order 2000, SI 2000/1116).

Welfare Reform and Pensions Act 1999[1]

****

Part III
Pensions on Divorce etc

Pension sharing orders

19[2]   Orders in England and Wales

Schedule 3 (which amends the Matrimonial Causes Act 1973 for the purpose of enabling the court to make pension sharing orders in connection with proceedings in England and Wales for divorce or nullity of marriage, and for supplementary purposes) shall have effect.

****

Sections 25B to 25D of the Matrimonial Causes Act 1973

21[3]   Amendments

Schedule 4 (which amends the sections about pensions inserted in the Matrimonial Causes Act 1973 by section 166 of the Pensions Act 1995) shall have effect.

22[4]   Extension to overseas divorces etc

(1)   Part III of the Matrimonial and Family Proceedings Act 1984 (financial relief in England and Wales after overseas divorce etc) shall be amended as follows.

(2)   In section 18 (matters to which the court is to have regard in exercising its powers to make orders for financial relief), after subsection (3) there shall be inserted –

'(3A)   The matters to which the court is to have regard under subsection (3) above –

(a)   so far as relating to paragraph (a) of section 25(2) of the 1973 Act, include any benefits under a pension arrangement which a party to the marriage has or is likely to have (whether or not in the foreseeable future), and

(b)   so far as relating to paragraph (h) of that provision, include any benefits under a pension arrangement which, by reason of the dissolution or annulment of the marriage, a party to the marriage will lose the chance of acquiring.'

(3)   In that section, at the end there shall be added –

'(7)   In this section –

(a)   "pension arrangement" has the meaning given by section 25D(3) of the 1973 Act, and

---

[1]   Act reference: 1999 c 30.
Royal assent: 11 November 1999.
Long title: An Act to make provision about pensions and social security; to make provision for reducing under-occupation of dwellings by housing benefit claimants; to authorise certain expenditure by the Secretary of State having responsibility for social security; and for connected purposes.

[2]   Commencement: 1 December 2000 (Welfare Reform and Pensions Act 1999 (Commencement No 5) Order 2000, SI 2000/1116).

[3]   Commencement: 1 December 2000 (Welfare Reform and Pensions Act 1999 (Commencement No 5) Order 2000, SI 2000/1116).

[4]   Commencement: 1 December 2000 (Welfare Reform and Pensions Act 1999 (Commencement No 5) Order 2000, SI 2000/1116).

(b)	references to benefits under a pension arrangement include any benefits by way of pension, whether under a pension arrangement or not.'

(4)	In section 21 (application of provisions of Part II of the Matrimonial Causes Act 1973), the existing provision shall become subsection (1) and, in that subsection, after paragraph (b) there shall be inserted –

'(bd)	section 25B(3) to (7B) (power, by financial provision order, to attach payments under a pension arrangement, or to require the exercise of a right of commutation under such an arrangement);

(be)	section 25C (extension of lump sum powers in relation to death benefits under a pension arrangement);'.

(5)	In that section, after subsection (1) there shall be inserted –

'(2)	Subsection (1)(bd) and (be) above shall not apply where the court has jurisdiction to entertain an application for an order for financial relief by reason only of the situation in England or Wales of a dwelling-house which was a matrimonial home of the parties.

(3)	Section 25D(1) of the 1973 Act (effect of transfers on orders relating to rights under a pension arrangement) shall apply in relation to an order made under section 17 above by virtue of subsection (1)(bd) or (be) above as it applies in relation to an order made under section 23 of that Act by virtue of section 25B or 25C of the 1973 Act.

(4)	The Lord Chancellor may by regulations make for the purposes of this Part of this Act provision corresponding to any provision which may be made by him under subsections (2) to (2B) of section 25D of the 1973 Act.

(5)	Power to make regulations under this section shall be exercisable by statutory instrument which shall be subject to annulment in pursuance of a resolution of either House of Parliament.'

Miscellaneous

## 23[1]	Supply of pension information in connection with divorce etc

(1)	The Secretary of State may by regulations –

(a)	make provision imposing on the person responsible for a pension arrangement, or on the Secretary of State, requirements with respect to the supply of information relevant to any power with respect to –

(i)	financial relief under Part II of the Matrimonial Causes Act 1973 or Part III of the Matrimonial and Family Proceedings Act 1984 (England and Wales powers in relation to domestic and overseas divorce etc),

(ii)	financial provision under the Family Law (Scotland) Act 1985 or Part IV of the Matrimonial and Family Proceedings Act 1984 (corresponding Scottish powers), or

(iii)	financial relief under Part III of the Matrimonial Causes (Northern Ireland) Order 1978 or Part IV of the Matrimonial and Family Proceedings (Northern Ireland) Order 1989 (corresponding Northern Ireland powers);

(b)	make provision about calculation and verification in relation to the valuation of –

(i)	benefits under a pension arrangement, or

(ii)	shareable state scheme rights,

for the purposes of regulations under paragraph (a)(i) or (iii);

(c)	make provision about calculation and verification in relation to –

[1]	Commencement: 11 November 1999, for the purpose only of the exercise of any power to make regulations (s 89(5)(a)); 1 December 2000, for remaining purposes (Welfare Reform and Pensions Act 1999 (Commencement No 4) Order 2000, SI 2000/1047).

(i)   the valuation of shareable rights under a pension arrangement or shareable state scheme rights for the purposes of regulations under paragraph (a)(ii), so far as relating to the making of orders for financial provision (within the meaning of the Family Law (Scotland) Act 1985), or

(ii)   the valuation of benefits under a pension arrangement for the purposes of such regulations, so far as relating to the making of orders under section 12A of that Act;

(d)   make provision for the purpose of enabling the person responsible for a pension arrangement to recover prescribed charges in respect of providing information in accordance with regulations under paragraph (a).

(2)   Regulations under subsection (1)(b) or (c) may include provision for calculation or verification in accordance with guidance from time to time prepared by a person prescribed by the regulations.

(3)   Regulations under subsection (1)(d) may include provision for the application in prescribed circumstances, with or without modification, of any provision made by virtue of section 41(2).

(4)   In subsection (1) –

(a)   the reference in paragraph (c)(i) to shareable rights under a pension arrangement is to rights in relation to which pension sharing is available under Chapter I of Part IV, or under corresponding Northern Ireland legislation, and

(b)   the references to shareable state scheme rights are to rights in relation to which pension sharing is available under Chapter II of Part IV, or under corresponding Northern Ireland legislation.

24[1]   Charges by pension arrangements in relation to earmarking orders

The Secretary of State may by regulations make provision for the purpose of enabling the person responsible for a pension arrangement to recover prescribed charges in respect of complying with –

(a)   an order under section 23 of the Matrimonial Causes Act 1973 (financial provision orders in connection with divorce etc), so far as it includes provision made by virtue of section 25B or 25C of that Act (powers to include provision about pensions),

(b)   an order under section 12A(2) or (3) of the Family Law (Scotland) Act 1985 (powers in relation to pensions lump sums when making a capital sum order), or

(c)   an order under Article 25 of the Matrimonial Causes (Northern Ireland) Order 1978, so far as it includes provision made by virtue of Article 27B or 27C of that Order (Northern Ireland powers corresponding to those mentioned in paragraph (a)).

Supplementary

25[2]   Power to make consequential amendments of Part III

(1)   If any amendment by the Family Law Act 1996 of Part II or IV of the Matrimonial Causes Act 1973 comes into force before the day on which any provision of this Part comes into force, the Lord Chancellor may by order make such consequential amendment of that provision as he thinks fit.

(2)   No order under this section may be made unless a draft of the order has been laid before and approved by resolution of each House of Parliament.

---

[1]   Commencement: 11 November 1999, for the purpose only of the exercise of any power to make regulations (s 89(5)(a)); 1 December 2000, for remaining purposes (Welfare Reform and Pensions Act 1999 (Commencement No 4) Order 2000, SI 2000/1047).

[2]   Commencement: 11 November 1999, for the purpose only of the exercise of any power to make regulations (s 89(5)(a)); to be appointed for remaining purposes.

26[1]   Interpretation of Part III

(1)   In this Part –

'occupational pension scheme' has the same meaning as in the Pension Schemes Act 1993;

'pension arrangement' means

(a)   an occupational pension scheme,

(b)   a personal pension scheme,

(c)   a retirement annuity contract,

(d)   an annuity or insurance policy purchased, or transferred, for the purpose of giving effect to rights under an occupational pension scheme or a personal pension scheme, and

(e)   an annuity purchased, or entered into, for the purpose of discharging liability in respect of a pension credit under section 29(1)(b) or under corresponding Northern Ireland legislation;

'personal pension scheme' has the same meaning as in the Pension Schemes Act 1993;

'prescribed' means prescribed by regulations made by the Secretary of State;

'retirement annuity contract' means a contract or scheme approved under Chapter III of Part XIV of the Income and Corporation Taxes Act 1988;

'trustees or managers', in relation to an occupational pension scheme or a personal pension scheme, means –

(a)   in the case of a scheme established under a trust, the trustees of the scheme, and

(b)   in any other case, the managers of the scheme.

(2)   References to the person responsible for a pension arrangement are –

(a)   in the case of an occupational pension scheme or a personal pension scheme, to the trustees or managers of the scheme,

(b)   in the case of a retirement annuity contract or an annuity falling within paragraph (d) or (e) of the definition of 'pension arrangement' above, the provider of the annuity, and

(c)   in the case of an insurance policy falling within paragraph (d) of the definition of that expression, the insurer.

Part IV
Pension Sharing

Chapter I
Sharing of Rights under Pension Arrangements

Pension sharing mechanism

27[2]   Scope of mechanism

(1)   Pension sharing is available under this Chapter in relation to a person's shareable rights under any pension arrangement other than an excepted public service pension scheme.

(2)   For the purposes of this Chapter, a person's shareable rights under a pension arrangement are any rights of his under the arrangement, other than rights of a description specified by regulations made by the Secretary of State.

---

[1]   Commencement: 1 December 2000 (Welfare Reform and Pensions Act 1999 (Commencement No 4) Order 2000, SI 2000/1047).

[2]   Commencement: 11 November 1999, for the purpose only of the exercise of any power to make regulations (s 89(5)(a)); 1 December 2000, for remaining purposes (Welfare Reform and Pensions Act 1999 (Commencement No 4) Order 2000, SI 2000/1047).

(3)   For the purposes of subsection (1), a public service pension scheme is excepted if it is specified by order made by such Minister of the Crown or government department as may be designated by the Treasury as having responsibility for the scheme.

28[1]   Activation of pension sharing

(1)   Section 29 applies on the taking effect of any of the following relating to a person's shareable rights under a pension arrangement –

    (a)   a pension sharing order under the Matrimonial Causes Act 1973,

    (b)   provision which corresponds to the provision which may be made by such an order and which –

        (i)   is contained in a qualifying agreement between the parties to a marriage, and

        (ii)   takes effect on the dissolution of the marriage under the Family Law Act 1996,

    (c)   provision which corresponds to the provision which may be made by such an order and which –

        (i)   is contained in a qualifying agreement between the parties to a marriage or former marriage, and

        (ii)   takes effect after the dissolution of the marriage under the Family Law Act 1996,

    (d)   an order under Part III of the Matrimonial and Family Proceedings Act 1984 (financial relief in England and Wales in relation to overseas divorce etc) corresponding to such an order as is mentioned in paragraph (a),

    (e)   a pension sharing order under the Family Law (Scotland) Act 1985,

    (f)   provision which corresponds to the provision which may be made by such an order and which –

        (i)   is contained in a qualifying agreement between the parties to a marriage,

        (ii)   is in such form as the Secretary of State may prescribe by regulations, and

        (iii)   takes effect on the grant, in relation to the marriage, of decree of divorce under the Divorce (Scotland) Act 1976 or of declarator of nullity,

    (g)   an order under Part IV of the Matrimonial and Family Proceedings Act 1984 (financial relief in Scotland in relation to overseas divorce etc) corresponding to such an order as is mentioned in paragraph (e),

    (h)   a pension sharing order under Northern Ireland legislation, and

    (i)   an order under Part IV of the Matrimonial and Family Proceedings (Northern Ireland) Order 1989 (financial relief in Northern Ireland in relation to overseas divorce etc) corresponding to such an order as is mentioned in paragraph (h).

(2)   For the purposes of subsection (1)(b) and (c), a qualifying agreement is one which –

    (a)   has been entered into in such circumstances as the Lord Chancellor may prescribe by regulations, and

    (b)   satisfies such requirements as the Lord Chancellor may so prescribe.

(3)   For the purposes of subsection (1)(f), a qualifying agreement is one which –

    (a)   has been entered into in such circumstances as the Secretary of State may prescribe by regulations, and

    (b)   is registered in the Books of Council and Session.

---

[1]   Commencement: 11 November 1999, for the purpose only of the exercise of any power to make regulations (s 89(5)(a)); 1 December 2000, for remaining purposes (Welfare Reform and Pensions Act 1999 (Commencement No 4) Order 2000, SI 2000/1047).

(4)   Subsection (1)(b) does not apply if –

    (a)   the pension arrangement to which the provision relates is the subject of a pension sharing order under the Matrimonial Causes Act 1973 in relation to the marriage, or

    (b)   there is in force a requirement imposed by virtue of section 25B or 25C of that Act (powers to include in financial provision orders requirements relating to benefits under pension arrangements) which relates to benefits or future benefits to which the party who is the transferor is entitled under the pension arrangement to which the provision relates.

(5)   Subsection (1)(c) does not apply if –

    (a)   the marriage was dissolved by an order under section 3 of the Family Law Act 1996 (divorce not preceded by separation) and the satisfaction of the requirements of section 9(2) of that Act (settlement of future financial arrangements) was a precondition to the making of the order,

    (b)   the pension arrangement to which the provision relates –

        (i)   is the subject of a pension sharing order under the Matrimonial Causes Act 1973 in relation to the marriage, or

        (ii)   has already been the subject of pension sharing between the parties, or

    (c)   there is in force a requirement imposed by virtue of section 25B or 25C of that Act which relates to benefits or future benefits to which the party who is the transferor is entitled under the pension arrangement to which the provision relates.

(6)   Subsection (1)(f) does not apply if there is in force an order under section 12A(2) or (3) of the Family Law (Scotland) Act 1985 which relates to benefits or future benefits to which the party who is the transferor is entitled under the pension arrangement to which the provision relates.

(7)   For the purposes of this section, an order or provision falling within subsection (1)(e), (f) or (g) shall be deemed never to have taken effect if the person responsible for the arrangement to which the order or provision relates does not receive before the end of the period of 2 months beginning with the relevant date –

    (a)   copies of the relevant matrimonial documents, and

    (b)   such information relating to the transferor and transferee as the Secretary of State may prescribe by regulations under section 34(1)(b)(ii).

(8)   The relevant date for the purposes of subsection (7) is –

    (a)   in the case of an order or provision falling within subsection (1)(e) or (f), the date of the extract of the decree or declarator responsible for the divorce or annulment to which the order or provision relates, and

    (b)   in the case of an order falling within subsection (1)(g), the date of disposal of the application under section 28 of the Matrimonial and Family Proceedings Act 1984.

(9)   The reference in subsection (7)(a) to the relevant matrimonial documents is –

    (a)   in the case of an order falling within subsection (1)(e) or (g), to copies of the order and the order, decree or declarator responsible for the divorce or annulment to which it relates, and

    (b)   in the case of provision falling within subsection (1)(f), to –

        (i)   copies of the provision and the order, decree or declarator responsible for the divorce or annulment to which it relates, and

        (ii)   documentary evidence that the agreement containing the provision is one to which subsection (3)(a) applies.

(10)   The sheriff may, on the application of any person having an interest, make an order –

    (a)   extending the period of 2 months referred to in subsection (7), and

(b)   if that period has already expired, providing that, if the person responsible for the arrangement receives the documents and information concerned before the end of the period specified in the order, subsection (7) is to be treated as never having applied.

(11)   In subsections (4)(b), (5)(c) and (6), the reference to the party who is the transferor is to the party to whose rights the provision relates.

29[1]   Creation of pension debits and credits

(1)   On the application of this section –

(a)   the transferor's shareable rights under the relevant arrangement become subject to a debit of the appropriate amount, and

(b)   the transferee becomes entitled to a credit of that amount as against the person responsible for that arrangement.

(2)   Where the relevant order or provision specifies a percentage value to be transferred, the appropriate amount for the purposes of subsection (1) is the specified percentage of the cash equivalent of the relevant benefits on the valuation day.

(3)   Where the relevant order or provision specifies an amount to be transferred, the appropriate amount for the purposes of subsection (1) is the lesser of –

(a)   the specified amount, and

(b)   the cash equivalent of the relevant benefits on the valuation day.

(4)   Where the relevant arrangement is an occupational pension scheme and the transferor is in pensionable service under the scheme on the transfer day, the relevant benefits for the purposes of subsections (2) and (3) are the benefits or future benefits to which he would be entitled under the scheme by virtue of his shareable rights under it had his pensionable service terminated immediately before that day.

(5)   Otherwise, the relevant benefits for the purposes of subsections (2) and (3) are the benefits or future benefits to which, immediately before the transfer day, the transferor is entitled under the terms of the relevant arrangement by virtue of his shareable rights under it.

(6)   The Secretary of State may by regulations provide for any description of benefit to be disregarded for the purposes of subsection (4) or (5).

(7)   For the purposes of this section, the valuation day is such day within the implementation period for the credit under subsection (1)(b) as the person responsible for the relevant arrangement may specify by notice in writing to the transferor and transferee.

(8)   In this section –

'relevant arrangement' means the arrangement to which the relevant order or provision relates;

'relevant order or provision' means the order or provision by virtue of which this section applies;

'transfer day' means the day on which the relevant order or provision takes effect;

'transferor' means the person to whose rights the relevant order or provision relates;

'transferee' means the person for whose benefit the relevant order or provision is made.

30[2]   Cash equivalents

(1)   The Secretary of State may by regulations make provision about the calculation and verification of cash equivalents for the purposes of section 29.

---

[1]   Commencement: 11 November 1999, for the purpose only of the exercise of any power to make regulations (s 89(5)(a)); 1 December 2000, for remaining purposes (Welfare Reform and Pensions Act 1999 (Commencement No 4) Order 2000, SI 2000/1047).

[2]   Commencement: 11 November 1999, for the purpose only of the exercise of any power to make regulations (s 89(5)(a)); 1 December 2000, for remaining purposes (Welfare Reform and Pensions Act 1999 (Commencement No 4) Order 2000, SI 2000/1047).

(2)   The power conferred by subsection (1) includes power to provide for calculation or verification –

    (a)   in such manner as may, in the particular case, be approved by a person prescribed by the regulations, or

    (b)   in accordance with guidance from time to time prepared by a person so prescribed.

Pension debits

31[1]   Reduction of benefit

(1)   Subject to subsection (2), where a person's shareable rights under a pension arrangement are subject to a pension debit, each benefit or future benefit –

    (a)   to which he is entitled under the arrangement by virtue of those rights, and

    (b)   which is a qualifying benefit,

is reduced by the appropriate percentage.

(2)   Where a pension debit relates to the shareable rights under an occupational pension scheme of a person who is in pensionable service under the scheme on the transfer day, each benefit or future benefit –

    (a)   to which the person is entitled under the scheme by virtue of those rights, and

    (b)   which corresponds to a qualifying benefit,

is reduced by an amount equal to the appropriate percentage of the corresponding qualifying benefit.

(3)   A benefit is a qualifying benefit for the purposes of subsections (1) and (2) if the cash equivalent by reference to which the amount of the pension debit is determined includes an amount in respect of it.

(4)   The provisions of this section override any provision of a pension arrangement to which they apply to the extent that the provision conflicts with them.

(5)   In this section –

'appropriate percentage', in relation to a pension debit, means –

    (a)   if the relevant order or provision specifies the percentage value to be transferred, that percentage;

    (b)   if the relevant order or provision specifies an amount to be transferred, the percentage which the appropriate amount for the purposes of subsection (1) of section 29 represents of the amount mentioned in subsection (3)(b) of that section;

'relevant order or provision', in relation to a pension debit, means the pension sharing order or provision on which the debit depends;

'transfer day', in relation to a pension debit, means the day on which the relevant order or provision takes effect.

32[2]   Effect on contracted-out rights

(1)   The Pension Schemes Act 1993 shall be amended as follows.

(2)   In section 10 (protected rights), in subsection (1), for 'subsections (2) and (3)' there shall be substituted 'the following provisions of this section', and at the end there shall be added –

---

[1]   Commencement: 1 December 2000 (Welfare Reform and Pensions Act 1999 (Commencement No 4) Order 2000, SI 2000/1047).

[2]   Commencement: 1 December 2000 (Welfare Reform and Pensions Act 1999 (Commencement No 4) Order 2000, SI 2000/1047).

'(4)   Where, in the case of a scheme which makes such provision as is mentioned in subsection (2) or (3), a member's rights under the scheme become subject to a pension debit, his protected rights shall exclude the appropriate percentage of the rights which were his protected rights immediately before the day on which the pension debit arose.

(5)   For the purposes of subsection (4), the appropriate percentage is –

(a)   if the order or provision on which the pension debit depends specifies the percentage value to be transferred, that percentage;

(b)   if the order or provision on which the pension debit depends specifies an amount to be transferred, the percentage which the appropriate amount for the purposes of subsection (1) of section 29 of the Welfare Reform and Pensions Act 1999 (lesser of specified amount and cash equivalent of transferor's benefits) represents of the amount mentioned in subsection (3)(b) of that section (cash equivalent of transferor's benefits).'

(3)   After section 15 there shall be inserted –

'15A   Reduction of guaranteed minimum in consequence of pension debit

(1)   Where –

(a)   an earner has a guaranteed minimum in relation to the pension provided by a scheme, and

(b)   his right to the pension becomes subject to a pension debit,

his guaranteed minimum in relation to the scheme is, subject to subsection (2), reduced by the appropriate percentage.

(2)   Where the earner is in pensionable service under the scheme on the day on which the order or provision on which the pension debit depends takes effect, his guaranteed minimum in relation to the scheme is reduced by an amount equal to the appropriate percentage of the corresponding qualifying benefit.

(3)   For the purposes of subsection (2), the corresponding qualifying benefit is the guaranteed minimum taken for the purpose of calculating the cash equivalent by reference to which the amount of the pension debit is determined.

(4)   For the purposes of this section the appropriate percentage is –

(a)   if the order or provision on which the pension debit depends specifies the percentage value to be transferred, that percentage;

(b)   if the order or provision on which the pension debit depends specifies an amount to be transferred, the percentage which the appropriate amount for the purposes of subsection (1) of section 29 of the Welfare Reform and Pensions Act 1999 (lesser of specified amount and cash equivalent of transferor's benefits) represents of the amount mentioned in subsection (3)(b) of that section (cash equivalent of transferor's benefits).'

(4)   In section 47 (entitlement to guaranteed minimum pensions for the purposes of the relationship with social security benefits), at the end there shall be added –

'(6)   For the purposes of section 46, a person shall be treated as entitled to any guaranteed minimum pension to which he would have been entitled but for any reduction under section 15A.'

(5)   In section 181(1), there shall be inserted at the appropriate place –

'"pension debit" means a debit under section 29(1)(a) of the Welfare Reform and Pensions Act 1999;'.

Pension credits

33[1] **Time for discharge of liability**

(1) A person subject to liability in respect of a pension credit shall discharge his liability before the end of the implementation period for the credit.

(2) Where the trustees or managers of an occupational pension scheme have not done what is required to discharge their liability in respect of a pension credit before the end of the implementation period for the credit –

    (a) they shall, except in such cases as the Secretary of State may prescribe by regulations, notify the Regulatory Authority of that fact within such period as the Secretary of State may so prescribe, and

    (b) section 10 of the Pensions Act 1995 (power of the Regulatory Authority to impose civil penalties) shall apply to any trustee or manager who has failed to take all such steps as are reasonable to ensure that liability in respect of the credit was discharged before the end of the implementation period for it.

(3) If trustees or managers to whom subsection (2)(a) applies fail to perform the obligation imposed by that provision, section 10 of the Pensions Act 1995 shall apply to any trustee or manager who has failed to take all reasonable steps to ensure that the obligation was performed.

(4) On the application of the trustees or managers of an occupational pension scheme who are subject to liability in respect of a pension credit, the Regulatory Authority may extend the implementation period for the credit for the purposes of this section if it is satisfied that the application is made in such circumstances as the Secretary of State may prescribe by regulations.

(5) In this section 'the Regulatory Authority' means the Occupational Pensions Regulatory Authority.

34[2] **'Implementation period'**

(1) For the purposes of this Chapter, the implementation period for a pension credit is the period of 4 months beginning with the later of –

    (a) the day on which the relevant order or provision takes effect, and

    (b) the first day on which the person responsible for the pension arrangement to which the relevant order or provision relates is in receipt of –

        (i) the relevant matrimonial documents, and

        (ii) such information relating to the transferor and transferee as the Secretary of State may prescribe by regulations.

(2) The reference in subsection (1)(b)(i) to the relevant matrimonial documents is to copies of –

    (a) the relevant order or provision, and

    (b) the order, decree or declarator responsible for the divorce or annulment to which it relates,

and, if the pension credit depends on provision falling within subsection (1)(f) of section 28, to documentary evidence that the agreement containing the provision is one to which subsection (3)(a) of that section applies.

(3) Subsection (1) is subject to any provision made by regulations under section 41(2)(a).

(4) The Secretary of State may by regulations –

---

[1] Commencement: 11 November 1999, for the purpose only of the exercise of any power to make regulations (s 89(5)(a)); 1 December 2000, for remaining purposes (Welfare Reform and Pensions Act 1999 (Commencement No 4) Order 2000, SI 2000/1047).

[2] Commencement: 11 November 1999, for the purpose only of the exercise of any power to make regulations (s 89(5)(a)); 1 December 2000, for remaining purposes (Welfare Reform and Pensions Act 1999 (Commencement No 4) Order 2000, SI 2000/1047).

(a)   make provision requiring a person subject to liability in respect of a pension credit to notify the transferor and transferee of the day on which the implementation period for the credit begins;

(b)   provide for this section to have effect with modifications where the pension arrangement to which the relevant order or provision relates is being wound up;

(c)   provide for this section to have effect with modifications where the pension credit depends on a pension sharing order and the order is the subject of an application for leave to appeal out of time.

(5)   In this section –

'relevant order or provision', in relation to a pension credit, means the pension sharing order or provision on which the pension credit depends;

'transferor' means the person to whose rights the relevant order or provision relates;

'transferee' means the person for whose benefit the relevant order or provision is made.

35[1]   Mode of discharge of liability

(1)   Schedule 5 (which makes provision about how liability in respect of a pension credit may be discharged) shall have effect.

(2)   Where the person entitled to a pension credit dies before liability in respect of the credit has been discharged –

(a)   Schedule 5 shall cease to have effect in relation to the discharge of liability in respect of the credit, and

(b)   liability in respect of the credit shall be discharged in accordance with regulations made by the Secretary of State.

Treatment of pension credit rights under schemes

36[2]   Safeguarded rights

After section 68 of the Pension Schemes Act 1993 there shall be inserted –

'Part IIIA
Safeguarded Rights

68A   Safeguarded rights

(1)   Subject to subsection (2), the safeguarded rights of a member of an occupational pension scheme or a personal pension scheme are such of his rights to future benefits under the scheme as are attributable (directly or indirectly) to a pension credit in respect of which the reference rights are, or include, contracted-out rights or safeguarded rights.

(2)   If the rules of an occupational pension scheme or a personal pension scheme so provide, a member's safeguarded rights are such of his rights falling within subsection (1) as –

(a)   in the case of rights directly attributable to a pension credit, represent the safeguarded percentage of the rights acquired by virtue of the credit, and

(b)   in the case of rights directly attributable to a transfer payment, represent the safeguarded percentage of the rights acquired by virtue of the payment.

---

[1]   Commencement: 11 November 1999, for the purpose only of the exercise of any power to make regulations (s 89(5)(a)); 1 December 2000, for remaining purposes (Welfare Reform and Pensions Act 1999 (Commencement No 4) Order 2000, SI 2000/1047).
[2]   Commencement: 11 November 1999, for the purpose only of the exercise of any power to make regulations (s 89(5)(a)); 1 December 2000, for remaining purposes (Welfare Reform and Pensions Act 1999 (Commencement No 4) Order 2000, SI 2000/1047).

(3)   For the purposes of subsection (2)(a), the safeguarded percentage is the percentage of the rights by reference to which the amount of the credit is determined which are contracted-out rights or safeguarded rights.

(4)   For the purposes of subsection (2)(b), the safeguarded percentage is the percentage of the rights in respect of which the transfer payment is made which are contracted-out rights or safeguarded rights.

(5)   In this section –

"contracted-out rights" means such rights under, or derived from –

(a)   an occupational pension scheme contracted-out by virtue of section 9(2) or (3), or

(b)   an appropriate personal pension scheme,

as may be prescribed;

"reference rights", in relation to a pension credit, means the rights by reference to which the amount of the credit is determined.

68B   Requirements relating to safeguarded rights

Regulations may prescribe requirements to be met in relation to safeguarded rights by an occupational pension scheme or a personal pension scheme.

68C   Reserve powers in relation to non-complying schemes

(1)   This section applies to –

(a)   any occupational pension scheme, other than a public service pension scheme, and

(b)   any personal pension scheme.

(2)   If any scheme to which this section applies does not comply with a requirement prescribed under section 68B and there are any persons who –

(a)   have safeguarded rights under the scheme, or

(b)   are entitled to any benefit giving effect to such rights under the scheme,

the Inland Revenue may direct the trustees or managers of the scheme to take or refrain from taking such steps as they may specify in writing for the purpose of safeguarding the rights of persons falling within paragraph (a) or (b).

(3)   A direction under subsection (2) shall be final and binding on the trustees or managers to whom the direction is given and any person claiming under them.

(4)   An appeal on a point of law shall lie to the High Court or, in Scotland, the Court of Session from a direction under subsection (2) at the instance of the trustees or managers, or any person claiming under them.

(5)   A direction under subsection (2) shall be enforceable –

(a)   in England and Wales, in a county court, as if it were an order of that court, and

(b)   in Scotland, by the sheriff, as if it were an order of the sheriff and whether or not the sheriff could himself have given such an order.

68D   Power to control transfer or discharge of liability

Regulations may prohibit or restrict the transfer or discharge of any liability under an occupational pension scheme or a personal pension scheme in respect of safeguarded rights except in prescribed circumstances or on prescribed conditions.'

37[1]   Requirements relating to pension credit benefit

After section 101 of the Pension Schemes Act 1993 there shall be inserted –

'Part IVA
Requirements Relating to Pension Credit Benefit

Chapter I
Pension Credit Benefit under Occupational Schemes

101A   Scope of Chapter I

(1)   This Chapter applies to any occupational pension scheme whose resources are derived in whole or part from –

   (a)   payments to which subsection (2) applies made or to be made by one or more employers of earners to whom the scheme applies, or

   (b)   such other payments by the earner or his employer, or both, as may be prescribed for different categories of scheme.

(2)   This subsection applies to payments –

   (a)   under an actual or contingent legal obligation, or

   (b)   in the exercise of a power conferred, or the discharge of a duty imposed, on a Minister of the Crown, government department or any other person, being a power or duty which extends to the disbursement or allocation of public money.

101B   Interpretation

In this Chapter –

"scheme" means an occupational pension scheme to which this Chapter applies;

"pension credit rights" means rights to future benefits under a scheme which are attributable (directly or indirectly) to a pension credit;

"pension credit benefit", in relation to a scheme, means the benefits payable under the scheme to or in respect of a person by virtue of rights under the scheme attributable (directly or indirectly) to a pension credit;

"normal benefit age", in relation to a scheme, means the earliest age at which a person who has pension credit rights under the scheme is entitled to receive a pension by virtue of those rights (disregarding any scheme rule making special provision as to early payment of pension on grounds of ill-health or otherwise).

101C   Basic principle as to pension credit benefit

(1)   Normal benefit age under a scheme must be between 60 and 65.

(2)   A scheme must not provide for payment of pension credit benefit in the form of a lump sum at any time before normal benefit age, except in such circumstances as may be prescribed.

101D   Form of pension credit benefit and its alternatives

(1)   Subject to subsection (2) and section 101E, a person's pension credit benefit under a scheme must be –

   (a)   payable directly out of the resources of the scheme, or

   (b)   assured to him by such means as may be prescribed.

(2)   Subject to subsections (3) and (4), a scheme may, instead of providing a person's pension credit benefit, provide –

---

[1]   Commencement: 11 November 1999, for the purpose only of the exercise of any power to make regulations (s 89(5)(a)); 1 December 2000, for remaining purposes (Welfare Reform and Pensions Act 1999 (Commencement No 4) Order 2000, SI 2000/1047).

(a)   for his pension credit rights under the scheme to be transferred to another occupational pension scheme or a personal pension scheme with a view to acquiring rights for him under the rules of the scheme, or

(b)   for such alternatives to pension credit benefit as may be prescribed.

(3)   The option conferred by subsection (2)(a) is additional to any obligation imposed by Chapter II of this Part.

(4)   The alternatives specified in subsection (2)(a) and (b) may only be by way of complete or partial substitute for pension credit benefit –

(a)   if the person entitled to the benefit consents, or

(b)   in such other cases as may be prescribed.

101E   Discharge of liability where pension credit or alternative benefits secured by insurance policies or annuity contracts

(1)   A transaction to which section 19 applies discharges the trustees or managers of a scheme from their liability to provide pension credit benefit or any alternative to pension credit benefit for or in respect of a member of the scheme if and to the extent that –

(a)   it results in pension credit benefit, or any alternative to pension credit benefit, for or in respect of the member being appropriately secured (within the meaning of that section),

(b)   the transaction is entered into with the consent of the member or, if the member has died, of the member's widow or widower, and

(c)   such requirements as may be prescribed are met.

(2)   Regulations may provide that subsection (1)(b) shall not apply in prescribed circumstances.

Chapter II
Transfer Values

101F   Power to give transfer notice

(1)   An eligible member of a qualifying scheme may by notice in writing require the trustees or managers of the scheme to use an amount equal to the cash equivalent of his pension credit benefit for such one or more of the authorised purposes as he may specify in the notice.

(2)   In the case of a member of an occupational pension scheme, the authorised purposes are –

(a)   to acquire rights allowed under the rules of an occupational pension scheme, or personal pension scheme, which is an eligible scheme,

(b)   to purchase from one or more insurance companies such as are mentioned in section 19(4)(a), chosen by the member and willing to accept payment on account of the member from the trustees or managers, one or more annuities which satisfy the prescribed requirements, and

(c)   in such circumstances as may be prescribed, to subscribe to other pension arrangements which satisfy prescribed requirements.

(3)   In the case of a member of a personal pension scheme, the authorised purposes are –

(a)   to acquire rights allowed under the rules of an occupational pension scheme, or personal pension scheme, which is an eligible scheme, and

(b)   in such circumstances as may be prescribed, to subscribe to other pension arrangements which satisfy prescribed requirements.

(4)   The cash equivalent for the purposes of subsection (1) shall –

(a)   in the case of a salary related occupational pension scheme, be taken to be the amount shown in the relevant statement under section 101H, and

(b)   in any other case, be determined by reference to the date the notice under that subsection is given.

(5)   The requirements which may be prescribed under subsection (2) or (3) include, in particular, requirements of the Inland Revenue.

(6)   In subsections (2) and (3), references to an eligible scheme are to a scheme –

(a)   the trustees or managers of which are able and willing to accept payment in respect of the member's pension credit rights, and

(b)   which satisfies the prescribed requirements.

(7)   In this Chapter, 'transfer notice' means a notice under subsection (1).

101G   Restrictions on power to give transfer notice

(1)   In the case of a salary related occupational pension scheme, the power to give a transfer notice may only be exercised if –

(a)   the member has been provided with a statement under section 101H, and

(b)   not more than 3 months have passed since the date by reference to which the amount shown in the statement is determined.

(2)   The power to give a transfer notice may not be exercised in the case of an occupational pension scheme if –

(a)   there is less than a year to go until the member reaches normal benefit age, or

(b)   the pension to which the member is entitled by virtue of his pension credit rights, or benefit in lieu of that pension, or any part of it has become payable.

(3)   Where an eligible member of a qualifying scheme –

(a)   is entitled to make an application under section 95 to the trustees or managers of the scheme, or

(b)   would be entitled to do so, but for the fact that he has not received a statement under section 93A in respect of which the guarantee date is sufficiently recent,

he may not, if the scheme so provides, exercise the power to give them a transfer notice unless he also makes an application to them under section 95.

(4)   The power to give a transfer notice may not be exercised if a previous transfer notice given by the member to the trustees or managers of the scheme is outstanding.

101H Salary related schemes: statements of entitlement

(1)   The trustees or managers of a qualifying scheme which is a salary related occupational pension scheme shall, on the application of an eligible member, provide him with a written statement of the amount of the cash equivalent of his pension credit benefit under the scheme.

(2)   For the purposes of subsection (1), the amount of the cash equivalent shall be determined by reference to a date falling within –

(a)   the prescribed period beginning with the date of the application, and

(b)   the prescribed period ending with the date on which the statement under that subsection is provided to the applicant.

(3)   Regulations may make provision in relation to applications under subsection (1) and may, in particular, restrict the making of successive applications.

(4)   If trustees or managers to whom subsection (1) applies fail to perform an obligation under that subsection, section 10 of the Pensions Act 1995 (power of the Regulatory Authority to impose civil penalties) shall apply to any trustee or manager who has failed to take all such steps as are reasonable to secure that the obligation was performed.

101I   Calculation of cash equivalents

Cash equivalents for the purposes of this Chapter shall be calculated and verified in the prescribed manner.

101J   Time for compliance with transfer notice

(1)   Trustees or managers of a qualifying scheme who receive a transfer notice shall comply with the notice –

   (a)   in the case of an occupational pension scheme, within 6 months of the valuation date or, if earlier, by the date on which the member to whom the notice relates reaches normal benefit age, and

   (b)   in the case of a personal pension scheme, within 6 months of the date on which they receive the notice.

(2)   The Regulatory Authority may, in prescribed circumstances, extend the period for complying with the notice.

(3)   If the Regulatory Authority are satisfied –

   (a)   that there has been a relevant change of circumstances since they granted an extension under subsection (2), or

   (b)   that they granted an extension under that subsection in ignorance of a material fact or on the basis of a mistake as to a material fact,

they may revoke or reduce the extension.

(4)   Where the trustees or managers of an occupational pension scheme have failed to comply with a transfer notice before the end of the period for compliance –

   (a)   they shall, except in prescribed cases, notify the Regulatory Authority of that fact within the prescribed period, and

   (b)   section 10 of the Pensions Act 1995 (power of the Regulatory Authority to impose civil penalties) shall apply to any trustee or manager who has failed to take all such steps as are reasonable to ensure that the notice was complied with before the end of the period for compliance.

(5)   If trustees or managers to whom subsection (4)(a) applies fail to perform the obligation imposed by that provision, section 10 of the Pensions Act 1995 shall apply to any trustee or manager who has failed to take all such steps as are reasonable to ensure that the obligation was performed.

(6)   Regulations may –

   (a)   make provision in relation to applications under subsection (2), and

   (b)   provide that subsection (4) shall not apply in prescribed circumstances.

(7)   In this section, "valuation date", in relation to a transfer notice given to the trustees or managers of an occupational pension scheme, means –

   (a)   in the case of a salary related scheme, the date by reference to which the amount shown in the relevant statement under section 101H is determined, and

   (b)   in the case of any other scheme, the date the notice is given.

101K   Withdrawal of transfer notice

(1)   Subject to subsections (2) and (3), a person who has given a transfer notice may withdraw it by giving the trustees or managers to whom it was given notice in writing that he no longer requires them to comply with it.

(2)   A transfer notice may not be withdrawn if the trustees or managers have already entered into an agreement with a third party to use the whole or part of the amount they are required to use in accordance with the notice.

(3)   If the giving of a transfer notice depended on the making of an application under section 95, the notice may only be withdrawn if the application is also withdrawn.

101L   Variation of the amount required to be used

(1)   Regulations may make provision for the amount required to be used under section 101F(1) to be increased or reduced in prescribed circumstances.

(2)   Without prejudice to the generality of subsection (1), the circumstances which may be prescribed include –

(a)   failure by the trustees or managers of a qualifying scheme to comply with a notice under section 101F(1) within 6 months of the date by reference to which the amount of the cash equivalent falls to be determined, and

(b)   the state of funding of a qualifying scheme.

(3)   Regulations under subsection (1) may have the effect of extinguishing an obligation under section 101F(1).

101M   Effect of transfer on trustees' duties

Compliance with a transfer notice shall have effect to discharge the trustees or managers of a qualifying scheme from any obligation to provide the pension credit benefit of the eligible member who gave the notice.

101N   Matters to be disregarded in calculations

In making any calculation for the purposes of this Chapter –

(a)   any charge or lien on, and

(b)   any set-off against,

the whole or part of a pension shall be disregarded.

101O   Service of notices

A notice under section 101F(1) or 101K(1) shall be taken to have been given if it is delivered to the trustees or managers personally or sent by post in a registered letter or by recorded delivery service.

101P   Interpretation of Chapter II

(1)   In this Chapter –

"eligible member", in relation to a qualifying scheme, means a member who has pension credit rights under the scheme;

"normal benefit age", in relation to an eligible member of a qualifying scheme, means the earliest age at which the member is entitled to receive a pension by virtue of his pension credit rights under the scheme (disregarding any scheme rule making special provision as to early payment of pension on grounds of ill-health or otherwise);

"pension credit benefit", in relation to an eligible member of a qualifying scheme, means the benefits payable under the scheme to or in respect of the member by virtue of rights under the scheme attributable (directly or indirectly) to a pension credit;

"pension credit rights", in relation to a qualifying scheme, means rights to future benefits under the scheme which are attributable (directly or indirectly) to a pension credit;

"qualifying scheme" means a funded occupational pension scheme and a personal pension scheme;

"transfer notice" has the meaning given by section 101F(7).

(2)   For the purposes of this Chapter, an occupational pension scheme is salary related if –

(a)   it is not a money purchase scheme, and

(b)   it does not fall within a prescribed class.

(3)   In this Chapter, references to the relevant statement under section 101H, in relation to a transfer notice given to the trustees or managers of a salary related occupational pension scheme, are to the statement under that section on which the giving of the notice depended.

(4)   For the purposes of this section, an occupational pension scheme is funded if it meets its liabilities out of a fund accumulated for the purpose during the life of the scheme.

101Q Power to modify Chapter II in relation to hybrid schemes

Regulations may apply this Chapter with prescribed modifications to occupational pension schemes –

(a)   which are not money purchase schemes, but

(b)   where some of the benefits that may be provided are money purchase benefits.'

38[1]   Treatment in winding up

(1)   In section 73 of the Pensions Act 1995 (treatment of rights on winding up of an occupational pension scheme to which section 56 of that Act (minimum funding requirement) applies), in subsection (3) (classification of liabilities), in paragraph (c) (accrued rights), at the end of sub-paragraph (i) there shall be inserted –

'(ia)   future pensions, or other future benefits, attributable (directly or indirectly) to pension credits (but excluding increases to pensions),'.

(2)   In the case of an occupational pension scheme which is not a scheme to which section 56 of the Pensions Act 1995 applies, rights attributable (directly or indirectly) to a pension credit are to be accorded in a winding up the same treatment –

(a)   if they have come into payment, as the rights of a pensioner member, and

(b)   if they have not come into payment, as the rights of a deferred member.

(3)   Subsection (2) overrides the provisions of a scheme to the extent that it conflicts with them, and the scheme has effect with such modifications as may be required in consequence.

(4)   In subsection (2) –

(a)   'deferred member' and 'pensioner member' have the same meanings as in Part I of the Pensions Act 1995,

(b)   'pension credit' includes a credit under Northern Ireland legislation corresponding to section 29(1)(b), and

(c)   references to rights attributable to a pension credit having come into payment are to the person to whom the rights belong having become entitled by virtue of the rights to the present payment of pension or other benefits.

Indexation

39[2]   Public service pension schemes

(1)   The Pensions (Increase) Act 1971 shall be amended as follows.

(2)   In section 3 (qualifying conditions), after subsection (2) there shall be inserted –

'(2A)   A pension attributable to the pensioner having become entitled to a pension credit shall not be increased unless the pensioner has attained the age of fifty-five years.'

(3)   In section 8, in subsection (1) (definition of 'pension'), in paragraph (a), the words from '(either' to 'person)' shall be omitted.

---

[1]   Commencement: 1 December 2000 (Welfare Reform and Pensions Act 1999 (Commencement No 4) Order 2000, SI 2000/1047).

[2]   Commencement: 1 December 2000 (Welfare Reform and Pensions Act 1999 (Commencement No 4) Order 2000, SI 2000/1047).

(4)   In that section, in subsection (2) (when pension deemed for purposes of the Act to begin), after 'pension', in the first place, there shall be inserted 'which is not attributable to a pension credit', and after that subsection there shall be inserted –

'(2A)   A pension which is attributable to a pension credit shall be deemed for purposes of this Act to begin on the day on which the order or provision on which the credit depends takes effect.'

(5)   In section 17(1) (interpretation) –

(a)   for the definitions of 'derivative pension' and 'principal pension' there shall be substituted –

'"derivative pension" means a pension which –

(a)   is not payable in respect of the pensioner's own services, and

(b)   is not attributable to the pensioner having become entitled to a pension credit;',

(b)   after the definition of 'pension' there shall be inserted –

'"pension credit" means a credit under section 29(1)(b) of the Welfare Reform and Pensions Act 1999 or under corresponding Northern Ireland legislation;

"principal pension" means a pension which –

(a)   is payable in respect of the pensioner's own services, or

(b)   is attributable to the pensioner having become entitled to a pension credit;', and

(c)   for the definition of 'widow's pension' there shall be substituted –

'"widow's pension" means a pension payable –

(a)   in respect of the services of the pensioner's deceased husband, or

(b)   by virtue of the pensioner's deceased husband having become entitled to a pension credit.'

40[1]   Other pension schemes

(1)   The Secretary of State may by regulations make provision for a pension to which subsection (2) applies to be increased, as a minimum, by reference to increases in the retail prices index, so far as not exceeding 5% per annum.

(2)   This subsection applies to –

(a)   a pension provided to give effect to eligible pension credit rights of a member under a qualifying occupational pension scheme, and

(b)   a pension provided to give effect to safeguarded rights of a member under a personal pension scheme.

(3)   In this section –

'eligible', in relation to pension credit rights, means of a description prescribed by regulations made by the Secretary of State;

'pension credit rights', in relation to an occupational pension scheme, means rights to future benefits under the scheme which are attributable (directly or indirectly) to a credit under section 29(1)(b) or under corresponding Northern Ireland legislation;

'qualifying occupational pension scheme' means an occupational pension scheme which is not a public service pension scheme;

'safeguarded rights' has the meaning given in section 68A of the Pension Schemes Act 1993.

---

[1]   Commencement: 11 November 1999, for the purpose only of the exercise of any power to make regulations (s 89(5)(a)); 1 December 2000, for remaining purposes (Welfare Reform and Pensions Act 1999 (Commencement No 4) Order 2000, SI 2000/1047).

Charges by pension arrangements

41¹   Charges in respect of pension sharing costs

(1)   The Secretary of State may by regulations make provision for the purpose of enabling the person responsible for a pension arrangement involved in pension sharing to recover from the parties to pension sharing prescribed charges in respect of prescribed descriptions of pension sharing activity.

(2)   Regulations under subsection (1) may include –

(a)   provision for the start of the implementation period for a pension credit to be postponed in prescribed circumstances;

(b)   provision, in relation to payments in respect of charges recoverable under the regulations, for reimbursement as between the parties to pension sharing;

(c)   provision, in relation to the recovery of charges by deduction from a pension credit, for the modification of Schedule 5;

(d)   provision for the recovery in prescribed circumstances of such additional amounts as may be determined in accordance with the regulations.

(3)   For the purposes of regulations under subsection (1), the question of how much of a charge recoverable under the regulations is attributable to a party to pension sharing is to be determined as follows –

(a)   where the relevant order or provision includes provision about the apportionment of charges under this section, there is attributable to the party so much of the charge as is apportioned to him by that provision;

(b)   where the relevant order or provision does not include such provision, the charge is attributable to the transferor.

(4)   For the purposes of subsection (1), a pension arrangement is involved in pension sharing if section 29 applies by virtue of an order or provision which relates to the arrangement.

(5)   In that subsection, the reference to pension sharing activity is to activity attributable (directly or indirectly) to the involvement in pension sharing.

(6)   In subsection (3) –

(a)   the reference to the relevant order or provision is to the order or provision which gives rise to the pension sharing, and

(b)   the reference to the transferor is to the person to whose rights that order or provision relates.

(7)   In this section 'prescribed' means prescribed in regulations under subsection (1).

Adaptation of statutory schemes

42²   Extension of scheme-making powers

(1)   Power under an Act to establish a pension scheme shall include power to make provision for the provision, by reference to pension credits which derive from rights under –

(a)   the scheme, or

(b)   a scheme in relation to which the scheme is specified as an alternative for the purposes of paragraph 2 of Schedule 5,

of benefits to or in respect of those entitled to the credits.

---

¹   Commencement: 11 November 1999, for the purpose only of the exercise of any power to make regulations (s 89(5)(a)); 1 December 2000, for remaining purposes (Welfare Reform and Pensions Act 1999 (Commencement No 4) Order 2000, SI 2000/1047).
²   Commencement: 1 December 2000 (Welfare Reform and Pensions Act 1999 (Commencement No 4) Order 2000, SI 2000/1047).

(2)   Subsection (1) is without prejudice to any other power.

(3)   Subsection (1) shall apply in relation to Acts whenever passed.

(4)   No obligation to consult shall apply in relation to the making, in exercise of a power under an Act to establish a pension scheme, of provision of a kind authorised by subsection (1).

(5)   Any provision of, or under, an Act which makes benefits under a pension scheme established under an Act a charge on, or payable out of –

   (a)   the Consolidated Fund,

   (b)   the Scottish Consolidated Fund, or

   (c)   the Consolidated Fund of Northern Ireland,

shall be treated as including any benefits under the scheme which are attributable (directly or indirectly) to a pension credit which derives from rights to benefits charged on, or payable out of, that fund.

(6)   In this section –

'pension credit' includes a credit under Northern Ireland legislation corresponding to section 29(1)(b);

'pension scheme' means a scheme or arrangement providing benefits, in the form of pensions or otherwise, payable on termination of service, or on death or retirement, to or in respect of persons to whom the scheme or arrangement applies.

43[1]   Power to extend judicial pension schemes

(1)   The appropriate minister may by regulations amend the Sheriffs' Pensions (Scotland) Act 1961, the Judicial Pensions Act 1981 or the Judicial Pensions and Retirement Act 1993 for the purpose of –

   (a)   extending a pension scheme under the Act to include the provision, by reference to pension credits which derive from rights under –

      (i)   the scheme, or

      (ii)   a scheme in relation to which the scheme is specified as an alternative for the purposes of paragraph 2 of Schedule 5,

   of benefits to or in respect of those entitled to the credits, or

   (b)   restricting the power of the appropriate minister to accept payments into a pension scheme under the Act, where the payments represent the cash equivalent of rights under another pension scheme which are attributable (directly or indirectly) to a pension credit.

(2)   Regulations under subsection (1) –

   (a)   may make benefits provided by virtue of paragraph (a) of that subsection a charge on, and payable out of, the Consolidated Fund;

   (b)   may confer power to make subordinate legislation, including subordinate legislation which provides for calculation of the value of rights in accordance with guidance from time to time prepared by a person specified in the subordinate legislation.

(3)   The appropriate minister for the purposes of subsection (1) is –

   (a)   in relation to a pension scheme whose ordinary members are limited to those who hold judicial office whose jurisdiction is exercised exclusively in relation to Scotland, the Secretary of State, and

   (b)   in relation to any other pension scheme, the Lord Chancellor.

(4)   In this section –

---

[1]   Commencement: 11 November 1999, for the purpose only of the exercise of any power to make regulations (s 89(5)(a)); 1 December 2000, for remaining purposes (Welfare Reform and Pensions Act 1999 (Commencement No 4) Order 2000, SI 2000/1047).

'pension credit' includes a credit under Northern Ireland legislation corresponding to section 29(1)(b);

'pension scheme' means a scheme or arrangement providing benefits, in the form of pensions or otherwise, payable on termination of service, or on death or retirement, to or in respect of persons to whom the scheme or arrangement applies.

****

Schedule 3
Pension Sharing Orders: England and Wales[1]

Section 19

1   The Matrimonial Causes Act 1973 is amended as follows.

2   [*Inserts Matrimonial Causes Act 1973, s 21A*]

3   [*Amends Matrimonial Causes Act 1973, s 24*]

4   [*Inserts Matrimonial Causes Act 1973, ss 24B –24D*]

5   [*Amends Matrimonial Causes Act 1973, s 25*]

6   [*Amends Matrimonial Causes Act 1973, s 25A*]

7   [*Amends Matrimonial Causes Act 1973, s 31*]

8   [*Amends Matrimonial Causes Act 1973, s 33A*]

9   [*Amends Matrimonial Causes Act 1973, s 37*]

10   [*Inserts Matrimonial Causes Act 1973, s 40A*]

11   [*Amends Matrimonial Causes Act 1973, s 52*]

Schedule 4
Amendments of Sections 25B to 25D of the
Matrimonial Causes Act 1973[2]

Section 21

1   [*Amends Matrimonial Causes Act 1973, s 25B*]

2   [*Amends Matrimonial Causes Act 1973, s 25C*]

3   [*Amends Matrimonial Causes Act 1973, s 25D*]

Schedule 5
Pension Credits: Mode of Discharge[3]

Section 35

Funded pension schemes

1—(1) This paragraph applies to a pension credit which derives from –

(a)   a funded occupational pension scheme, or

---

[1]   Commencement: 1 December 2000 (Welfare Reform and Pensions Act 1999 (Commencement No 5) Order 2000, SI 2000/1116).

[2]   Commencement: 1 December 2000 (Welfare Reform and Pensions Act 1999 (Commencement No 5) Order 2000, SI 2000/1116).

[3]   Commencement: 11 November 1999, for the purpose only of the exercise of any power to make regulations (s 89(5)(a)); 1 December 2000, for remaining purposes (Welfare Reform and Pensions Act 1999 (Commencement No 4) Order 2000, SI 2000/1047).

(b)   a personal pension scheme.

(2)   The trustees or managers of the scheme from which a pension credit to which this paragraph applies derives may discharge their liability in respect of the credit by conferring appropriate rights under that scheme on the person entitled to the credit –

    (a)   with his consent, or

    (b)   in accordance with regulations made by the Secretary of State.

(3)   The trustees or managers of the scheme from which a pension credit to which this paragraph applies derives may discharge their liability in respect of the credit by paying the amount of the credit to the person responsible for a qualifying arrangement with a view to acquiring rights under that arrangement for the person entitled to the credit if –

    (a)   the qualifying arrangement is not disqualified as a destination for the credit,

    (b)   the person responsible for that arrangement is able and willing to accept payment in respect of the credit, and

    (c)   payment is made with the consent of the person entitled to the credit, or in accordance with regulations made by the Secretary of State.

(4)   For the purposes of sub-paragraph (2), no account is to be taken of consent of the person entitled to the pension credit unless –

    (a)   it is given after receipt of notice in writing of an offer to discharge liability in respect of the credit by making a payment under sub-paragraph (3), or

    (b)   it is not withdrawn within 7 days of receipt of such notice.

Unfunded public service pension schemes

2—(1)   This paragraph applies to a pension credit which derives from an occupational pension scheme which is –

    (a)   not funded, and

    (b)   a public service pension scheme.

(2)   The trustees or managers of the scheme from which a pension credit to which this paragraph applies derives may discharge their liability in respect of the credit by conferring appropriate rights under that scheme on the person entitled to the credit.

(3)   If such a scheme as is mentioned in sub-paragraph (1) is closed to new members, the appropriate authority in relation to that scheme may by regulations specify another public service pension scheme as an alternative to it for the purposes of this paragraph.

(4)   Where the trustees or managers of a scheme in relation to which an alternative is specified under sub-paragraph (3) are subject to liability in respect of a pension credit, they may –

    (a)   discharge their liability in respect of the credit by securing that appropriate rights are conferred on the person entitled to the credit by the trustees or managers of the alternative scheme, and

    (b)   for the purpose of so discharging their liability, require the trustees or managers of the alternative scheme to take such steps as may be required.

(5)   In sub-paragraph (3), 'the appropriate authority', in relation to a public service pension scheme, means such Minister of the Crown or government department as may be designated by the Treasury as having responsibility for the scheme.

Other unfunded occupational pension schemes

3—(1)   This paragraph applies to a pension credit which derives from an occupational pension scheme which is –

    (a)   not funded, and

(b)   not a public service pension scheme.

(2)   The trustees or managers of the scheme from which a pension credit to which this paragraph applies derives may discharge their liability in respect of the credit by conferring appropriate rights under that scheme on the person entitled to the credit.

(3)   The trustees or managers of the scheme from which a pension credit to which this paragraph applies derives may discharge their liability in respect of the credit by paying the amount of the credit to the person responsible for a qualifying arrangement with a view to acquiring rights under that arrangement for the person entitled to the credit if –

   (a)   the qualifying arrangement is not disqualified as a destination for the credit,

   (b)   the person responsible for that arrangement is able and willing to accept payment in respect of the credit, and

   (c)   payment is made with the consent of the person entitled to the credit, or in accordance with regulations made by the Secretary of State.

Other pension arrangements

4—(1) This paragraph applies to a pension credit which derives from –

   (a)   a retirement annuity contract,

   (b)   an annuity or insurance policy purchased or transferred for the purpose of giving effect to rights under an occupational pension scheme or a personal pension scheme, or

   (c)   an annuity purchased, or entered into, for the purpose of discharging liability in respect of a pension credit.

(2)   The person responsible for the pension arrangement from which a pension credit to which this paragraph applies derives may discharge his liability in respect of the credit by paying the amount of the credit to the person responsible for a qualifying arrangement with a view to acquiring rights under that arrangement for the person entitled to the credit if –

   (a)   the qualifying arrangement is not disqualified as a destination for the credit,

   (b)   the person responsible for that arrangement is able and willing to accept payment in respect of the credit, and

   (c)   payment is made with the consent of the person entitled to the credit, or in accordance with regulations made by the Secretary of State.

(3)   The person responsible for the pension arrangement from which a pension credit to which this paragraph applies derives may discharge his liability in respect of the credit by entering into an annuity contract with the person entitled to the credit if the contract is not disqualified as a destination for the credit.

(4)   The person responsible for the pension arrangement from which a pension credit to which this paragraph applies derives may, in such circumstances as the Secretary of State may prescribe by regulations, discharge his liability in respect of the credit by assuming an obligation to provide an annuity for the person entitled to the credit.

(5)   In sub-paragraph (1)(c), 'pension credit' includes a credit under Northern Ireland legislation corresponding to section 29(1)(b).

Appropriate rights

5—For the purposes of this Schedule, rights conferred on the person entitled to a pension credit are appropriate if –

   (a)   they are conferred with effect from, and including, the day on which the order, or provision, under which the credit arises takes effect, and

   (b)   their value, when calculated in accordance with regulations made by the Secretary of State, equals the amount of the credit.

Qualifying arrangements

6—(1) The following are qualifying arrangements for the purposes of this Schedule –

    (a)   an occupational pension scheme,

    (b)   a personal pension scheme,

    (c)   an appropriate annuity contract,

    (d)   an appropriate policy of insurance, and

    (e)   an overseas arrangement within the meaning of the Contracting-out (Transfer and Transfer Payment) Regulations 1996.

(2)   An annuity contract or policy of insurance is appropriate for the purposes of sub-paragraph (1) if, at the time it is entered into or taken out, the [insurer][1] with which it is entered into or taken out –

    (a)   is carrying on ...[2] long-term insurance business in the United Kingdom or any other member State, and

    (b)   satisfies such requirements as the Secretary of State may prescribe by regulations.

[(3)   'Insurer' and 'long-term insurance business' have the meaning given in section 180A of the Pension Schemes Act 1993.][3]

Disqualification as destination for pension credit

7—(1) If a pension credit derives from a pension arrangement which is approved for the purposes of Part XIV of the Income and Corporation Taxes Act 1988, an arrangement is disqualified as a destination for the credit unless –

    (a)   it is also approved for those purposes, or

    (b)   it satisfies such requirements as the Secretary of State may prescribe by regulations.

(2)   If the rights by reference to which the amount of a pension credit is determined are or include contracted-out rights or safeguarded rights, an arrangement is disqualified as a destination for the credit unless –

    (a)   it is of a description prescribed by the Secretary of State by regulations, and

    (b)   it satisfies such requirements as he may so prescribe.

(3)   An occupational pension scheme is disqualified as a destination for a pension credit unless the rights to be acquired under the arrangement by the person entitled to the credit are rights whose value, when calculated in accordance with regulations made by the Secretary of State, equals the credit.

(4)   An annuity contract or insurance policy is disqualified as a destination for a pension credit in such circumstances as the Secretary of State may prescribe by regulations.

(5)   The requirements which may be prescribed under sub-paragraph (1)(b) include, in particular, requirements of the Inland Revenue.

(6)   In sub-paragraph (2) –

'contracted-out rights' means such rights under, or derived from –

    (a)   an occupational pension scheme contracted-out by virtue of section 9(2) or (3) of the Pension Schemes Act 1993, or

    (b)   a personal pension scheme which is an appropriate scheme for the purposes of that Act,

---

[1]   Word substituted: Financial Services and Markets Act 2000 (Consequential Amendments and Repeals) Order 2001, SI 2001/3649, with effect from 1 December 2001.

[2]   Word repealed: Financial Services and Markets Act 2000 (Consequential Amendments and Repeals) Order 2001, SI 2001/3649, with effect from 1 December 2001.

[3]   Sub-paragraph substituted: Financial Services and Markets Act 2000 (Consequential Amendments and Repeals) Order 2001, SI 2001/3649, with effect from 1 December 2001.

as the Secretary of State may prescribe by regulations;

'safeguarded rights' has the meaning given by section 68A of the Pension Schemes Act 1993.

Adjustments to amount of pension credit

8—(1) If –

    (a)   a pension credit derives from an occupational pension scheme,

    (b)   the scheme is one to which section 56 of the Pensions Act 1995 (minimum funding requirement for funded salary related schemes) applies,

    (c)   the scheme is underfunded on the valuation day, and

    (d)   such circumstances as the Secretary of State may prescribe by regulations apply,

paragraph 1(3) shall have effect in relation to the credit as if the reference to the amount of the credit were to such lesser amount as may be determined in accordance with regulations made by the Secretary of State.

(2)   Whether a scheme is underfunded for the purposes of sub-paragraph (1)(c) shall be determined in accordance with regulations made by the Secretary of State.

(3)   For the purposes of that provision, the valuation day is the day by reference to which the cash equivalent on which the amount of the pension credit depends falls to be calculated.

9—If –

    (a)   a person's shareable rights under a pension arrangement have become subject to a pension debit, and

    (b)   the person responsible for the arrangement makes a payment which is referable to those rights without knowing of the pension debit,

this Schedule shall have effect as if the amount of the corresponding pension credit were such lesser amount as may be determined in accordance with regulations made by the Secretary of State.

10   The Secretary of State may by regulations make provision for paragraph 1(3), 3(3) or 4(2) to have effect, where payment is made after the end of the implementation period for the pension credit, as if the reference to the amount of the credit were to such larger amount as may be determined in accordance with the regulations.

General

11   Liability in respect of a pension credit shall be treated as discharged if the effect of paragraph 8(1) or 9 is to reduce it to zero.

12   Liability in respect of a pension credit may not be discharged otherwise than in accordance with this Schedule.

13   Regulations under paragraph 5(b) or 7(3) may provide for calculation of the value of rights in accordance with guidance from time to time prepared by a person specified in the regulations.

14   In this Schedule –

'funded', in relation to an occupational pension scheme, means that the scheme meets its liabilities out of a fund accumulated for the purpose during the life of the scheme;

'public service pension scheme' has the same meaning as in the Pension Schemes Act 1993.

Schedule 6
Effect of State Scheme Pension Debits and Credits[1]

Section 50

1   The Contributions and Benefits Act is amended as follows.

2   After section 45A there is inserted –

'45B   Reduction of additional pension in Category A retirement pension: pension sharing

(1)   The weekly rate of the additional pension in a Category A retirement pension shall be reduced as follows in any case where –

     (a)   the pensioner has become subject to a state scheme pension debit, and

     (b)   the debit is to any extent referable to the additional pension.

(2)   If the pensioner became subject to the debit in or after the final relevant year, the weekly rate of the additional pension shall be reduced by the appropriate weekly amount.

(3)   If the pensioner became subject to the debit before the final relevant year, the weekly rate of the additional pension shall be reduced by the appropriate weekly amount multiplied by the relevant revaluation percentage.

(4)   The appropriate weekly amount for the purposes of subsections (2) and (3) above is the weekly rate, expressed in terms of the valuation day, at which the cash equivalent, on that day, of the pension mentioned in subsection (5) below is equal to so much of the debit as is referable to the additional pension.

(5)   The pension referred to above is a notional pension for the pensioner by virtue of section 44(3)(b) above which becomes payable on the later of –

     (a)   his attaining pensionable age, and

     (b)   the valuation day.

(6)   For the purposes of subsection (3) above, the relevant revaluation percentage is the percentage specified, in relation to earnings factors for the tax year in which the pensioner became subject to the debit, by the last order under section 148 of the Administration Act to come into force before the end of the final relevant year.

(7)   Cash equivalents for the purposes of this section shall be calculated in accordance with regulations.

(8)   In this section –

"final relevant year" means the tax year immediately preceding that in which the pensioner attains pensionable age;

"state scheme pension debit" means a debit under section 49(1)(a) of the Welfare Reform and Pensions Act 1999 (debit for the purposes of this Part of this Act);

"valuation day" means the day on which the pensioner became subject to the state scheme pension debit.'

3   After section 55 there is inserted –

'Shared additional pension

55A   Shared additional pension

(1)   A person shall be entitled to a shared additional pension if he is –

     (a) over pensionable age, and

     (b) entitled to a state scheme pension credit.

---

[1]   Commencement: 11 November 1999, for the purpose only of the exercise of any power to make regulations (s 89(5)(a)); 1 December 2000, for remaining purposes (Welfare Reform and Pensions Act 1999 (Commencement No 4) Order 2000, SI 2000/1047).

(2)   A person's entitlement to a shared additional pension shall continue throughout his life.

(3)   The weekly rate of a shared additional pension shall be the appropriate weekly amount, unless the pensioner's entitlement to the state scheme pension credit arose before the final relevant year, in which case it shall be that amount multiplied by the relevant revaluation percentage.

(4)   The appropriate weekly amount for the purposes of subsection (3) above is the weekly rate, expressed in terms of the valuation day, at which the cash equivalent, on that day, of the pensioner's entitlement, or prospective entitlement, to the shared additional pension is equal to the state scheme pension credit.

(5)   The relevant revaluation percentage for the purposes of that subsection is the percentage specified, in relation to earnings factors for the tax year in which the entitlement to the state scheme pension credit arose, by the last order under section 148 of the Administration Act to come into force before the end of the final relevant year.

(6)   Cash equivalents for the purposes of this section shall be calculated in accordance with regulations.

(7)   In this section –

'final relevant year' means the tax year immediately preceding that in which the pensioner attains pensionable age;

'state scheme pension credit' means a credit under section 49(1)(b) of the Welfare Reform and Pensions Act 1999 (credit for the purposes of this Part of this Act);

'valuation day' means the day on which the pensioner becomes entitled to the state scheme pension credit.

55B   Reduction of shared additional pension: pension sharing

(1)   The weekly rate of a shared additional pension shall be reduced as follows in any case where –

    (a)   the pensioner has become subject to a state scheme pension debit, and

    (b)   the debit is to any extent referable to the pension.

(2)   If the pensioner became subject to the debit in or after the final relevant year, the weekly rate of the pension shall be reduced by the appropriate weekly amount.

(3)   If the pensioner became subject to the debit before the final relevant year, the weekly rate of the additional pension shall be reduced by the appropriate weekly amount multiplied by the relevant revaluation percentage.

(4)   The appropriate weekly amount for the purposes of subsections (2) and (3) above is the weekly rate, expressed in terms of the valuation day, at which the cash equivalent, on that day, of the pension mentioned in subsection (5) below is equal to so much of the debit as is referable to the shared additional pension.

(5)   The pension referred to above is a notional pension for the pensioner by virtue of section 55A above which becomes payable on the later of –

    (a)   his attaining pensionable age, and

    (b)   the valuation day.

(6)   For the purposes of subsection (3) above, the relevant revaluation percentage is the percentage specified, in relation to earnings factors for the tax year in which the pensioner became subject to the debit, by the last order under section 148 of the Administration Act to come into force before the end of the final relevant year.

(7)   Cash equivalents for the purposes of this section shall be calculated in accordance with regulations.

(8)   In this section –

"final relevant year" means the tax year immediately preceding that in which the pensioner attains pensionable age;

"state scheme pension debit", means a debit under section 49(1)(a) of the Welfare Reform and Pensions Act 1999 (debit for the purposes of this Part of this Act);

"valuation day" means the day on which the pensioner became subject to the state scheme pension debit.

55C   Increase of shared additional pension where entitlement is deferred

(1)   For the purposes of this section, a person's entitlement to a shared additional pension is deferred –

    (a)   where he would be entitled to a Category A or Category B retirement pension but for the fact that his entitlement to such a pension is deferred, if and so long as his entitlement to such a pension is deferred, and

    (b)   otherwise, if and so long as he does not become entitled to the shared additional pension by reason only of not satisfying the conditions of section 1 of the Administration Act (entitlement to benefit dependent on claim),

and, in relation to a shared additional pension, "period of deferment" shall be construed accordingly.

(2)   Where a person's entitlement to a shared additional pension is deferred, the rate of his shared additional pension shall be increased by an amount equal to the aggregate of the increments to which he is entitled under subsection (3) below, but only if that amount is enough to increase the rate of the pension by at least 1 per cent.

(3)   A person is entitled to an increment under this subsection for each complete incremental period in his period of enhancement.

(4)   The amount of the increment for an incremental period shall be $^1/_7$th per cent of the weekly rate of the shared additional pension to which the person would have been entitled for the period if his entitlement had not been deferred.

(5)   Amounts under subsection (4) above shall be rounded to the nearest penny, taking any ½p as nearest to the next whole penny.

(6)   Where an amount under subsection (4) above would, apart from this subsection, be a sum less than ½p, the amount shall be taken to be zero, notwithstanding any other provision of this Act, the Pensions Act 1995 or the Administration Act.

(7)   Where one or more orders have come into force under section 150 of the Administration Act during the period of enhancement, the rate for any incremental period shall be determined as if the order or orders had come into force before the beginning of the period of enhancement.

(8)   The sums which are the increases in the rates of shared additional pensions under this section are subject to alteration by order made by the Secretary of State under section 150 of the Administration Act.

(9)   In this section –

"incremental period" means any period of six days which are treated by regulations as days of increment for the purposes of this section in relation to the person and pension in question; and

"period of enhancement", in relation to that person and that pension, means the period which –

    (a)   begins on the same day as the period of deferment in question, and

    (b)   ends on the same day as that period or, if earlier, on the day before the 5th anniversary of the beginning of that period.'

****

Divorce etc (Pensions) Regulations 2000[1]

1[2]   Citation, commencement and transitional provisions

(1)   These Regulations may be cited as the Divorce etc (Pensions) Regulations 2000 and shall come into force on 1st December 2000.

(2)   These Regulations shall apply to any proceedings for divorce, judicial separation or nullity of marriage commenced on or after 1st December 2000, and any such proceedings commenced before that date shall be treated as if these Regulations had not come into force.

2[3]   Interpretation

In these Regulations:

(a)   a reference to a section by number alone means the section so numbered in the Matrimonial Causes Act 1973;

(b)   'the 1984 Act' means the Matrimonial and Family Proceedings Act 1984;

(c)   expressions defined in sections 21A and 25D(3) have the meanings assigned by those sections;

(d)   every reference to a rule by number alone means the rule so numbered in the Family Proceedings Rules 1991.

3[4]   Valuation

(1)   For the purposes of the court's functions in connection with the exercise of any of its powers under Part II of the Matrimonial Causes Act 1973, benefits under a pension arrangement shall be calculated and verified in the manner set out in regulation 3 of the Pensions on Divorce etc (Provision of Information) Regulations 2000, and –

(a)   the benefits shall be valued as at a date to be specified by the court (being not earlier than one year before the date of the petition and not later than the date on which the court is exercising its power);

(b)   in determining that value the court may have regard to information furnished by the person responsible for the pension arrangement pursuant to any of the provisions set out in paragraph (2); and

(c)   in specifying a date under sub-paragraph (a) above the court may have regard to the date specified in any information furnished as mentioned in sub-paragraph (b) above.

(2)   The relevant provisions for the purposes of paragraph (1)(b) above are:

(a)   the Pensions on Divorce etc (Provision of Information) Regulations 2000;

(b)   regulation 5 of and Schedule 2 to the Occupational Pension Schemes (Disclosure of Information) Regulations 1996 and regulation 11 of and Schedule 1 to the Occupational Pension Schemes (Transfer Value) Regulations 1996;

(c)   section 93A or 94(1)(a) or (aa) of the Pension Schemes Act 1993;

(d)   section 94(1)(b) of the Pension Schemes Act 1993 or paragraph 2(a) (or, where applicable, 2(b)) of Schedule 2 to the Personal Pension Schemes (Disclosure of Information) Regulations 1987.

---

[1]   SI reference: SI 2000/1123.
   Made under: Matrimonial Causes Act 1973, ss 24C, 25D(1)(b), (2), (3) and 31(4C) and Matrimonial and Family Proceedings Act 1984, s 21(4).
[2]   Commencement: 1 December 2000 (reg 1(1)).
[3]   Commencement: 1 December 2000 (reg 1(1)).
[4]   Commencement: 1 December 2000 (reg 1(1)).

4[1]   Pension attachment: notices

(1)   This regulation applies in the circumstances set out in section 25D(1)(a) (transfers of pension rights).

(2)   Where this regulation applies, the person responsible for the first arrangement shall give notice in accordance with the following paragraphs of this regulation to

(a)   the person responsible for the new arrangement, and

(b)   the other party.

(3)   The notice to the person responsible for the new arrangement shall include copies of the following documents:

(a)   every order made under section 23 imposing any requirement on the person responsible for the first arrangement in relation to the rights transferred;

(b)   any order varying such an order;

(c)   all information or particulars which the other party has been required to supply under any provision of rule 2.70 for the purpose of enabling the person responsible for the first arrangement: –

(i)   to provide information, documents or representations to the court to enable it to decide what if any requirement should be imposed on that person; or

(ii)   to comply with any order imposing such a requirement;

(d)   any notice given by the other party to the person responsible for the first arrangement under regulation 6;

(e)   where the pension rights under the first arrangement were derived wholly or partly from rights held under a previous pension arrangement, any notice given to the person responsible for the previous arrangement under paragraph (2) of this regulation on the occasion of that acquisition of rights.

(4)   The notice to the other party shall contain the following particulars:

(a)   the fact that the pension rights have been transferred;

(b)   the date on which the transfer takes effect;

(c)   the name and address of the person responsible for the new arrangement;

(d)   the fact that the order made under section 23 is to have effect as if it had been made in respect of the person responsible for the new arrangement.

(5)   Both notices shall be given:

(a)   within the period provided by section 99 of the Pension Schemes Act 1993 for the person responsible for the first arrangement to carry out what the member requires; and

(b)   before the expiry of 21 days after the person responsible for the first arrangement has made all required payments to the person responsible for the new arrangement.

5[2]   Pension attachment: reduction in benefits

(1)   This regulation applies where:

(a)   an order under section 23 or under section 17 of the 1984 Act has been made by virtue of section 25B or 25C imposing any requirement on the person responsible for a pension arrangement;

(b)   an event has occurred which is likely to result in a significant reduction in the benefits payable under the arrangement, other than:

---

[1]   Commencement: 1 December 2000 (reg 1(1)).
[2]   Commencement: 1 December 2000 (reg 1(1)).

(i)   the transfer from the arrangement of all the rights of the party with pension rights in the circumstances set out in section 25D(1)(a), or

(ii)   a reduction in the value of assets held for the purposes of the arrangement by reason of a change in interest rates or other market conditions.

(2)   Where this regulation applies, the person responsible for the arrangement shall, within 14 days of the occurrence of the event mentioned in paragraph (1)(b), give notice to the other party of:

(a)   that event;

(b)   the likely extent of the reduction in the benefits payable under the arrangement.

(3)   Where the event mentioned in paragraph (1)(b) consists of a transfer of some but not all of the rights of the party with pension rights from the arrangement, the person responsible for the first arrangement shall, within 14 days of the transfer, give notice to the other party of the name and address of the person responsible for any pension arrangement under which the party with pension rights has acquired rights as a result of that event.

6[1]   Pension attachment: change of circumstances

(1)   This regulation applies where:

(a)   an order under section 23 or under section 17 of the 1984 Act has been made by virtue of section 25B or 25C imposing any requirement on the person responsible for a pension arrangement; and

(b)   any of the events set out in paragraph (2) has occurred.

(2)   Those events are:

(a)   any of the particulars supplied by the other party under rule 2.70 for any purpose mentioned in regulation 4(3)(c) has ceased to be accurate; or

(b)   by reason of the remarriage of the other party or otherwise, the order has ceased to have effect.

(3)   Where this regulation applies, the other party shall, within 14 days of the event, give notice of it to the person responsible for the pension arrangement.

(4)   Where, because of the inaccuracy of the particulars supplied by the other party under rule 2.70 or because the other party has failed to give notice of their having ceased to be accurate, it is not reasonably practicable for the person responsible for the pension arrangement to make a payment to the other party as required by the order:

(a)   it may instead make that payment to the party with pension rights, and

(b)   it shall then be discharged of liability to the other party to the extent of that payment.

(5)   Where an event set out in paragraph (2)(b) has occurred and, because the other party has failed to give notice in accordance with paragraph (3), the person responsible for the pension arrangement makes a payment to the other party as required by the order:

(a)   its liability to the party with pension rights shall be discharged to the extent of that payment, and

(b)   the other party shall, within 14 days of the payment being made, make a payment to the party with pension rights to the extent of that payment.

7[2]   Pension attachment: transfer of rights

(1)   This regulation applies where:

(a)   a transfer of rights has taken place in the circumstances set out in section 25D(1)(a);

(b)   notice has been given in accordance with regulation 4(2)(a) and (b);

---

[1]   Commencement: 1 December 2000 (reg 1(1)).
[2]   Commencement: 1 December 2000 (reg 1(1)).

(c)   any of the events set out in regulation 6(2) has occurred; and

(d)   the other party has not, before receiving notice under regulation 4(2)(b), given notice of that event to the person responsible for the first arrangement under regulation 6(3).

(2)   Where this regulation applies, the other party shall, within 14 days of the event, give notice of it to the person responsible for the new arrangement.

(3)   Where, because of the inaccuracy of the particulars supplied by the other party under rule 2.70 for any purpose mentioned in regulation 4(3)(c) or because the other party has failed to give notice of their having ceased to be accurate, it is not reasonably practicable for the person responsible for the new arrangement to make a payment to the other party as required by the order:

(a)   it may instead make that payment to the party with pension rights, and

(b)   it shall then be discharged of liability to the other party to the extent of that payment.

(4)   Subject to paragraph (5), where this regulation applies and the other party, within one year from the transfer, gives to the person responsible for the first arrangement notice of the event set out in regulation 6(2) in purported compliance with regulation 7(2), the person responsible for the first arrangement shall:

(a)   send that notice to the person responsible for the new arrangement, and

(b)   give the other party a second notice under regulation 4(2)(b);

and the other party shall be deemed to have given notice under regulation 7(2) to the person responsible for the new arrangement.

(5)   Upon complying with paragraph (4) above, the person responsible for the first arrangement shall be discharged from any further obligation under regulation 4 or 7(4), whether in relation to the event in question or any further event set out in regulation 6(2) which may be notified to it by the other party.

8[1]   Service

A notice under regulation 4, 5, 6 or 7 may be sent by fax or by ordinary first class post to the last known address of the intended recipient and shall be deemed to have been received on the seventh day after the day on which it was sent.

9[2]   Pension sharing order not to take effect pending appeal

(1)   No pension sharing order under section 24B or variation of a pension sharing order under section 31 shall take effect earlier than 7 days after the end of the period for filing notice of appeal against the order.

(2)   The filing of a notice of appeal within the time allowed for doing so prevents the order taking effect before the appeal has been dealt with.

10[3]   Revocation

The Divorce etc (Pensions) Regulations 1996 and the Divorce etc (Pensions) (Amendment) Regulations 1997 are revoked.

---

[1]   Commencement: 1 December 2000 (reg 1(1)).
[2]   Commencement: 1 December 2000 (reg 1(1)).
[3]   Commencement: 1 December 2000 (reg 1(1)).

Family Proceedings Rules 1991[1]

Part I
Preliminary

****

1.2[2]　Interpretation

(1)　In these rules, unless the context otherwise requires –

'the Act of 1973' means the Matrimonial Causes Act 1973;

'the Act of 1984' means the Matrimonial and Family Proceedings Act 1984;

'the Act of 1986' means the Family Law Act 1986;

'the Act of 1989' means the Children Act 1989;

['the Act of 1991' means the Child Support Act 1991;][3]

'ancillary relief ' means –

(a)　an avoidance of disposition order,

(b)　a financial provision order,

(c)　an order for maintenance pending suit,

(d)　a property adjustment order, ...[4]

(e)　a variation order; [or

(f)　a pension sharing order;][5]

'avoidance of disposition order' means an order under section 37(2)(b) or (c) of the Act of 1973;

'business day' has the meaning assigned to it by rule 1.5(6);

'cause' means a matrimonial cause as defined by section 32 of the Act of 1984 or proceedings under section 19 of the Act of 1973 (presumption of death and dissolution of marriage);

'child' and 'child of the family' have, except in Part IV, the meanings respectively assigned to them by section 52(1) of the Act of 1973;

'consent order' means an order under section 33A of the Act of 1973;

['Contracting State' means –

(a)　one of the original parties to the Council Regulation, that is to say Belgium, Germany, Greece, Spain, France, Ireland, Italy, Luxembourg, the Netherlands, Austria, Portugal, Finland, Sweden and the United Kingdom, and

(b)　a party which has subsequently adopted the Council Regulation;

'the Council Regulation' means Council Regulation (EC) No 1347/2000 of 29th May 2000 on jurisdiction and the recognition and enforcement of judgments in matrimonial matters and in matters of parental responsibility for children of both spouses;][6]

'court' means a judge or the district judge;

---

[1]　SI reference: SI 1991/1247.
　　Made under: Matrimonial and Family Proceedings Act 1984, s 40(1).
[2]　Commencement: 14 October 1991 (r 1.1).
[3]　Definition inserted: Family Proceedings (Amendment) Rules 1993, SI 1993/295, with effect from 5 April 1993.
[4]　Word revoked: Family Proceedings (Amendment) Rules 2000, SI 2000/2267, with effect from 1 December 2000.
[5]　Definition inserted: Family Proceedings (Amendment) Rules 2000, SI 2000/2267, with effect from 1 December 2000.
[6]　Definitions inserted: Family Proceedings (Amendment) Rules 2001, SI 2001/821, with effect from 1 April 2001.

'court of trial' means a divorce county court designated by the Lord Chancellor as a court of trial pursuant to section 33(1) of the Act of 1984 and, in relation to matrimonial proceedings pending in a divorce county court, the principal registry shall be treated as a court of trial having its place of sitting at the Royal Courts of Justice;

'defended cause' means a cause not being an undefended cause;

'district judge', in relation to proceedings in the principal registry, a district registry or a county court, means the district judge or one of the district judges of that registry or county court, as the case may be;

'district registry'[, except in rule 4.22(2A),]¹ means any district registry having a divorce county court within its district;

'divorce county court' means a county court so designated by the Lord Chancellor pursuant to section 33(1) of the Act of 1984;

'divorce town', in relation to any matrimonial proceedings, means a place at which sittings of the High Court are authorised to be held outside the Royal Courts of Justice for the hearing of such proceedings or proceedings of the class to which they belong;

'document exchange' means any document exchange for the time being approved by the Lord Chancellor;

'family proceedings' has the meaning assigned to it by section 32 of the Act of 1984;

'financial provision order' means any of the orders mentioned in section 21(1) of the Act of 1973 except an order under section 27(6) of that Act;

'financial relief' has the same meaning as in section 37 of the Act of 1973;

'judge' does not include a district judge;

'notice of intention to defend' has the meaning assigned to it by rule 10.8;

['officer of the service' has the same meaning as in the Criminal Justice and Court Services Act 2000;]²

'order for maintenance pending suit' means an order under section 22 of the Act of 1973;

'person named' includes a person described as 'passing under the name of A.B.';

'the President' means the President of the Family Division or, in the case of his absence or incapacity through illness or otherwise or of a vacancy in the office of President, the senior puisne judge of that Division;

'principal registry' means the Principal Registry of the Family Division;

'proper officer' means –

(a)   in relation to the principal registry, the [family proceedings department manager],³ and

(b)   in relation to any other court or registry, the [court manager],⁴

or other officer of the court or registry acting on his behalf in accordance with directions given by the Lord Chancellor;

'property adjustment order' means any of the orders mentioned in section 21(2) of the Act of 1973;

'registry for the divorce town' shall be construed in accordance with rule 2.32(6);

'Royal Courts of Justice', in relation to matrimonial proceedings pending in a divorce county court, means such place, being the Royal Courts of Justice or elsewhere, as may be specified in directions given by the Lord Chancellor pursuant to section 42(2)(a) of the Act of 1984;

---

[1]   Words inserted: Family Proceedings (Amendment No 2) Rules 1992, SI 1992/2067, with effect from 5 October 1992.

[2]   Definition inserted: Family Proceedings (Amendment) Rules 2001, SI 2001/821, with effect from 1 April 2001.

[3]   Words substituted: Family Proceedings (Amendment No 2) Rules 1997, SI 1997/1056, with effect from 21 April 1997.

[4]   Words substituted: Family Proceedings (Amendment No 2) Rules 1997, SI 1997/1056, with effect from 21 April 1997.

'senior district judge' means the senior district judge of the Family Division or, in his absence from the principal registry, the senior of the district judges in attendance at the registry;

'special procedure list' has the meaning assigned to it by rule 2.24(3);

'undefended cause' means –

(i)　　a cause in which no answer has been filed or any answer filed has been struck out, or

(ii)　　a cause which is proceeding only on the respondent's answer and in which no reply or answer to the respondent's answer has been filed or any such reply or answer has been struck out, or

(iii)　　a cause to which rule 2.12(4) applies and in which no notice has been given under that rule or any notice so given has been withdrawn, or

(iv)　　a cause in which an answer has been filed claiming relief but in which no pleading has been filed opposing the grant of a decree on the petition or answer or any pleading or part of a pleading opposing the grant of such relief has been struck out, or

(v)　　any cause not within (i) to (iv) above in which a decree has been pronounced;

'variation order' means an order under section 31 of the Act of 1973.

(2)　　Unless the context otherwise requires, a cause begun by petition shall be treated as pending for the purposes of these rules notwithstanding that a final decree or order has been made on the petition.

(3)　　Unless the context otherwise requires, a rule or Part referred to by number means the rule or Part so numbered in these rules.

(4)　　In these rules a form referred to by number means the form so numbered in Appendix 1 [or 1A][1] to these rules with such variation as the circumstances of the particular case may require.

(5)　　In these rules any reference to an Order and rule is –

(a)　　if prefixed by the letters 'CCR', a reference to that Order and rule in the County Court Rules 1981, and

(b)　　if prefixed by the letters 'RSC', a reference to that Order and rule in the Rules of the Supreme Court 1965.

[(5A)　In these rules a reference to a Part or rule, if prefixed by the letters 'CPR', is a reference to that Part or rule in the Civil Procedure Rules 1998.][2]

(6)　　References in these rules to a county court shall, in relation to matrimonial proceedings, be construed as reference to a divorce county court.

(7)　　In this rule and in rule 1.4, 'matrimonial proceedings' means proceedings of a kind with respect to which divorce county courts have jurisdiction by or under section 33, 34 or 35 of the Act of 1984.

****

Part II
Matrimonial Causes

****

2.53[3]　Application by petitioner or respondent for ancillary relief

(1)　　Any application by a petitioner, or by a respondent who files an answer claiming relief, for –

(a)　　an order for maintenance pending suit,

---

[1]　　Words inserted: Family Proceedings (Amendment No 2) Rules 1999, SI 1999/3491, with effect from 5 June 2000.

[2]　　Paragraph inserted: Family Proceedings (Amendment No 2) Rules 1999, SI 1999/3491, with effect from 5 June 2000.

[3]　　Commencement: 14 October 1991 (r 1.1).

  (b) a financial provision order,

  (c) a property adjustment order,

  [(d) a pension sharing order][1]

shall be made in the petition or answer, as the case may be.

(2) Notwithstanding anything in paragraph (1), an application for ancillary relief which should have been made in the petition or answer may be made subsequently –

  (a) by leave of the court, either by notice in [Form A][2] or at the trial, or

  (b) where the parties are agreed upon the terms of the proposed order, without leave by notice in [Form A].[3]

(3) An application by a petitioner or respondent for ancillary relief, not being an application which is required to be made in the petition or answer, shall be made by notice in [Form A].[4]

****

2.61[5] Information on application for consent order for financial relief

(1) Subject to paragraphs (2) and (3), there shall be lodged with every application for a consent order under any of sections 23, 24 or 24A of the Act of 1973 two copies of a draft of the order in the terms sought, one of which shall be indorsed with a statement signed by the respondent to the application signifying his agreement, and a statement of information (which may be made in more than one document) which shall include –

  (a) the duration of the marriage, the age of each party and of any minor or dependent child of the family;

  (b) an estimate in summary form of the approximate amount or value of the capital resources and net income of each party and of any minor child of the family;

  (c) what arrangements are intended for the accommodation of each of the parties and any minor child of the family;

  (d) whether either party has remarried or has any present intention to marry or to cohabit with another person;

  [(dd) where the order [includes provision to be made under section 24B,][6] 25B or 25C of the Act of 1973, a statement confirming that [the person responsible for the pension arrangement in question has been served with the documents required by rule 2.70(11)][7] and that no objection to such an order has been made by [that person][8] within 14 days from such service;][9]

  (e) where the terms of the order provide for a transfer of property, a statement confirming that any mortgagee of that property has been served with notice of the application and that no objection to such a transfer has been made by the mortgagee within 14 days from such service; and

  (f) any other especially significant matters.

---

[1] Sub-paragraph inserted: Family Proceedings (Amendment) Rules 2000, SI 2000/2267, with effect from 1 December 2000.

[2] Words substituted: Family Proceedings (Amendment No 2) Rules 1999, SI 1999/3491, with effect from 5 June 2000.

[3] Words substituted: Family Proceedings (Amendment No 2) Rules 1999, SI 1999/3491, with effect from 5 June 2000.

[4] Words substituted: Family Proceedings (Amendment No 2) Rules 1999, SI 1999/3491, with effect from 5 June 2000.

[5] Commencement: 14 October 1991 (r 1.1).

[6] Words substituted: Family Proceedings (Amendment) Rules 2000, SI 2000/2267, with effect from 1 December 2000.

[7] Words substituted: Family Proceedings (Amendment) Rules 2000, SI 2000/2267, with effect from 1 December 2000.

[8] Words substituted: Family Proceedings (Amendment) Rules 2000, SI 2000/2267, with effect from 1 December 2000.

[9] Paragraph inserted: Family Proceedings (Amendment) (No 2) Rules 1996, SI 1996/1674, with effect from 1 August 1996.

(2)   Where an application is made for a consent order varying an order for periodical payments paragraph (1) shall be sufficiently complied with if the statement of information required to be lodged with the application includes only the information in respect of net income mentioned in paragraph (1)(b) [(and, where appropriate, a statement under paragraph (1)(dd))],[1] and an application for a consent order for interim periodical payments pending the determination of an application for ancillary relief may be made in like manner.

(3)   Where all or any of the parties attend the hearing of an application for financial relief the court may dispense with the lodging of a statement of information in accordance with paragraph (1) and give directions for the information which would otherwise be required to be given in such a statement to be given in such a manner as it sees fit.

[2.61A Application for ancillary relief

(1)   A notice of intention to proceed with an application for ancillary relief made in the petition or answer or an application for ancillary relief must be made by notice in Form A.

(2)   The notice must be filed:

  (a)   if the case is pending in a divorce county court, in that court; or

  (b)   if the case is pending in the High Court, in the registry in which it is proceeding.

(3)   Where the applicant requests an order for ancillary relief that includes provision to be made by virtue of section [24B,][2] 25B or 25C of the Act of 1973 the terms of the order requested must be specified in the notice in Form A.

(4)   Upon the filing of Form A the court must:

  (a)   fix a first appointment not less than 12 weeks and not more than 16 weeks after the date of the filing of the notice and give notice of that date;

  (b)   serve a copy on the respondent within 4 days of the date of the filing of the notice.

(5)   The date fixed under paragraph (4) for the first appointment, or for any subsequent appointment, must not be cancelled except with the court's permission and, if cancelled, the court must immediately fix a new date.][3]

[2.61B Procedure before the first appointment

(1)   Both parties must, at the same time, exchange with each other, and each file with the court, a statement in Form E, which –

  (a)   is signed by the party who made the statement;

  (b)   is sworn to be true, and

  (c)   contains the information and has attached to it the documents required by that Form.

(2)   Form E must be exchanged and filed not less than 35 days before the date of the first appointment.

(3)   Form E must have attached to it:

  (a)   any documents required by Form E; ...[4]

  (b)   any other documents necessary to explain or clarify any of the information contained in Form E [; and

  (c)   any documents furnished to the party producing the form by a person responsible for a pension arrangement, either following a request under rule 2.70(2) or as part of a 'relevant valuation' as defined in rule 2.70(4).][5]

---

[1]   Words inserted: Family Proceedings (Amendment) (No 2) Rules 1996, SI 1996/1674, with effect from 1 August 1996.

[2]   Definition inserted: Family Proceedings (Amendment) Rules 2000, SI 2000/2267, with effect from 1 December 2000.

[3]   Rule inserted: Family Proceedings (Amendment No 2) Rules 1999, SI 1999/3491, with effect from 5 June 2000.

[4]   Word revoked: Family Proceedings (Amendment) Rules 2000, SI 2000/2267, with effect from 1 December 2000.

[5]   Paragraph and preceding word inserted: Family Proceedings (Amendment) Rules 2000, SI 2000/2267, with effect from 1 December 2000.

(4)   Form E must have no documents attached to it other than the documents referred to in paragraph (3).

(5)   Where a party was unavoidably prevented from sending any document required by Form E, that party must at the earliest opportunity:

    (a)   serve copies of that document on the other party, and

    (b)   file a copy of that document with the court, together with a statement explaining the failure to send it with Form E.

(6)   No disclosure or inspection of documents may be requested or given between the filing of the application for ancillary relief and the first appointment, except –

    (a)   copies sent with Form E, or in accordance with paragraph (5); or

    (b)   in accordance with paragraph (7).

(7)   At least 14 days before the hearing of the first appointment, each party must file with the court and serve on the other party –

    (a)   a concise statement of the issues between the parties;

    (b)   a chronology;

    (c)   a questionnaire setting out by reference to the concise statement of issues any further information and documents requested from the other party or a statement that no information and documents are required;

    (d)   a notice in Form G stating whether that party will be in a position at the first appointment to proceed on that occasion to a FDR appointment.

(8)   ...[1]

(9)   At least 14 days before the hearing of the first appointment, the applicant must file with the court and serve on the respondent, confirmation of the names of all persons served in accordance with rule 2.59(3) and (4), and that there are no other persons who must be served in accordance with those paragraphs.][2]

****

[2.70   Pensions

(1)   This rule applies where an application for ancillary relief has been made, or notice of intention to proceed with the application has been given, in Form A, or an application has been made in Form B, and the applicant or respondent has or is likely to have any benefits under a pension arrangement.

(2)   When the court fixes a first appointment as required by rule 2.61A(4)(a), the party with pension rights shall, within seven days after receiving notification of the date of that appointment, request the person responsible for each pension arrangement under which he has or is likely to have benefits to furnish the information referred to in regulation 2(2) and (3)(b) to (f) of the Pensions on Divorce etc (Provision of Information) Regulations 2000.

(3)   Within seven days of receiving information under paragraph (2) the party with pension rights shall send a copy of it to the other party, together with the name and address of the person responsible for each pension arrangement.

(4)   A request under paragraph (2) above need not be made where the party with pension rights is in possession of, or has requested, a relevant valuation of the pension rights or benefits accrued under the pension arrangement in question.

---

[1]   Paragraph revoked: Family Proceedings (Amendment) Rules 2000, SI 2000/2267, with effect from 1 December 2000.

[2]   Rule inserted: Family Proceedings (Amendment No 2) Rules 1999, SI 1999/3491, with effect from 5 June 2000.

(5)   In this rule, a relevant valuation means a valuation of pension rights or benefits as at a date not more than twelve months earlier than the date fixed for the first appointment which has been furnished or requested [for the purposes of][1] any of the following provisions: –

(a)   the Pensions on Divorce etc (Provision of Information) Regulations 2000;

(b)   regulation 5 of and Schedule 2 to the Occupational Pension Schemes (Disclosure of Information) Regulations 1996 and regulation 11 of and Schedule 1 to the Occupational Pension Schemes (Transfer Value) Regulations 1996;

(c)   section 93A or 94(1)(a) or (aa) of the Pension Schemes Act 1993;

(d)   section 94(1)(b) of the Pension Schemes Act 1993 or paragraph 2(a) (or, where applicable, 2(b)) of Schedule 2 to the Personal Pension Schemes (Disclosure of Information) Regulations 1987.

(6)   Upon making or giving notice of intention to proceed with an application for ancillary relief including provision to be made under section 24B (pension sharing) of the Act of 1973, or upon adding a request for such provision to an existing application for ancillary relief, the applicant shall send to the person responsible for the pension arrangement concerned a copy of Form A.

(7)   Upon making or giving notice of intention to proceed with an application for ancillary relief including provision to be made under section 25B or 25C (pension attachment) of the Act of 1973, or upon adding a request for such provision to an existing application for ancillary relief, the applicant shall send to the person responsible for the pension arrangement concerned –

(a)   a copy of Form A;

(b)   an address to which any notice which the person responsible is required to serve on the applicant under the Divorce etc (Pensions) Regulations 2000 is to be sent;

(c)   an address to which any payment which the person responsible is required to make to the applicant is to be sent; and

(d)   where the address in sub-paragraph (c) is that of a bank, a building society or the Department of National Savings, sufficient details to enable payment to be made into the account of the applicant.

(8)   A person responsible for a pension arrangement on whom a copy of a notice under paragraph (7) is served may, within 21 days after service, require the applicant to provide him with a copy of section 2.16 of the statement in Form E supporting his application; and the applicant must then provide that person with the copy of that section of the statement within the time limited for filing it by rule 2.61B(2), or 21 days after being required to do so, whichever is the later.

(9)   A person responsible for a pension arrangement who receives a copy of section 2.16 of Form E as required pursuant to paragraph (8) may within 21 days after receipt send to the court, the applicant and the respondent a statement in answer.

(10)   A person responsible for a pension arrangement who files a statement in answer pursuant to paragraph (9) shall be entitled to be represented at the first appointment, and the court must within 4 days of the date of filing of the statement in answer give the person notice of the date of the first appointment.

(11)   Where the parties have agreed on the terms of an order including provision under section 25B or 25C (pension attachment) of the Act of 1973, then unless service has already been effected under paragraph (7), they shall serve on the person responsible for the pension arrangement concerned –

(a)   the notice of application for a consent order under rule 2.61(1);

(b)   a draft of the proposed order under rule 2.61(1), complying with paragraph (13) below; and

(c)   the particulars set out in sub-paragraphs (b), (c) and (d) of paragraph (7) above.

(12)   No consent order under paragraph (11) shall be made unless either –

---

[1]   Words substituted: Family Proceedings (Amendment) Rules 2001, SI 2001/821, with effect from 1 April 2001.

(a) the person responsible has not made any objection within 21 days after the service on him of such notice; or

(b) the court has considered any such objection

and for the purpose of considering any objection the court may make such direction as it sees fit for the person responsible to attend before it or to furnish written details of his objection.

(13) An order for ancillary relief, whether by consent or not, including provision under section 24B (pension sharing), 25B or 25C (pension attachment) of the Act of 1973, shall –

(a) in the body of the order, state that there is to be provision by way of pension sharing or pension attachment in accordance with the annex or annexes to the order; and

(b) be accompanied by an annex containing the information set out in paragraph (14) or paragraph (15) as the case may require; and if provision is made in relation to more than one pension arrangement there shall be one annex for each pension arrangement.

(14) Where provision is made under section 24B (pension sharing) of the Act of 1973, the annex shall state –

(a) the name of the court making the order, together with the case number and the title of the proceedings;

(b) that it is a pension sharing order made under Part IV of the Welfare Reform and Pensions Act 1999;

(c) the names of the transferor and the transferee;

(d) the national insurance number of the transferor;

(e) sufficient details to identify the pension arrangement concerned and the transferor's rights or benefits from it (for example a policy reference number);

(f) the specified percentage, or where appropriate the specified amount, required in order to calculate the appropriate amount for the purposes of section 29(1) of the Welfare Reform and Pensions Act 1999 (creation of pension debits and credits);

(g) how the pension sharing charges are to be apportioned between the parties or alternatively that they are to be paid in full by the transferor;

(h) that the person responsible for the pension arrangement has furnished the information required by regulation 4 of the Pensions on Divorce etc (Provision of Information) Regulations 2000 and that it appears from that information that there is power to make an order including provision under section 24B (pension sharing) of the Act of 1973;

(i) the day on which the order or provision takes effect; and

(j) that the person responsible for the pension arrangement concerned must discharge his liability in respect of the pension credit within a period of 4 months beginning with the day on which the order or provision takes effect or, if later, with the first day on which the person responsible for the pension arrangement concerned is in receipt of –

(i) the order for ancillary relief, including the annex;

(ii) the decree of divorce or nullity of marriage; and

(iii) the information prescribed by regulation 5 of the Pensions on Divorce etc (Provision of Information) Regulations 2000;

provided that if the court knows that the implementation period is different from that stated in sub-paragraph (j) by reason of regulations under section 34(4) or 41(2)(a) of the Welfare Reform and Pensions Act 1999, the annex shall contain details of the implementation period as determined by those regulations instead of the statement in sub-paragraph (j).

(15) Where provision is made under section 25B or 25C (pension attachment) of the Act of 1973, the annex shall state –

(a) the name of the court making the order, together with the case number and the title of the proceedings;

(b)   that it is an order making provision under section 25B or 25C, as the case may be, of the Act of 1973;

(c)   the names of the party with pension rights and the other party;

(d)   the national insurance number of the party with pension rights;

(e)   sufficient details to identify the pension arrangement concerned and the rights or benefits from it to which the party with pension rights is or may become entitled (for example a policy reference number);

(f)   in the case of an order including provision under section 25B(4) of the Act of 1973, what percentage of any payment due to the party with pension rights is to be paid for the benefit of the other party;

(g)   in the case of an order including any other provision under section 25B or 25C of the Act of 1973, what the person responsible for the pension arrangement is required to do;

(h)   the address to which any notice which the person responsible for the pension arrangement is required to serve on the other party under the Divorce etc (Pensions) Regulations 2000 is to be sent, if not notified under paragraph (7)(b);

(i)   an address to which any payment which the person responsible for the pension arrangement is required to make to the other party is to be sent, if not notified under paragraph (7)(c);

(j)   where the address in sub-paragraph (i) is that of a bank, a building society or the Department of National Savings, sufficient details to enable payment to be made into the account of the other party, if not notified under paragraph (7)(d); and

(k)   where the order is made by consent, that no objection has been made by the person responsible for the pension arrangement, or that an objection has been received and considered by the court, as the case may be.

(16)   A court which makes, varies or discharges an order including provision under section 24B (pension sharing), 25B or 25C (pension attachment) of the Act of 1973, shall send to the person responsible for the pension arrangement concerned –

(a)   a copy of the decree of divorce, nullity of marriage or judicial separation;

(b)   in the case of divorce or nullity of marriage, a copy of the certificate under rule 2.51 that the decree has been made absolute; and

(c)   a copy of that order, or as the case may be of the order varying or discharging that order, including any annex to that order relating to that pension arrangement but no other annex to that order.

(17)   The documents referred to in paragraph (16) shall be sent within 7 days after the making of the relevant order, or within 7 days after the decree absolute of divorce or nullity or decree of judicial separation, whichever is the later.

(18)   In this rule –

(a)   all words and phrases defined in sections 25D(3) and (4) of the Act of 1973 have the meanings assigned by those subsections;

(b)   all words and phrases defined in section 46 of the Welfare Reform and Pensions Act 1999 have the meanings assigned by that section.][1]

****

---

[1]   Rule substituted: Family Proceedings (Amendment) Rules 2000, SI 2000/2267, with effect from 1 December 2000.

Pensions on Divorce etc (Charging) Regulations 2000[1]

1[2]   **Citation, commencement and interpretation**

(1)   These Regulations may be cited as the Pensions on Divorce etc (Charging) Regulations 2000 and shall come into force on 1st December 2000.

(2)   In these Regulations, unless the context otherwise requires –

'the 1999 Act' means the Welfare Reform and Pensions Act 1999;

'the Provision of Information Regulations' means the Pensions on Divorce etc (Provision of Information) Regulations 2000;

'day' means any day other than –

(a) Christmas Day or Good Friday; or

(b) a bank holiday, that is to say, a day which is, or is to be observed as, a bank holiday or a holiday under Schedule 1 to the Banking and Financial Dealings Act 1971;

'implementation period' has the meaning given by section 34(1) of the 1999 Act;

['normal pension age' has the meaning given by section 180 of the Pension Schemes Act 1993;][3]

'notice of implementation' has the meaning given by regulation 1(2) of the Provision of Information Regulations;

'pension arrangement' has the meaning given to that expression in section 46(1) of the 1999 Act;

'pension credit' means a credit under section 29(1)(b) of the 1999 Act;

'pension credit benefit' has the meaning given by section 101B of the Pensions Schemes Act 1993;

'pension credit rights' has the meaning given by section 101B of the Pension Schemes Act 1993;

'pension sharing activity' has the meaning given by section 41(5) of the 1999 Act;

'pension sharing order or provision' means an order or provision which is mentioned in section 28(1) of the 1999 Act;

'person responsible for a pension arrangement' has the meaning given to that expression in section 46(2) of the 1999 Act;

'the Regulatory Authority' means the Occupational Pensions Regulatory Authority;

'the relevant date' has the meaning given by section 10(3) of the Family Law (Scotland) Act 1985;

'trustees or managers' has the meaning given by section 46(1) of the 1999 Act.

2[4]   **General requirements as to charges**

(1)   Subject to paragraph (8), a person responsible for a pension arrangement shall not recover any charges incurred in connection with –

(a)   the provision of information under –

(i)   regulation 2 of the Provision of Information Regulations (basic information about pensions and divorce);

---

[1]   SI reference: SI 2000/1049.
    Made under: Pension Schemes Act 1993, ss 168(1), (4), 181(1), 182(2), (3); Welfare Reform and Pensions Act 1999, ss 23(1)(a), (b)(i), (c)(i), (2), 34(1)(b)(ii), 45(1), 83(4), (6).
[2]   Commencement: 1 December 2000 (reg 1(1)).
[3]   Amendment: Definition inserted: Pension Sharing (Consequential and Miscellaneous Amendments) Regulations 2000, SI 2000/2691, with effect from 1 December 2000.
[4]   Commencement: 1 December 2000 (reg 1(1)).

(ii)   regulation 4 of those Regulations (provision of information in response to a notification that a pension sharing order or provision may be made); or

(iii)   regulation 10 of those Regulations (provision of information after receipt of an earmarking order);

(b)   complying with any order specified in section 24 of the 1999 Act (charges by pension arrangements in relation to earmarking orders); or

(c)   any description of pension sharing activity specified in regulation 5 of these Regulations,

unless he has complied with the requirements of paragraphs (2) to (5).

(2)   The requirements mentioned in paragraph (1) are that the person responsible for a pension arrangement shall, before a pension sharing order or provision is made –

(a)   inform the member or his spouse, as the case may be, in writing of his intention to recover costs incurred in connection with any of the matters specified in sub-paragraph (a), (b) or (c) of paragraph (1); and

(b)   provide the member or his spouse, as the case may be, with a written schedule of charges in accordance with paragraphs (3) and (4) in respect of those matters specified in sub-paragraph (a) or (c) of paragraph (1) for which a charge may be recoverable.

(3)   No charge shall be recoverable in respect of any of the items mentioned in paragraph (4) unless the person responsible for a pension arrangement has specified in the written schedule of charges mentioned in paragraph (2)(b) that a charge may be recoverable in respect of that item.

(4)   The items referred to in paragraph (3) are –

(a)   the provision of a cash equivalent other than one which is provided in accordance with the provisions of –

(i)   section 93A or 94 of the 1993 Act (salary related schemes: right to statement of entitlement, and right to cash equivalent);

(ii)   regulation 11(1) of the Occupational Pension Schemes (Transfer Values) Regulations 1996 (disclosure); or

(iii)   regulation 5 (information to be made available to individuals) of, and paragraph 2(b) of Schedule 2 (provision of cash equivalent) to the Personal Pension Schemes (Disclosure of Information) Regulations 1987;

(b)   subject to regulation 3(2)(b) or (c), as the case may be, the provision of a valuation in accordance with regulation 2(2) of the Provision of Information Regulations;

(c)   whether a person responsible for a pension arrangement intends to recover the cost of providing membership of the pension arrangement to the person entitled to a pension credit, before or after the pension sharing order is implemented;

(d)   whether the person responsible for a pension arrangement intends to recover additional charges in the circumstances prescribed in regulation 6 of these Regulations in respect of pension sharing activity described in regulation 5 of these Regulations;

(e)   whether the charges are inclusive or exclusive of value added tax, where the person responsible for a pension arrangement is required to charge value added tax in accordance with the provisions of the Value Added Tax Act 1994;

(f)   periodical charges in respect of pension sharing activity which the person responsible for a pension arrangement may make when a person entitled to a pension credit becomes a member of the pension arrangement from which the pension credit is derived;

(g)   whether the person responsible for a pension arrangement intends to recover charges specified in regulation 10 of these Regulations.

(5)   In the case of the cost referred to in paragraph (4)(c) or the charges to be imposed in respect of pension sharing activity described in regulation 5 of these Regulations, the person responsible for a pension arrangement shall provide –

(a) a single estimate of the overall cost of the pension sharing activity;

(b) a range of estimates of the overall cost of the pension sharing activity which is dependent upon the complexity of an individual case; or

(c) a breakdown of the cost of each element of pension sharing activity for which a charge shall be made.

(6) Subject to regulation 9(3) and (4), a person responsible for a pension arrangement shall recover only those sums which represent the reasonable administrative expenses which he has incurred or is likely to incur in connection with any of the activities mentioned in paragraph (1), or in relation to a pension sharing order having been made the subject of an application for leave to appeal out of time.

(7) The requirements of paragraph (2) do not apply in connection with the recovery by a person responsible for a pension arrangement of costs incurred in relation to a pension sharing order having been made the subject of an application for leave to appeal out of time.

[(8) The information specified in regulation 2(2) and (3) of the Provision of Information Regulations shall be provided to the member or his spouse without charge unless –

(a) the person responsible for the pension arrangement has furnished the information to the member, his spouse or the court within a period of 12 months immediately prior to the date of the request or the court order for the provision of that information;

(b) the member has reached normal pension age on or before the date of the request or the court order for the provision of the information;

(c) the request or the court order for the provision of the information is made within 12 months prior to the member reaching normal pension age; or

(d) the circumstances referred to in regulation 3(2)(b)(i) apply.][1]

3[2] Charges recoverable in respect of the provision of basic information

(1) Subject to paragraph (2), the charges prescribed for the purposes of section 23(1)(d) of the 1999 Act (charges which a person responsible for a pension arrangement may recover in respect of supplying pension information in connection with divorce etc) are any charges incurred by the person responsible for the pension arrangement in connection with the provision of any of the information set out in –

(a) regulation 2 of the Provision of Information Regulations which may be recovered in accordance with regulation 2(8) of these Regulations;

(b) regulation 4 of those Regulations; or

(c) regulation 10 of those Regulations.

(2) The charges mentioned in paragraph (1) shall not include any costs incurred by a person responsible for a pension arrangement in respect of the matters specified in sub-paragraphs (a) to (f) –

(a) any costs incurred by the person responsible for a pension arrangement which are directly related to the fulfilment of his obligations under regulation 2(3) of the Provision of Information Regulations, other than charges which may be recovered in the circumstances described in regulation 2(8) of these Regulations;

(b) any costs incurred by the person responsible for the pension arrangement as a result of complying with a request for, or an order of the court requiring, a valuation under regulation 2(2) of the Provision of Information Regulations, unless –

---

[1] Amendment: Paragraph substituted: Pension Sharing (Consequential and Miscellaneous Amendments) Regulations 2000, SI 2000/2691, with effect from 1 December 2000.

[2] Commencement: 1 December 2000 (reg 1(1)).

(i)   he is required by a member or a court to provide that valuation in less than 3 months beginning with the date the person responsible for the pension arrangement receives that request or order for the valuation;

(ii)   the valuation is requested by a member who is not entitled to a cash equivalent under any of the provisions referred to in regulation 2(4)(a);

(iii)   a member has requested a cash equivalent in accordance with any of those provisions within 12 months immediately prior to the date of the request for a valuation under regulation 2(2) of the Provision of Information Regulations;

(c)   any costs incurred by the person responsible for the pension arrangement as a result of providing a valuation of benefits calculated and verified in accordance with regulation 3 of the Divorce etc (Pensions) (Scotland) Regulations 2000 (valuation), unless –

(i)   he is required by the court to provide that valuation in less than 3 months beginning with the date the person responsible for the pension arrangement receives that order;

(ii)   the valuation is requested by a member who is not entitled to a cash equivalent under any of the provisions referred to in regulation 2(4)(a);

(iii)   a member has requested a cash equivalent in accordance with any of those provisions within 12 months immediately prior to the date of the request for a valuation under regulation 2(2) of the Provision of Information Regulations; or

(iv)   the relevant date is more than 12 months immediately prior to the date the person responsible for the pension arrangement receives the request for the valuation;

(d)   any costs incurred by the trustees or managers of –

(i)   an occupational pension scheme in connection with the provision of information under regulation 4 of the Occupational Pension Schemes (Disclosure of Information) Regulations 1996 (basic information about the scheme); or

(ii)   a personal pension scheme in connection with the provision of information under regulation 4 of the Personal Pension Schemes (Disclosure of Information) Regulations 1987 (basic information about the scheme),

which the trustees or managers shall provide to the member free of charge under those Regulations;

(e)   any costs incurred by the trustees or managers of an occupational pension scheme, or a personal pension scheme, as the case may be, in connection with the provision of a transfer value in accordance with the provisions of –

(i)   section 93A or 94 of the 1993 Act;

(ii)   regulation 11(1) of the Occupational Pension Schemes (Transfer Values) Regulations 1996; or

(iii)   regulation 5 of, and paragraph 2(b) of Schedule 2 to, the Personal Pension Schemes (Disclosure of Information) Regulations 1987; or

(f)   any costs not specified by the person responsible for a pension arrangement in the information on charges provided to the member pursuant to regulation 2 of the Provision of Information Regulations with the exception of any additional amounts under regulation 6(1)(a) of these Regulations.

4[1]   Charges in respect of the provision of information - method of recovery

(1)   A person responsible for a pension arrangement may recover the charges specified in regulation 3(1) by using either of the methods described in sub-paragraph (a) or (b) –

(a)   requiring payment of charges at any specified time between the request for basic information and the completion of the implementation of a pension sharing order or

---

[1]   Commencement: 1 December 2000 (reg 1(1)).

provision, or the compliance with an order specified in section 24 of the 1999 Act, as the case may be; or

(b)   subject to paragraph (2), requiring as a condition of providing information in accordance with –

    (i)   regulation 2 of the Provision of Information Regulations; or

    (ii)   regulation 10 of those Regulations,

that payment of the charges to which regulation 3(1) refers shall be made in full by the member before the person responsible for the pension arrangement becomes obliged to provide the information.

(2)   Paragraph (1)(b) shall not apply –

(a)   where a court has ordered a member to obtain the information specified in regulation 2 of the Provision of Information Regulations;

(b)   where, in accordance with regulation 2(8) of these Regulations, the person responsible for the pension arrangement shall provide that information without charge; or

(c)   where the person responsible for the pension arrangement is required to supply that information by virtue of regulation 4 of the Provision of Information Regulations.

5[1]   Charges in respect of pension sharing activity

(1)   The charges prescribed in respect of prescribed descriptions of pension sharing activity for the purposes of section 41(1) of the 1999 Act (charges in respect of pension sharing costs) are any costs reasonably incurred by the person responsible for the pension arrangement in connection with pension sharing activity other than those costs specified in paragraph (3).

(2)   The descriptions of pension sharing activity prescribed for the purposes of section 41(1) of the 1999 Act are any type of activity which fulfils the requirements of section 41(5) of the 1999 Act.

(3)   The costs specified in this paragraph are any costs which are not directly related to the costs which arise in relation to an individual case.

6[2]   Additional amounts recoverable in respect of pension sharing activity

(1)   The circumstances in which a person responsible for a pension arrangement may recover additional amounts are –

(a)   where a period of more than 12 months has elapsed between the person responsible for the pension arrangement supplying information in accordance with regulation 2 of the Provision of Information Regulations and the taking effect of an order or provision specified in subsection (1) of section 28 of the 1999 Act (activation of pension sharing); or

(b)   in the case of an occupational pension scheme, where the trustees or managers of that scheme undertake activity from time to time associated with pension credit rights or pension credit benefit in that scheme which belong to a member.

(2)   For the purposes of section 41(2)(d) of the 1999 Act, the additional amounts are –

(a)   in the circumstances described in paragraph (1)(a), interest calculated at a rate not exceeding increases in the retail prices index on the amounts of any charges not yet due, or of any charges requested but yet to be recovered, which are specified in the schedule of charges issued to the member in accordance with regulation 2(2)(b) of these Regulations; and

(b)   in the circumstances described in paragraph (1)(b), an amount not exceeding an increase calculated by reference to increases in the retail prices index on the amounts which relate to the costs referred to in regulation 2(4)(d) and which are specified in the schedule of charges provided to the member and his spouse in accordance with regulation 2(2)(b).

---

[1]   Commencement: 1 December 2000 (reg 1(1)).
[2]   Commencement: 1 December 2000 (reg 1(1)).

(3)   Where a person responsible for a pension arrangement intends to recover an additional amount specified in paragraph (2)(a) in the circumstances described in paragraph (1)(a), he shall set out this intention, the rate of interest to be used, and the total costs recoverable in the notice of implementation and final costs issued in accordance with regulation 7 of the Provision of Information Regulations (provision of information after receiving a pension sharing order or provision).

(4)   Where the trustees or managers of an occupational pension scheme intend to recover an additional amount specified in paragraph (2)(b) in the circumstances described in paragraph (1)(b), they shall inform the parties involved in pension sharing in writing of this intention in the schedule of charges issued in accordance with regulation 2(2)(b) of these Regulations.

7[1] Charges in respect of pension sharing activity – postponement of implementation period

(1)   The circumstances when the start of the implementation period may be postponed are when a person responsible for a pension arrangement –

    (a)   issues a notice to the member and the person entitled to the pension credit no later than 21 days after the day on which the person responsible for the pension arrangement receives the pension sharing order or provision; and

    (b)   in that notice, requires the charges specified in regulation 3, 5 or 6 to be paid before the implementation of the pension sharing order or provision is commenced.

(2)   Paragraph (1) shall apply only if the person responsible for the pension arrangement has specified at a stage no later than in his response to the notification that a pension sharing order or provision may be made, issued in accordance with regulation 4 of the Provision of Information Regulations

    (a)   that he requires the charges mentioned in paragraph (1) to be paid before the implementation period is commenced; and either

    (b)   whether he requires those charges to be paid in full; or

    (c)   the proportion of those charges which he requires to be paid as full settlement of those charges.

(3)   Once payment of the charges mentioned in paragraph (1) has been made in accordance with the requirements of the person responsible for the pension arrangement –

    (a)   that person shall

        (i)   issue the notice of implementation in accordance with regulation 7(1)(c) of the Provision of Information Regulations, and

        (ii)   begin the implementation period for the pension credit,

        within 21 days from the date the charges are paid, provided that the person responsible for the pension arrangement would otherwise be able to begin to implement the pension sharing order or provision, and

    (b)   subject to paragraph (4), that person shall not be entitled to recover any further charges in respect of the pension sharing order or provision in question.

(4)   Paragraph (3)(b) shall not apply –

    (a)   in relation to the recovery of charges referred to in regulations 2(4)(d) and 6(2)(b); or

    (b)   where the pension credit depends on a pension sharing order and the order is the subject of an application for leave to appeal out of time.

---

[1]   Commencement: 1 December 2000 (reg 1(1)).

8[1]   Charges in respect of pension sharing activity – reimbursement as between the parties to pension sharing

A payment in respect of charges recoverable under regulation 3, 5 or 6 made by one party to pension sharing on behalf of the other party to pension sharing, shall be recoverable by the party who made the payment from that other party as a debt.

9[2]   Charges in respect of pension sharing activity – method of recovery

(1)   Subject to paragraphs (7) and (8), a person responsible for a pension arrangement may recover the charges specified in regulations 3, 5 and 6 by using any of the methods described in paragraph (2).

(2)   The methods of recovery described in this paragraph are –

(a)   subject to regulation 7 requiring the charges referred to in paragraph (1) to be paid before the implementation period for the pension sharing order or provision is commenced;

(b)   deduction from a pension credit;

(c)   deduction from the accrued rights of the member;

(d)   where a pension sharing order or provision is made in respect of a pension which is in payment, deduction from the member's pension benefits;

(e)   where liability in respect of a pension credit is discharged by the person responsible for the pension arrangement in accordance with paragraph 1(2), 2(2), or 3(2) of Schedule 5 to the 1999 Act (mode of discharge of liability for pension credits), deduction from payments of pension credit benefit; or

(f)   deduction from the amount of a transfer value which is calculated in accordance with –

(i)   regulation 7 of the Occupational Pension Schemes (Transfer Values) Regulations 1996 (manner of calculation and verification of cash equivalents); or

(ii)   regulation 3 of the Personal Pension Schemes (Transfer Values) Regulations 1987 (manner of calculation and verification of cash equivalents).

(3)   A person responsible for a pension arrangement shall not recover charges referred to in paragraph (1) by using any of the methods described in paragraph (2)(b), (c), (d), (e) or (f) unless –

(a)   a pension sharing order or provision corresponding to any order or provision specified in subsection (1) of section 28 of the 1999 Act has been made;

(b)   the implementation period has commenced;

(c)   where a pension sharing order has been made, the person responsible for a pension arrangement is not aware of an appeal against the order having begun on or after the day on which the order takes effect;

(d)   there are charges which are unpaid and for which the party, to whom paragraph (2)(b), (c), (d), (e) or (f) applies, is liable;

(e)   the person responsible for the pension arrangement has issued a notice of implementation in accordance with regulation 7 of the Provision of Information Regulations;

(f)   the person responsible for a pension arrangement specifies in the notice of implementation that recovery of the charges may be made by using any of those methods; and

(g)   21 days have elapsed since the notice of implentation was issued to the parties to pension sharing in accordance with the requirements of regulation 7 of the Provision of Information Regulations.

(4)   If a pension sharing order or provision includes provision about the apportionment between the parties to pension sharing of any charge under section 41 of the 1999 Act or under corresponding Northern Ireland legislation, by virtue of section 24D of the Matrimonial Causes Act 1973 (pension

---

[1]   Commencement: 1 December 2000 (reg 1(1)).
[2]   Commencement: 1 December 2000 (reg 1(1)).

sharing orders: apportionment of charges) or section 8A of the Family Law (Scotland) Act 1985 (pension sharing orders: apportionment of charges), the recovery of charges using any of the methods described in paragraph (2) by the person responsible for the pension arrangement shall comply with the terms of the order or provision.

(5)   A person responsible for a pension arrangement shall not recover charges referred to in paragraph (1) by using any of the methods described in paragraph (2), from a party to pension sharing, if that party has paid in full the proportion of the charges for which he is liable.

(6)   A person responsible for a pension arrangement may recover charges by using any of the methods described in paragraph (2)(b), (c) or (d) –

    (a)   at any time within the implementation period prescribed by section 34 of the 1999 Act ('implementation period');

    (b)   following an application by the trustees or managers of an occupational pension scheme, such longer period as the Regulatory Authority may allow in accordance with section 33(4) of the 1999 Act (extension of time for discharge of liability); or

    (c)   within 21 days after the end of the period referred to in sub-paragraph (a) or (b).

(7)   Where the commencement of the implementation period is postponed, or its operation ceases in accordance with regulation 4 of the Pension Sharing (Implementation and Discharge of Liability) Regulations 2000 (postponement or cessation of implementation period where an application is made for leave to appeal out of time) a person responsible for a pension arrangement may require any outstanding charges referred to in paragraph (1) to be paid immediately, in respect of –

    (a)   all costs which have been incurred prior to the date of postponement or cessation; or

    (b)   any reasonable costs related to –

        (i)   the application for leave to appeal out of time; or

        (ii)   the appeal out of time itself.

(8)   Paragraph (7) applies even if, prior to receiving the notification of the application for leave to appeal out of time, a person responsible for a pension arrangement has indicated to the parties to pension sharing that he will not be using the method of recovery specified in paragraph (2)(a).

10[1]   Charges in relation to earmarking orders

The prescribed charges which a person responsible for a pension arrangement may recover in respect of complying with an order specified in section 24 of the 1999 Act are those charges which represent the reasonable administrative expenses which he has incurred or is likely to incur by reason of the order.

---

[1]   Commencement: 1 December 2000 (reg 1(1)).

Pensions on Divorce etc (Provision of Information) Regulations 2000[1]

1[2]   **Citation, commencement and interpretation**

(1)   These Regulations may be cited as the Pensions on Divorce etc (Provision of Information) Regulations 2000 and shall come into force on 1st December 2000.

(2)   In these Regulations –

'the 1993 Act' means the Pension Schemes Act 1993;

'the 1995 Act' means the Pensions Act 1995;

'the 1999 Act' means the Welfare Reform and Pensions Act 1999;

'the Charging Regulations' means the Pensions on Divorce etc (Charging) Regulations 2000;

'the Implementation and Discharge of Liability Regulations' means the Pension Sharing (Implementation and Discharge of Liability) Regulations 2000;

'the Valuation Regulations' means the Pension Sharing (Valuation) Regulations 2000;

'active member' has the meaning given by section 124(1) of the 1995 Act;

'day' means any day other than –

(a)   Christmas Day or Good Friday; or

(b)   a bank holiday, that is to say, a day which is, or is to be observed as, a bank holiday or a holiday under Schedule 1 to the Banking and Financial Dealings Act 1971;

'deferred member' has the meaning given by section 124(1) of the 1995 Act;

'implementation period' has the meaning given by section 34(1) of the 1999 Act;

'member' means a person who has rights to future benefits, or has rights to benefits payable, under a pension arrangement;

'money purchase benefits' has the meaning given by section 181(1) of the 1993 Act;

'normal benefit age' has the meaning given by section 101B of the 1993 Act;

'notice of discharge of liability' means a notice issued to the member and his former spouse by the person responsible for a pension arrangement when that person has discharged his liability in respect of a pension credit in accordance with Schedule 5 to the 1999 Act;

'notice of implementation' means a notice issued by the person responsible for a pension arrangement to the member and his former spouse at the beginning of the implementation period notifying them of the day on which the implementation period for the pension credit begins;

'occupational pension scheme' has the meaning given by section 1 of the 1993 Act;

'the party with pension rights' and 'the other party' have the meanings given by section 25D(3) of the Matrimonial Causes Act 1997;

'pension arrangement' has the meaning given in section 46(1) of the 1999 Act;

'pension credit' means a credit under section 29(1)(b) of the 1999 Act;

'pension credit benefit' means the benefits payable under a pension arrangement or a qualifying arrangement to or in respect of a person by virtue of rights under the arrangement in question which are attributable (directly or indirectly) to a pension credit;

---

[1]   SI reference: SI 2000/1048.

Made under: Pension Schemes Act 1993, ss 168(1), (4), 181(1), 182(2), (3); Welfare Reform and Pensions Act 1999, ss 23(1)(a), (b)(i), (c)(i), (2), 34(1)(b)(ii), 45(1), 83(4), (6).

[2]   Commencement: 1 December 2000 (reg 1(1)).

'pension credit rights' means rights to future benefits under a pension arrangement or a qualifying arrangement which are attributable (directly or indirectly) to a pension credit;

'pension sharing order or provision' means an order or provision which is mentioned in section 28(1) of the 1999 Act;

'pensionable service' has the meaning given by section 124(1) of the 1995 Act;

'person responsible for a pension arrangement' has the meaning given by section 46(2) of the 1999 Act;

'personal pension scheme' has the meaning given by section 1 of the 1993 Act;

'qualifying arrangement' has the meaning given by paragraph 6 of Schedule 5 to the 1999 Act;

...[1]

'retirement annuity contract' means a contract or scheme approved under Chapter III of Part XIV of the Income and Corporation Taxes Act 1988;

'salary related occupational pension scheme' has the meaning given by regulation 1A of the Occupational Pension Schemes (Transfer Values) Regulations 1996;

'the Regulatory Authority' means the Occupational Pensions Regulatory Authority;

'transfer day' has the meaning given by section 29(8) of the 1999 Act;

'transferee' has the meaning given by section 29(8) of the 1999 Act;

'transferor' has the meaning given by section 29(8) of the 1999 Act;

'trustees or managers' has the meaning given by section 46(1) of the 1999 Act.

2[2]   Basic information about pensions and divorce

(1)   The requirements imposed on a person responsible for a pension arrangement for the purposes of section 23(1)(a) of the 1999 Act (supply of pension information in connection with divorce etc.) are that he shall furnish –

   (a)   on request from a member, the information referred to in paragraphs (2) and (3)(b) to (f);

   (b)   on request from the spouse of a member, the information referred to in paragraph (3); or

   (c)   pursuant to an order of the court, the information referred to in paragraph (2), (3) or (4),

   to the member, the spouse of the member, or, as the case may be, to the court.

(2)   The information in this paragraph is a valuation of pension rights or benefits accrued under that member's pension arrangement.

(3)   The information in this paragraph is –

   (a)   a statement that on request from the member, or pursuant to an order of the court, a valuation of pension rights or benefits accrued under that member's pension arrangement, will be provided to the member, or, as the case may be, to the court;

   (b)   a statement summarising the way in which the valuation referred to in paragraph (2) and sub-paragraph (a) is calculated;

   (c)   the pension benefits which are included in a valuation referred to in paragraph (2) and sub-paragraph (a);

   (d)   whether the person responsible for the pension arrangement offers membership to a person entitled to a pension credit, and if so, the types of benefits available to pension credit members under that arrangement;

---

[1]   Definition 'relevant date' revoked: Pension Sharing (Consequential and Miscellaneous Amendments) Regulations 2000, SI 2000/2691, with effect from 1 December 2000.

[2]   Commencement: 1 December 2000 (reg 1(1)).

(e) whether the person responsible for the pension arrangements intends to discharge his liability for a pension credit other than by offering membership to a person entitled to a pension credit; and

(f) the schedule of charges which the person responsible for the pension arrangement will levy in accordance with regulation 2(2) of the Charging Regulations (general requirements as to charges).

(4) The information in this paragraph is any other information relevant to any power with respect to the matters specified in section 23(1)(a) of the 1999 Act and which is not specified in Schedule 1 or 2 to the Occupational Pension Schemes (Disclosure of Information) Regulations 1996 (basic information about the scheme and information to be made available to individuals), or in Schedule 1 or 2 to the Personal Pension Schemes (Disclosure of Information) Regulations 1987 (basic information about the scheme and information to be made available to individuals), in a case where either of those Regulations applies.

(5) Where the member's request for, or the court order for the provision of, information includes a request for, or an order for the provision of, a valuation under paragraph (2), the person responsible for the pension arrangement shall furnish all the information requested, or ordered, to the member –

(a) within 3 months beginning with the date the person responsible for the pension arrangement receives that request or order for the provision of the information;

(b) within 6 weeks beginning with the date the person responsible for the pension arrangement receives the request, or order, for the provision of the information, if the member has notified that person on the date of the request or order that the information is needed in connection with proceedings commenced under any of the provisions referred to in section 23(1)(a) of the 1999 Act; or

(c) within such shorter period specified by the court in an order requiring the person responsible for the pension arrangement to provide a valuation in accordance with paragraph (2).

(6) Where –

(a) the member's request for, or the court order for the provision of, information does not include a request or an order for a valuation under paragraph (2); or

(b) the member's spouse requests the information specified in paragraph (3),

the person responsible for the pension arrangement shall furnish that information to the member, his spouse, or the court, as the case may be, within one month beginning with the date that person responsible for the pension arrangement receives the request for, or the court order for the provision of, the information.

(7) At the same time as furnishing the information referred to in paragraph (1), the person responsible for a pension arrangement may furnish the information specified in regulation 4(2) (provision of information in response to a notification that a pension sharing order or provision may be made).

3[1]   Information about pensions and divorce: valuation of pension benefits

(1) Where an application for financial relief under any of the provisions referred to in section 23(1)(a)(i) or (iii) of the 1999 Act (supply of pension information in connection with domestic and overseas divorce etc in England and Wales and corresponding Northern Ireland powers) has been made or is in contemplation, the valuation of benefits under a pension arrangement shall be calculated and verified for the purposes of regulation 2 of these Regulations in accordance with –

(a) paragraph (3), if the person with pension rights is a deferred member of an occupational pension scheme;

(b) paragraph (4), if the person with pension rights is an active member of an occupational pension scheme;

---

[1]   Commencement: 1 December 2000 (reg 1(1)).

    (c)   paragraphs (5) and (6), if –

          (i)   the person with pension rights is a member of a personal pension scheme; or

          (ii)   those pension rights are contained in a retirement annuity contract; or

    (d)   paragraphs (7) to (9), if –

          (i)   the pension of the person with pension rights is in payment;

          (ii)   the rights of the person with pension rights are contained in an annuity contract other than a retirement annuity contract; or

          (iii)   the rights of the person with pension rights are contained in a deferred annuity contract other than a retirement annuity contract.

(2)   Where an application for financial provision under any of the provisions referred to in section 23(1)(a)(ii) of the 1999 Act (corresponding Scottish powers) has been made, or is in contemplation, the valuation of benefits under a pension arrangement shall be calculated and verified for the purposes of regulation 2 of these Regulations in accordance with regulation 3 of the Divorce etc (Pensions) (Scotland) Regulations 2000 (valuation).

(3)   Where the person with pension rights is a deferred member of an occupational pension scheme, the value of the benefits which he has under that scheme shall be taken to be –

    (a)   in the case of an occupational pension scheme other than a salary related scheme, the cash equivalent to which he acquired a right under section 94(1)(a) of the 1993 Act (right to cash equivalent) on the termination of his pensionable service, calculated on the assumption that he has made an application under section 95 of that Act (ways of taking right to cash equivalent) on the date on which the request for the valuation was received; or

    (b)   in the case of a salary related occupational pension scheme, the guaranteed cash equivalent to which he would have acquired a right under section 94(1)(aa) of the 1993 Act if he had made an application under section 95(1) of that Act, calculated on the assumption that he has made such an application on the date on which the request for the valuation was received.

(4)   Where the person with pension rights is an active member of an occupational pension scheme, the valuation of the benefits which he has accrued under that scheme shall be calculated and verified –

    (a)   on the assumption that the member had made a request for an estimate of the cash equivalent that would be available to him were his pensionable service to terminate on the date on which the request for the valuation was received; and

    (b)   in accordance with regulation 11 of and Schedule 1 to the Occupational Pension Schemes (Transfer Values) Regulations 1996 (disclosure).

(5)   Where the person with pension rights is a member of a personal pension scheme, or those rights are contained in a retirement annuity contract, the value of the benefits which he has under that scheme or contract shall be taken to be the cash equivalent to which he would have acquired a right under section 94(1)(b) of the 1993 Act, if he had made an application under section 95(1) of that Act on the date on which the request for the valuation was received.

(6)   In relation to a personal pension scheme which is comprised in a retirement annuity contract made before 4th January 1988, paragraph (5) shall apply as if such a scheme were not excluded from the scope of Chapter IV of Part IV of the 1993 Act by section 93(1)(b) of that Act (scope of Chapter IV).

(7)   Except in a case to which, or to the extent to which, paragraph (9) applies, the cash equivalent of benefits in respect of a person referred to in paragraph (1)(d) shall be calculated and verified in such manner as may be approved in a particular case by –

    (a)   a Fellow of the Institute of Actuaries;

    (b)   a Fellow of the Faculty of Actuaries; or

    (c)   a person with other actuarial qualifications who is approved by the Secretary of State, at the request of the person responsible for the pension arrangement in question, as being a proper person to act for the purposes of this regulation in connection with that arrangement.

(8)   Except in a case to which paragraph (9) applies, cash equivalents are to be calculated and verified by adopting methods and making assumptions which –

    (a)   if not determined by the person responsible for the pension arrangement in question, are notified to him by an actuary referred to in paragraph (7); and

    (b)   are certified by the actuary to the person responsible for the pension arrangement in question as being consistent with 'Retirement Benefit Schemes – Transfer Values (GN11)' published by the Institute of Actuaries and the Faculty of Actuaries and current at the date on which the request for the valuation is received.

(9)   Where the cash equivalent, or any portion of it represents rights to money purchase benefits under the pension arrangement in question of the person with pension rights, and those rights do not fall, either wholly or in part, to be valued in a manner which involves making estimates of the value of benefits, then that cash equivalent, or that portion of it, shall be calculated and verified in such manner as may be approved in a particular case by the person responsible for the pension arrangement in question, and by adopting methods consistent with the requirements of Chapter IV of Part IV of the 1993 Act (protection for early leavers - transfer values).

(10)   Where paragraph (3), (4) or (9) has effect by reference to provisions of Chapter IV of Part IV of the 1993 Act, section 93(1)(a)(i) of that Act (scope of Chapter IV) shall apply to those provisions as if the words 'at least one year' had been omitted from section 93(1)(a)(i).

4[1]   Provision of information in response to a notification that a pension sharing order or provision may be made

(1)   A person responsible for a pension arrangement shall furnish the information specified in paragraph (2) to the member or to the court, as the case may be –

    (a)   within 21 days beginning with the date that the person responsible for the pension arrangement received the notification that a pension sharing order or provision may be made; or

    (b)   if the court has specified a date which is outside the 21 days referred to in sub-paragraph (a), by that date.

(2)   The information referred to in paragraph (1) is –

    (a)   the full name of the pension arrangement and address to which any order or provision referred to in section 28(1) of the 1999 Act (activation of pension sharing) should be sent;

    (b)   in the case of an occupational pension scheme, whether the scheme is winding up, and, if so, –

        (i)   the date on which the winding up commenced; and

        (ii)   the name and address of the trustees who are dealing with the winding up;

    (c)   in the case of an occupational pension scheme, whether a cash equivalent of the member's pension rights, if calculated on the date the notification referred to in paragraph (1)(a) was received by the trustees or managers of that scheme, would be reduced in accordance with the provisions of regulation 8(4), (6) or (12) of the Occupational Pension Schemes (Transfer Values) Regulations 1996 (further provisions as to reductions of cash equivalents);

    (d)   whether the person responsible for the pension arrangement is aware that the member's rights under the pension arrangement are subject to any, and if so, to specify which, of the following –

        (i)   any order or provision specified in section 28(1) of the 1999 Act;

        (ii)   an order under section 23 of the Matrimonial Causes Act 1973 (financial provision orders in connection with divorce etc.), so far as it includes provision made by virtue of section 25B or 25C of that Act (powers to include provisions about pensions);

---

[1]   Commencement: 1 December 2000 (reg 1(1)).

(iii)   an order under section 12A(2) or (3) of the Family Law (Scotland) Act 1985 (powers in relation to pensions lump sums when making a capital sum order) which relates to benefits or future benefits to which the member is entitled under the pension arrangement;

(iv)   an order under Article 25 of the Matrimonial Causes (Northern Ireland) Order 1978, so far as it includes provision made by virtue of Article 27B or 27C of that Order (Northern Ireland powers corresponding to those mentioned in paragraph (2)(d)(ii));

(v)   a forfeiture order;

(vi)   a bankruptcy order;

(vii)   an award of sequestration on a member's estate or the making of the appointment on his estate of a judicial factor under section 41 of the Solicitors (Scotland) Act 1980 (appointment of judicial factor);

(e)   whether the member's rights under the pension arrangement include rights specified in regulation 2 of the Valuation Regulations (rights under a pension arrangement which are not shareable);

(f)   if the person responsible for the pension arrangement has not at an earlier stage provided the following information, whether that person requires the charges specified in regulation 3 (charges recoverable in respect of the provision of basic information), 5 (charges in respect of pension sharing activity), or 6 (additional amounts recoverable in respect of pension sharing activity) of the Charging Regulations to be paid before the commencement of the implementation period, and if so, –

(i)   whether that person requires those charges to be paid in full; or

(ii)   the proportion of those charges which he requires to be paid;

(g)   whether the person responsible for the pension arrangement may levy additional charges specified in regulation 6 of the Charging Regulations, and if so, the scale of the additional charges which are likely to be made;

(h)   whether the member is a trustee of the pension arrangement;

(i)   whether the person responsible for the pension arrangement may request information about the member's state of health from the member if a pension sharing order or provision were to be made;

(j)   ...;[1] and

(k)   whether the person responsible for the pension arrangement requires information additional to that specified in regulation 5 (information required by the person responsible for the pension arrangement before the implementation period may begin) in order to implement the pension sharing order or provision.

5[2]   Information required by the person responsible for the pension arrangement before the implementation period may begin

The information prescribed for the purposes of section 34(1)(b) of the 1999 Act (information relating to the transferor and the transferee which the person responsible for the pension arrangement must receive) is –

(a)   in relation to the transferor –

(i)   all names by which the transferor has been known;

(ii)   date of birth;

(iii)   address;

---

[1]   Sub-paragraph deleted: Pension Sharing (Consequential and Miscellaneous Amendments) Regulations 2000, SI 2000/2691, with effect from 1 December 2000.

[2]   Commencement: 1 December 2000 (reg 1(1)).

(iv)   National Insurance number;

(v)   the name of the pension arrangement to which the pension sharing order or provision relates; and

(vi)   the transferor's membership or policy number in that pension arrangement;

(b)   in relation to the transferee –

(i)   all names by which the transferee has been known;

(ii)   date of birth;

(iii)   address;

(iv)   National Insurance number; and

(v)   if the transferee is a member of the pension arrangement from which the pension credit is derived, his membership or policy number in that pension arrangement;

(c)   where the transferee has given his consent in accordance with paragraph 1(3)(c), 3(3)(c) or 4(2)(c) of Schedule 5 to the 1999 Act (mode of discharge of liability for a pension credit) to the payment of the pension credit to the person responsible for a qualifying arrangement –

(i)   the full name of that qualifying arrangement;

(ii)   its address;

(iii)   if known, the transferee's membership number or policy number in that arrangement; and

(iv)   the name or title, business address, business telephone number, and, where available, the business facsimile number and electronic mail address of a person who may be contacted in respect of the discharge of liability for the pension credit;

(d)   where the rights from which the pension credit is derived are held in an occupational pension scheme which is being wound up, whether the transferee has given an indication whether he wishes to transfer his pension credit rights which may have been reduced in accordance with the provisions of regulation 16(1) of the Implementation and Discharge of Liability Regulations (adjustments to the amount of the pension credit – occupational pension schemes which are underfunded on the valuation day) to a qualifying arrangement; and

(e)   any information requested by the person responsible for the pension arrangement in accordance with regulation 4(2)(i) or (k).

6[1]   Provision of information after the death of the person entitled to the pension credit before liability in respect of the pension credit has been discharged

[(1)   Where the person entitled to the pension credit dies before the person responsible for the pension arrangement has discharged his liability in respect of the pension credit, the person responsible for the pension arrangement shall, within 21 days of the date of receipt of the notification of the death of the person entitled to the pension credit, notify in writing any person whom the person responsible for the pension arrangement considers should be notified of the matters specified in paragraph (2).][2]

(2)   The matters specified in this paragraph are –

(a)   how the person responsible for the pension arrangement intends to discharge his liability in respect of the pension credit;

(b)   whether the person responsible for the pension arrangement intends to recover charges from the person nominated to receive pension credit benefits, in accordance with regulations 2 to 9 of the Charging Regulations, and if so, a copy of the schedule of charges

---

[1]   Commencement: 1 December 2000 (reg 1(1)).

[2]   Paragraph substituted: Pension Sharing (Consequential and Miscellaneous Amendments) Regulations 2000, SI 2000/2691, with effect from 1 December 2000.

issued to the parties to pension sharing in accordance with regulation 2(2)(b) of the Charging Regulations (general requirements as to charges); and

(c) a list of any further information which the person responsible for the pension arrangement requires in order to discharge his liability in respect of the pension credit.

7[1] Provision of information after receiving a pension sharing order or provision

(1) A person responsible for a pension arrangement who is in receipt of a pension sharing order or provision relating to that arrangement shall provide in writing to the transferor and transferee, or, where regulation 6(1) applies, to the person other than the person entitled to the pension credit referred to in regulation 6 of the Implementation and Discharge of Liability Regulations (discharge of liability in respect of a pension credit following the death of the person entitled to the pension credit), as the case may be, –

    (a) a notice in accordance with the provisions of regulation 7(1) of the Charging Regulations (charges in respect of pension sharing activity - postponement of implementation period);

    (b) a list of information relating to the transferor or the transferee, or, where regulation 6(1) applies, the person other than the person entitled to the pension credit referred to in regulation 6 of the Implementation and Discharge of Liability Regulations, as the case may be, which –

        (i) has been requested in accordance with regulation 4(2)(i) and (k), or, where appropriate, 6(2)(c), or should have been provided in accordance with regulation 5;

        (ii) the person responsible for the pension arrangement considers he needs in order to begin to implement the pension sharing order or provision; and

        (iii) remains outstanding;

    (c) a notice of implementation; or

    (d) a statement by the person responsible for the pension arrangement explaining why he is unable to implement the pension sharing order or agreement.

(2) The information specified in paragraph (1) shall be furnished in accordance with that paragraph within 21 days beginning with –

    (a) in the case of sub-paragraph (a), (b) or (d) of that paragraph, the day on which the person responsible for the pension arrangement receives the pension sharing order or provision; or

    (b) in the case of sub-paragraph (c) of that paragraph, the later of the days specified in section 34(1)(a) and (b) of the 1999 Act (implementation period).

8[2] Provision of information after the implementation of a pension sharing order or provision

(1) The person responsible for the pension arrangement shall issue a notice of discharge of liability to the transferor and the transferee, or, as the case may be, the person entitled to the pension credit by virtue of regulation 6 of the Implementation and Discharge of Liability Regulations no later than the end of the period of 21 days beginning with the day on which the discharge of liability in respect of the pension credit is completed.

(2) In the case of a transferor whose pension is not in payment, the notice of discharge of liability shall include the following details –

    (a) the value of the transferor's accrued rights as determined by reference to the cash equivalent value of those rights calculated and verified in accordance with regulation 3 of the Valuation Regulations (calculation and verification of cash equivalents for the purposes of the creation of pension debits and credits);

    (b) the value of the pension debit;

---

[1] Commencement: 1 December 2000 (reg 1(1)).
[2] Commencement: 1 December 2000 (reg 1(1)).

(c)   any amount deducted from the value of the pension rights in accordance with regulation 9(2)(c) of the Charging Regulations (charges in respect of pension sharing activity – method of recovery);

(d)   the value of the transferor's rights after the amounts referred to in sub-paragraphs (b) and (c) have been deducted; and

(e)   the transfer day.

(3)   In the case of a transferor whose pension is in payment, the notice of discharge of liability shall include the following details –

(a)   the value of the transferor's benefits under the pension arrangement as determined by reference to the cash equivalent value of those rights calculated and verified in accordance with regulation 3 of the Valuation Regulations;

(b)   the value of the pension debit;

(c)   the amount of the pension which was in payment before liability in respect of the pension credit was discharged;

(d)   the amount of pension which is payable following the deduction of the pension debit from the transferor's pension benefits;

(e)   the transfer day;

(f)   if the person responsible for the pension arrangement intends to recover charges, the amount of any unpaid charges –

    (i)   not prohibited by regulation 2 of the Charging Regulations (general requirements as to charges); and

    (ii)   specified in regulations 3 and 6 of those Regulations;

(g)   how the person responsible for the pension arrangement will recover the charges referred to in sub-paragraph (f), including –

    (i)   whether the method of recovery specified in regulation 9(2)(d) of the Charging Regulations will be used;

    (ii)   the date when payment of those charges in whole or in part is required; and

    (iii)   the sum which will be payable by the transferor, or which will be deducted from his pension benefits, on that date.

(4)   In the case of a transferee –

(a)   whose pension is not in payment; and

(b)   who will become a member of the pension arrangement from which the pension credit rights were derived,

the notice of discharge of liability to the transferee shall include the following details –

    (i)   the value of the pension credit;

    (ii)   any amount deducted from the value of the pension credit in accordance with regulation 9(2)(b) of the Charging Regulations;

    (iii)   the value of the pension credit after the amount referred to in sub-paragraph (b)(ii) has been deducted;

    (iv)   the transfer day;

    (v)   any periodical charges the person responsible for the pension arrangement intends to make, including how and when those charges will be recovered from the transferee; and

    (vi)   information concerning membership of the pension arrangement which is relevant to the transferee as a pension credit member.

(5)   In the case of a transferee who is transferring his pension credit rights out of the pension arrangement from which those rights were derived, the notice of discharge of liability to the transferee shall include the following details –

    (a)   the value of the pension credit;

    (b)   any amount deducted from the value of the pension credit in accordance with regulation 9(2)(b) of the Charging Regulations;

    (c)   the value of the pension credit after the amount referred to in sub-paragraph (b) has been deducted;

    (d)   the transfer day; and

    (e)   details of the pension arrangement, including its name, address, reference number, telephone number, and, where available, the business facsimile number and electronic mail address, to which the pension credit has been transferred.

(6)   In the case of a transferee, who has reached normal benefit age on the transfer day, and in respect of whose pension credit liability has been discharged in accordance with paragraph 1(2), 2(2), 3(2) or 4(4) of Schedule 5 to the 1999 Act (pension credits: mode of discharge – funded pension schemes, unfunded public service pension schemes, other unfunded pension schemes, or other pension arrangements), the notice of discharge of liability to the transferee shall include the following details –

    (a)   the amount of pension credit benefit which is to be paid to the transferee;

    (b)   the date when the pension credit benefit is to be paid to the transferee;

    (c)   the transfer day;

    (d)   if the person responsible for the pension arrangement intends to recover charges, the amount of any unpaid charges –

        (i)   not prohibited by regulation 2 of the Charging Regulations; and

        (ii)   specified in regulations 3 and 6 of those Regulations; and

    (e)   how the person responsible for the pension arrangement will recover the charges referred to in sub-paragraph (d), including –

        (i)   whether the method of recovery specified in regulation 9(2)(e) of the Charging Regulations will be used;

        (ii)   the date when payment of those charges in whole or in part is required; and

        (iii)   the sum which will be payable by the transferee, or which will be deducted from his pension credit benefits, on that date.

(7)   In the case of a person entitled to the pension credit by virtue of regulation 6 of the Implementation and Discharge of Liability Regulations, the notice of discharge of liability shall include the following details –

    (a)   the value of the pension credit rights as determined in accordance with regulation 10 of the Implementation and Discharge of Liability Regulations (calculation of the value of appropriate rights);

    (b)   any amount deducted from the value of the pension credit in accordance with regulation 9(2)(b) of the Charging Regulations;

    (c)   the value of the pension credit;

    (d)   the transfer day; and

    (e)   any periodical charges the person responsible for the pension arrangement intends to make, including how and when those charges will be recovered from the payments made to the person entitled to the pension credit by virtue of regulation 6 of the Implementation and Discharge of Liability Regulations.

9[1]   Penalties

Where any trustee or manager of an occupational pension scheme fails, without reasonable excuse, to comply with any requirement imposed under regulation 6, 7 or 8, the Regulatory Authority may require that trustee or manager to pay within 28 days from the date of its imposition, a penalty which shall not exceed –

(a)   £200 in the case of an individual, and

(b)   £1,000 in any other case.

10[2]   Provision of information after receipt of an earmarking order

(1)   The person responsible for the pension arrangement shall, within 21 days beginning with the day that he receives –

(a)   an order under section 23 of the Matrimonial Causes Act 1973, so far as it includes provision made by virtue of section 25B or 25C of that Act (powers to include provision about pensions);

(b)   an order under section 12A(2) or (3) of the Family Law (Scotland) Act 1985; or

(c)   an order under Article 25 of the Matrimonial Causes (Northern Ireland) Order 1978, so far as it includes provision made by virtue of Article 27B or 27C of that Order (Northern Ireland powers corresponding to those mentioned in sub-paragraph (a)),

issue to the party with pension rights and the other party a notice which includes the information specified in paragraphs (2) and (5), or (3), (4) and (5), as the case may be.

(2)   Where an order referred to in paragraph (1)(a), (b) or (c) is made in respect of the pension rights or benefits of a party with pension rights whose pension is not in payment, the notice issued by the person responsible for a pension arrangement to the party with pension rights and the other party shall include a list of the circumstances in respect of any changes of which the party with pension rights or the other party must notify the person responsible for the pension arrangement.

(3)   Where an order referred to in paragraph (1)(a) or (c) is made in respect of the pension rights or benefits of a party with pension rights whose pension is in payment, the notice issued by the person responsible for a pension arrangement to the party with pension rights and the other party shall include –

(a)   the value of the pension rights or benefits of the party with pension rights;

(b)   the amount of the pension of the party with pension rights after the order has been implemented;

(c)   the first date when a payment pursuant to the order is to be made; and

(d)   a list of the circumstances, in respect of any changes of which the party with pension rights or the other party must notify the person responsible for the pension arrangement.

(4)   Where an order referred to in paragraph (1)(a) or (c) is made in respect of the pension rights of a party with pension rights whose pension is in payment, the notice issued by the person responsible for a pension arrangement to the party with pension rights shall, in addition to the items specified in paragraph (3), include –

(a)   the amount of the pension of the party with pension rights which is currently in payment; and

(b)   the amount of pension which will be payable to the party with pension rights after the order has been implemented.

---

[1]   Commencement: 1 December 2000 (reg 1(1)).
[2]   Commencement: 1 December 2000 (reg 1(1)).

(5)   Where an order referred to in paragraph (1)(a), (b) or (c) is made the notice issued by the person responsible for a pension arrangement to the party with pension rights and the other party shall include –

(a)   the amount of any charges which remain unpaid by –

(i)   the party with pension rights; or

(ii)   the other party,

in respect of the provision by the person responsible for the pension arrangement of information about pensions and divorce pursuant to regulation 3 of the Charging Regulations, and in respect of complying with an order referred to in paragraph (1)(a), (b) or (c); and

(b)   information as to the manner in which the person responsible for the pension arrangement will recover the charges referred to in sub-paragraph (a), including –

(i)   the date when payment of those charges in whole or in part is required;

(ii)   the sum which will be payable by the party with pension rights or the other party, as the case may be; and

(iii)   whether the sum will be deducted from payments of pension to the party with pension rights, or, as the case may be, from payments to be made to the other party pursuant to an order referred to in paragraph (1)(a), (b) or (c).

APPENDIX 2

SPECIMEN LETTER TO PENSION PROVIDER

Dear Sirs

[Party with pension rights]
[Name and reference number for pension arrangement]

We act for [*party with pension rights*] in divorce proceedings and would be grateful if you would supply us with the following information in relation to the above pension arrangement pursuant to the Family Proceedings Rules 1991, r 2.70(2):

1   The CETV value of pension rights or benefits accrued under the above arrangement;

2   A statement summarising the way in which the valuation referred to in paragraph 1 is calculated;

3   The pension benefits, which are included in the valuation referred to in paragraph 1;

4   Whether you offer membership to a person entitled to a pension credit and, if so, the types of benefits available to pension credit members under that arrangement;

5   Whether you intend to discharge your liability for a pension credit other than by offering membership to a person entitled to a pension credit; and

6   The schedule of charges which you will levy in accordance with the Pensions on Divorce etc (Charging) Regulations 2000, reg 2(2).

Under the Pensions on Divorce etc (Provision of Information) Regulations 2000, reg 2[(5)/(6)], the information must be provided within [♦ see note 2] of the date of this request.

We would also be grateful for the following additional information, which our client is also required by the Family Proceedings Rules 1991, r 2.61B to provide to the court and [*his wife/her husband*]:

7   The lump sum payable on death in service before retirement;

8   The lump sum payable on death in deferment before retirement;

9   The lump sum payable on death after retirement;

10   The earliest date when benefit can be paid;

11   The estimated lump sum and monthly pension payable on retirement, assuming that the maximum lump sum is taken;

12   The estimated monthly pension without taking any lump sum;

13   The spouse's benefit on death in service;

14   The spouse's benefit on death in deferment;

15   The spouse's benefit on death in retirement;

16   The dependant's benefit on death in service;

17   The dependant's benefit on death in deferment;

18   The dependant's benefit on death in retirement.

We look forward to hearing from you. Please quote our above reference.

Yours faithfully

Notes:

(1)   This specimen letter attempts to collate the information required by section 2.16 of Form E (Appendix 8) and FPR 1991, r 2.70(2). It is submitted that section 2.16 (which predates the Family Proceedings (Amendment) Rules 2000, SI 2000/2267) requires revision.

(2)   The time-limit for supplying the information required by FPR 1991, r 2.70(2) is within 3 months of the request or (if needed in connection with proceedings) 6 weeks (or such shorter period as may be specified by the court). Where the request relates to information other than a valuation, the time-limit is one month.

APPENDIX 3

PR4 – TRACING REQUEST

The following pages of this Appendix include a selection of pages from Form PR4 'Tracing your old pension scheme', published by the Pension Schemes Registry.

the
pension
schemes
registry

What you should do

| Are you trying to trace an occupational pension scheme? | Yes ☐ | If 'Yes', please tell us how many schemes you are trying to trace and answer the questions on page 2 and pages 3 to 7 if you need to. Then go to page 15.

Number of schemes |
|---|---|---|
| | No ☐ | If 'No', please see below. |

| Are you trying to trace a personal pension scheme or a 'group personal pension scheme' (GPP)? | Yes ☐ | If 'Yes', please tell us how many schemes you are trying to trace and answer the questions on page 8 and pages 9 to 13 if you need to. Then go to page 15.

Number of schemes |
|---|---|---|
| | No ☐ | If 'No', please see above. |

Please turn over ➡

TRACE 1
About the occupational pension scheme
employer details

a	What was the name of your employer or the company you worked for?	
b	When did you work for this employer?	
c	If the employer traded under a different name, please give the trading name.	
d	What was the employer's address (including postcode)?	
e	What type of business did the employer run?	
f	What was your job title?	
g	If the employer was known under a different name at any time, please give their other name.	
h	If the employer changed address at any time, please give their old address (including postcode).	
i	If the employer's company was part of a larger organisation or group of companies, please give the name of that organisation.	
j	If the employer's company was part of a larger organisation or group of companies, please give the address of that organisation (including postcode).	

If you have any extra information which might help us to trace your pension scheme, please use page 14 and then go to page 16.

If you do not have any extra information, go straight to page 16.

TRACE 1
About the personal pension scheme

a | What was the name of your personal pension scheme?

b | What was the name of the insurance company involved with the personal pension scheme?

c | What address was the personal pension scheme run from (including postcode)?

d | If the personal pension scheme ever changed names, please give the old name.

e | If the address where the personal pension scheme was run from ever changed, please give the old address (including postcode).

If you have any extra information which might help us to trace your pension scheme, please use page 14 and then go to page 16.

If you do not have any extra information, go straight to page 16.

What to do now

Please check that you have filled in the form properly, then sign it.

Please send the form to the address shown at the bottom of this page.

Declaration	Please tick the appropriate box.
	(a) I am the person who is, or may become, entitled to benefits under the scheme which I am trying to trace. ☐
Your name	
Your address (including postcode)	
Your signature	Date: / /
	(b) I am representing the person named below. ☐
The name of the person you are representing	
The name of your organisation (where appropriate)	
Your name (please use capitals)	
If you are representing someone and you want us to send the reply to this application to you, please give your address (including postcode).	
Your phone number	
Your signature	Date: / /

Crystal Mark
Clarity approved by
Plain English Campaign

PR4

Send this form to:

**Opra
Pension Schemes Registry**
PO Box 1NN
**Newcastle upon Tyne
NE99 1NN.**
Phone: 0191 225 6316
Typetalk registered

www.opra.gov.uk

INVESTOR IN PEOPLE

APPENDIX 4

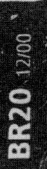

BR20 12/00

How to get a State Earnings Related Pension Scheme (SERPS) valuation

Please fill in this form if you want us to provide you with the lump sum value of your Additional Pension earned to date under the State Earnings Related Pension Scheme (SERPS).

This information may be required for any financial settlement on divorce.

The Additional Pension is the part of your State Retirement Pension that is earnings related. It is based on earnings on which you have paid National Insurance (NI) Contributions since April 1978.

■ About you

Your National Insurance (NI) number	☐☐ ☐☐ ☐☐ ☐☐ ☐
Your title	Mr/Mrs/Miss/Ms
Your surname	
Your first names	
Any other surnames you have had	
Your date of birth	/ /
Your address	
	Postcode
Daytime phone number	Code Number
Will you be divorced under Scottish law?	No ☐
	Yes ☐
If Yes, please give the relevant date	/ /

The *relevant date* is
- the date you and your spouse stopped living together, or
- the date the summons or initial writ in the action for divorce was served

whichever is earlier.

Please turn over ▶

benefits agency

An Executive Agency of
the Department of Social Security

■ About your marriage

Date of marriage	/ /
Spouse's surname	
Spouse's first names	
Spouse's date of birth	/ /
Spouse's National Insurance (NI) number	☐☐ ☐☐ ☐☐ ☐☐ ☐☐ ☐
Spouse's last address	
	Postcode

If you want your SERPS valuation to be sent to someone else, please tell us about them below.

Their full name	Mr/Mrs/Miss/Ms
Their address	
	Postcode

■ Your signature

Please sign and date this form.

Your signature	
Date	/ /

■ What to do now

When you have filled in this form, please send it to us at the address below

    Benefits Agency
    Pensions and Overseas Benefits Directorate
    RPFA Unit
    Newcastle upon Tyne
    NE98 1YX

If you have a problem with hearing or speaking, we have a textphone service. Just ring **0191 218 2160**. If you do not have your own textphone system, they are available in some libraries or Citizens Advice Bureau offices.

■ What happens next

We will send you your SERPS valuation as soon as we can.

Once we have received your application form, it takes an average of 40 working days to prepare a valuation.

If it will take us longer to prepare your valuation, we will let you know.

APPENDIX 5

FORM P1 – PENSION SHARING ANNEX

Pension Sharing Annex under Section 24B of the Matrimonial Causes Act 1973

(Rule 2.70 (14) FPR 1991)

In the	
	*[County Court]
*[Principal Registry of the Family Division]	
Case No. *Always quote this*	
Applicant's Solicitor's reference	
Respondent's Solicitors' reference	

The marriage of

Take Notice that:

On [*date*] the court

- made a pension sharing order under Part IV of the Welfare Reform and Pensions Act 1999.

- [varied] [discharged] an order which included provision for pension sharing made under Part IV of the Welfare Reform and Pensions Act 1999 and dated [*date*].

This annex to the order provides the person responsible for the pension arrangement with the information required by virtue of The Family Proceedings Rules 1991 as amended.

1. Name of the Transferor:

2. Name of the Transferee:

3. The Transferor's National Insurance Number:

4. Details of the Pension Arrangement and Policy Reference Number:

   (or such other details to enable the pension arrangement to be identified).

5. The specified percentage value of the pension arrangement to be transferred:

(The specified amount required in order to create a pension credit and debit should only be inserted where specifically ordered by the court).

In accordance with The Divorce etc. (Pensions) Regulations 2000 the court has specified that the benefits shall be valued as at the following date:

6. Pension Sharing Charges:

(*Delete as appropriate)

It is directed that:

*The pension sharing charges be apportioned between the parties as follows:

*The pension sharing charges be paid in full by the transferor.

The court is satisfied that the person responsible for the pension arrangement has furnished the information required by Regulation 4 of the Pensions on Divorce etc. (Provision of Information) Regulations 2000 and that it appears from the information that there is power to make an order including provision under section 24B (pension sharing) of the 1973 Act.

THIS [ORDER] [PROVISION] TAKES EFFECT FROM

To the person responsible for the pension arrangement:
(*Delete as appropriate)

1. *Take notice that you must discharge your liability within the period of 4 months beginning with the later of:
   - the day on which this order or provision takes effect; or,
   - the first day on which you are in receipt of –

   a. this [order] [provision] for ancillary relief, including the annex;

   b. the decree of divorce or nullity of marriage; and

   c. the information prescribed by Regulation 5 of the Pensions on Divorce etc. (Provision of Information) Regulations 2000.

2. *The court directs that the implementation period for discharging your liability should be determined by regulations made under section 34(4) or 41(2)(a) of the Welfare Reform and Pensions Act 1999, in that:

APPENDIX 6

PENSION ATTACHMENT ANNEX

Pension Attachment Annex under
Section 25B or 25C of the
Matrimonial Causes Act 1973
(Rule 2.70 (15) FPR 1991)

In the	
	*[County Court]
*[Principal Registry of the Family Division]	
Case No. *Always quote this*	
Applicant's Solicitor's reference	
Respondent's Solicitors' reference	

The marriage of

Take Notice that:

On [*date*] the court

- made an order including provision under section [25B] [25C]* of the Matrimonial Causes Act 1973.

- [varied] [discharged] an order which included provision under section [25B] [25C]* of the Matrimonial Causes Act 1973 and dated [*date*].

(*delete as appropriate*)

This annex to the order provides the person responsible for the pension arrangement with the information required by virtue of The Family Proceedings Rules 1991 as amended.

1. Name of the party with the pension rights:

2. Name of the other party:

3. The National Insurance Number of the party with pension rights:

4. Details of the Pension Arrangement and Policy Reference Number:

   (or such other details to enable the pension arrangement to be identified).

5.   *The specified percentage of any payment due to the party with pension rights that is to be paid for the benefit of the other party:

*The person responsible for the pension arrangement is required to:

(*delete as appropriate)

In accordance with The Divorce etc. (Pensions) Regulations 2000 the court has specified that the benefits shall be valued as at the following date:

To the person responsible for the pension arrangement:

(*Delete if this information had already been provided to the person responsible for the pension arrangement with Form A or pursuant to FPR 2.70(11))

1.   *You are required to serve any notice under the Divorce etc. (Pensions) Regulations 2000 on the other party at the following address:

2.   *You are required to make any payments due under the pension arrangement to the other party at the following address:

3.   *If the address at 2. above is that of a bank, building society or the Department of National Savings the following details will enable you to make payment into the account of the other party (e.g. Account Name, Number, Bank/Building Society/etc. Sort code):

Note: Where the order to which this annex applies was made by consent the following section should also be completed.

The court also confirms:
(*Delete as appropriate)

• *That notice under Rule 2.70(11) of the Family Proceedings Rules 1991 has been served on the person responsible for the pension arrangement and that no objection has been received under Rule 2.70(12).

• *That notice under Rule 2.70(11) of the Family Proceedings Rules 1991 has been served on the person responsible for the pension arrangement and that the court has considered any objection received under Rule 2.70(12)(b).

APPENDIX 7

EXPLAINING THE PROS AND CONS: A MODEL ADVICE LETTER

Dear [*Client*]

At our meeting yesterday, we discussed the possibility of a pension sharing order being made in your case. We discussed the advantages and disadvantages of such an order and I am writing to summarise those points to help you consider what future action we should take:

- Pension sharing is a type of order which the court can make at the time of divorce (or more unusually nullity), which enables a pension to be shared (in other words, split). It cannot be ordered on a legal separation. Proceedings must have been commenced after 1 December 2000.

- Sharing does not automatically mean that it has to be 50%: it can be any percentage between 1% and 100%.

- Pension sharing requires a court order (which may be made by agreement).

- It is possible to share a pension which is already in payment.

- We need to make sure that the pension sharing order will reliably meet your future needs [and enable a clean break to take place on that basis].

- To this end, we need projections from an independent financial adviser as to the likely pension and lump sum which you will receive at age [   ].

- We need to bear in mind that your husband may seek to argue that he should retain a greater share of the net proceeds of sale of the family home if a pension sharing order is made in your favour against him.

- If a pension sharing order is made in your favour, you will have a pension which will benefit you regardless of your husband's death or retirement date. It does not matter if you remarry in the future; the pension will remain yours. Your husband cannot go back to the court to vary the pension sharing order once it has been implemented. You will be able to make a nomination under your new pension arrangement to benefit a person of your own choosing in the event that you die before taking your pension benefits.

- The lump sum payable under your new pension will be tax free. However, the monthly pension payable to you will be subject to income tax in just the same way as any other pension.

- You will only be able to make further contributions into your pension from earnings, unless the part of your husband's pension to be shared with you is paid into a new type of pension called a stakeholder pension or a new-style personal pension, in which event you will be able to make further contributions from your maintenance income up to £2,808 per year. The Inland Revenue will top this up with a notional tax rebate to £3,600 per year.

- [As you are already over 50, you will be able to draw the benefits of your new pension immediately. However, by doing this, the available benefits will not be as great as they would be if you deferred drawing the pension.]

- If we decide that a pension sharing order is right for you, we need to decide whether you should become a member of your husband's pension scheme or whether you should transfer your share of his pension into a scheme of your own choosing. This is a matter about which I am not qualified to advise you and I would recommend that we involve [   ], who are independent financial advisers. If, on their recommendation, we decide to transfer your share into an alternative pension arrangement, they will be able to advise on the appropriate choice of new arrangement. [*Explanation of IFA's charges*].

Yours sincerely

APPENDIX 8

FORM E: para 2.16

Part 2 Financial Details   *Capital: Pensions (including SERPS but excluding basic state pensions)*

2.16 Give details of your pension interests.

If you have been provided with a valuation of your pension rights by the trustees or managers of the pension scheme, you must attach it. Where the information is not available, give the estimated date when it will be available and attach the letter to pension company or administrators from whom the information was sought. If you have more than one pension plan or scheme, you must provide the information in respect of each one, continuing, if necessary, on a separate piece of paper. If you have made Additional Voluntary Contributions or any Free Standing Additional Voluntary Contributions to any plan or scheme, you must give the information separately if the benefits referable to such contributions are separately recorded or paid. Please include any SERPS.

Information about the scheme(s)

Name and address of scheme, plan or policy	
Your national insurance number	
Number of scheme, plan or policy	
Type of scheme, plan or policy (e.g. final salary, money purchase or other)	

CETV - Cash Equivalent Transfer Value

CETV Value	
The lump sum payable on death in service before retirement	
The lump sum payable on death in deferment before retirement	
The lump sum payable on death after retirement	

Retirement Benefits

Earliest date when benefit can be paid	
The estimated lump sum and monthly pension payable on retirement, assuming you take the maximum lump sum	
The estimated monthly pension without taking any lump sum	

Spouse's Benefit

On death in service	
On death in deferment	
On death in retirement	

Dependant's Benefit

On death in service	
On death in deferment	
On death in retirement	

TOTAL value of your pension assets (F)